AI and the Future of the Public Sector

AI and the Future of the Public Sector

The Creation of Public Sector 4.0

TONY BOOBIER

WILEY

This edition first published 2022

Copyright © 2022 by John Wiley & Sons, Ltd.

Registered office

John Wiley & Sons Ltd, The Atrium, Southern Gate, Chichester, West Sussex, PO19 8SQ, United Kingdom

For details of our global editorial offices, for customer services and for information about how to apply for permission to reuse the copyright material in this book please see our website at www.wiley.com.

Library of Congress Cataloging-in-Publication Data is Available:

ISBN 9781119868101 (Hardback)
ISBN 9781119868118 (ePDF)
ISBN 9781119868125 (ePub)

Cover Design: Wiley
Cover Image: © oxygen/Getty Images

SKY10035215_071322

This book is dedicated to all the public sector workers who not only performed miracles but kept society running during the pandemic.

Contents

Acknowledgments

The acknowledgment section is principally about saying thank you. My first point of call is to thank Gemma Valler at Wiley, who has constantly believed in me and allowed me to write about this most important of subject areas. Thank you also to the remainder of the Wiley team.

Closer to home, I must of course acknowledge my wife Michelle and the rest of the family who have supported me.

George Orwell once said that he wrote for four reasons:

1. Sheer egotism, which for him was the joy of being talked about and remembered.
2. Aesthetic enthusiasm, which was about choosing and arranging the words and chapters in the right order.
3. Historical impulse, which is about storing information up for posterity.
4. Political purpose, with "politics" being used in the widest possible sense, which is about pushing the world in a particular direction.

Focusing especially on the final point, this book was written not only in recognition of the very great importance of the public sector in current times but also to recognize the challenges of that sector going forward. These are pressures of cost, political will, and the continued need of the citizen for public services, as well as the impact of technology.

Throughout the text, I have relied on many different opinions, as evidenced by the number of references contained within this book. I would also like to thank those contributors for their insight and inspiration. Where specific products and services are mentioned within the text, this is by way of example and although doubtless they are fine organizations, there are no commercial relationships between them and the author, and no recommendation should be inferred from their inclusion.

About the Author

Tony Boobier is an independent advisor with over 40 years of broad-based international experience who supports startups, established organizations, and individual executives. Qualified in engineering, marketing, insurance, and supply chain management, and having held several fellowships, he has a deep understanding of the practical applications of advanced analytics and AI for improving the management and delivery of products and services.

A frequent public speaker and commentator on industry matters, especially the use of AI, he is a strong advocate for the use of business-led, enterprise-wide analytics and AI to enhance service and reduce cost. He is the author of *Analytics for Insurance: The Real Business of Big Data* (2016); *Advanced Analytics and AI: Impact, Implementation, and the Future of Work* (2018); and *AI and the Future of Banking* (2020), all published by Wiley. He lives near London, UK.

Introduction

There is a price to be paid for everything. The enormous payments made by individual governments around the world to support economies as a result of the COVID-19 pandemic will need somehow to be funded. The additional impact of other subsequent world events also cannot be discounted.

Cutting the costs of the public sector budget is inevitably in the cards, sooner or later. Even so, previous experience has shown that an approach of austerity to control costs isn't always best. Austerity as a solution has historically been seen as a major contributor to political tension, as evidenced by governmental approaches following the global financial crisis of 2007–2008. Some suggest that austerity could be the best and perhaps only way forward, especially when we are in a low-interest-rate environment; low interest rates are usually only a temporary relief, and higher interest rates do not normally provide a panacea.

The mood to managing debt has changed from a decade ago. Then, Germany's Chancellor Angela Merkel pressured the European states to reduce their debt levels to preserve the integrity of the Euro. Nowadays, economists such as Ulrik Knudsen, appointed Deputy Secretary General of the Organisation for Economic Co-operation and Development (OECD) in 2019, are calling austerity "an old-fashioned way of thinking" and one that leads ultimately to isolationism.

Although perhaps in a less dramatic form, it is almost certain that there will be a financial impact on the public purse as a result of the pandemic. Savings will have to be made. For many sectors of society, and despite political reassurances, essential reductions will be made in public funding. While the proverbial barrel is not yet dry, the amounts available from governments to prop up public services are likely to diminish. This scarcity will affect services as diverse as policing, social services, medical care, and public administration. It will also affect both national and regional strategies. At an individual level, it will affect the funding of leisure services for the public, as well as how we are policed. It will also have an impact on matters as mundane as how often the streets are cleaned.

All of these effects, and others, will force us to find ways of providing services at lower cost. Budgetary costs will inevitably translate into manpower reduction and possibly higher levels of unemployment. For many sectors, there is likely to be a struggle to maintain the level of current services, and the potential is for the frequency and quality of public services to start to fall below our expected standards.

We should not underestimate the size of the public sector. In the majority of countries, public sector expenditure represents 35 to 60% of their GDP. At a global level, between 14% and 19% of all employees are paid from the public purse. Indirectly they are funded by the taxpayer. While one simple argument is to increase the taxpayers' contribution, invariably there are political pressures that relate to that option as a remedy, not least that few political parties have been successful at reelection on a ticket that promises to increase taxation.

The aspect of politics equally cannot be overlooked – although this is not meant to be a book that is political in nature. Rather, governments need to prioritize public services so that funding can be appropriately allocated. This in itself is no small task. How might a government prioritize policing over healthcare, or street cleaning over the care of the elderly? The reality is that all these sectors will need to be maintained in one way or another.

Having created a dark picture for the future, I've written this book as an antithesis to that situation. It aims to provide insight and a way forward, whereby the quality and efficiency of almost all types of public services can be improved through the effective use of data, advanced analytics, and artificial intelligence. It helps provide a road map for an analytically infused future in public services, where improvements can occur (or, at the very least, the quality of services can be maintained) at no additional cost (or maybe even at a reduced cost) to the taxpayer.

Recent developments in analytics and AI are timely. They coincide with our time of greatest need. The advent of ubiquitous devices providing multiple data points, together with new forms of analysis, helps create new insights that will inevitably affect the way in which public services are undertaken. The advent of 5G and ultimately quantum computing will also improve the quantity and quality of data collection and its analysis. However, we need to recognize that this will not be a world taken over by data scientists and computer systems, but rather that there is a need for experienced and trusted practitioners (who might be called "traditionalists") to ensure that there remains a balance between essential services and effective technology.

Effective implementation requires experts in their fields to be able to interpret the output from data, and from this to create new business models and working practices. This is not simply a matter of digitalizing the present, but also one of reimagining the future.

This book has been written principally for three groups.

First, it is for those directly employed in the public sector who will be faced with the challenge of maintaining and in some cases even improving public services, yet are concerned about or maybe even have a fear about the technologies likely to be used. Those people in this group are key stakeholders, as it will be their knowledge and experience that will play an essential part in the transformation. The range of those involved will extend from those at an operational level to those who act at an executive level. Both of these groups, and all those in between, will benefit from having a single reference point into a complex area.

Second, the book is for those data scientists and AI experts who, while having a knowledge of the "pure" elements of data management and AI will nevertheless have limited appreciation of the key business drivers of various public sector activities, and without whom it will be more difficult to understand how technologies might be best implemented. The nature of the advanced analytics and AI boom will necessarily require a great increase in those who have requisite technology skills. This second group may comprise mature candidates who have decided to retrain to keep up with the times, and also comprise new entrants who have chosen technology as their preferred career.

The third group is a critical component to the process of transformation. These people are those who sit in the Office of Finance and whose job it will be to identify likely returns of investment and also to measure the benefits that accrue. Although effective implementation of AI will bring a combination of hard and soft benefits, it is this group that is most likely to want to measure the financial benefit of AI transformation, especially as the greatest pressure will be on financial control and constraints. For many organizations, the topic of risk management also sits within the Office of Finance, usually assisted by additional forms of governance.

Despite there being many different elements within the public sector, which might be described as "vertical components," there are also key generic features that apply across almost all of them. Better understanding of these generic features or "horizontal components" leads to greater improvement in knowledge transfer and facilitates a move away from what is seen by many to be a siloed mentality, toward what will be a more holistic approach to the provision of public services.

The scope and breadth of public services is so wide as to render it virtually impossible to cover each and every service in complete detail. Therefore the book will consider some of the key public services, which are dealt with as individual chapters, such as healthcare and defense, but otherwise bundles together other services. This bundling is not arbitrary but rather follows the grouping of public services in the UK Government, which, while not perfect, suffices to provide a framework for the text.

Throughout the book, progress to date in different public sectors will be evidenced where possible by documented case studies that are already in the public domain.

Beyond all this, there are also geographical and demographical issues to consider. The topic of public services has international scope, which is overlaid by cultural aspects and differing types of governmental attitudes. This potentially leads to different nuances in terms of implementation and adoption. Invariably there will also be a different response to some of these ideas dependent on the demography and attitude of the citizen themselves.

The book adopts three key precepts: First and foremost, that it is the citizen who needs to be the overriding concern in these transformations. All that will happen going forward must necessarily be in the interest of the citizen who has to engage with the process, either directly or indirectly. This level of engagement might demand that the citizen needs to undergo some shifts in thinking, and to have a change of mindset. One of these changes will necessarily relate to the topic of data capture, its security, and how this data is used. Some citizens, perhaps even a sizeable proportion, will be concerned about this development. The book will necessarily reflect on the role of the State, dealing with some of the implications that attach to that consideration, and how this particular challenge might be addressed going forward.

Public opinion is mixed on the use of AI in the public sector. A 2019 YouGov survey reported that nearly half of people (45%) don't like the idea of humans not being involved in decisions that affect them:

- 49% thought that the public sector should understand AI more before they start to use it.
- 24% think it will lead to job losses.
- 23% think that there won't be any benefits for local authorities if they use AI.

- 25% worry about public accountability.
- 23% worry about decisions being made logically rather than ethically.[1]

In social services, according to feedback from the survey, practitioners believe, for example, that they "need to see the whites of their clients' eyes" rather than rely on algorithms.

The second precept is that it is possible to maintain and almost certainly improve service at the same time costs are being reduced. This may seem to be a paradox to many, yet the reality is that public services are not only often frictional in operation, but also comprise unnecessary management layers that technology will reduce. In other words, public services of the future will comprise a flatter, data-driven, and overall more efficient "friction-free" service. According to former UK Government chief operating officer Stephen Kelly, "The best way to protect the future of local council services and communities is through the smart use of technology."[2]

The third precept is that some of the changes discussed here may require an abandonment of traditional ideas. In a 2021 newspaper article, author Daniel Kahneman reinforced that point, and commented on the potential difficulties, saying, "When linear people are faced with exponential change, they're not going to be able to adapt to that very easily. So clearly, something is coming. . . . And clearly AI is going to win [against human intelligence]. It's not even close. How people are going to adjust to this is a fascinating problem – but one for my children and grandchildren, not me."[3]

The likelihood is that this isn't a matter that will wait for those future generations but rather that the need is more pressing in terms of the timescale involved. It will not only affect Kahneman's children and grandchildren, but almost certainly will affect him (and you) as well.

In a future for public services that has some degree of uncertainty, there are inevitable risks. It's a topic that will reemerge throughout this book. These risks were captured in the 2019 report for Zurich Municipal, entitled "Artificial Intelligence in the Public Sector," and are reinterpreted in Table I.1.

Many of these elements are relatively straightforward, but one of these, the Paradox of Automation, requires a little more explanation. The term originates from the book *Messy* by Tim Harford, based on the crash of Air France Flight 447 in June 2009. In it, Harford writes ". . . the more efficient the automated system, the more crucial the human contribution of the operators. . . . If an automated system has an error, it will multiply that error until it's fixed or shut down. This is where human operators come in. Efficient automation makes humans more important, not less "[4,5]

The Paradox of Automation considers the idea that it is unreasonable for humans to leave matters to automated systems for most of the time, and then pay attention only when there is an emergency or when things go wrong. It suggests that if and when human intervention is needed in a world that is more automated, then humans will find it difficult to take appropriate corrective action because of their absence of experience. The development of autonomous vehicles is referenced, for example, as a potential area of concern, as humans might only be needed when an emergency happens, but the principle also extends to the public sector, where matters of life and death could be involved.

TABLE I.1   Possible Risk Implications of AI in Public Services

Physical risks will continue to exist	Can appropriate skills and capabilities be developed quickly enough?	Accountability – who is at fault for failure in complex AI ecosystems?	Do policy makers really understand the technology and its impact?	"Dumb" vs. "Intelligent" AI/"Soft" vs. "Hard" AI
How will change affect employee well-being, their rights, and the nature of employment?	What is the best regulatory framework and how will the Government implement it?	Does the technology need to be owned, or is access to the technology enough?	How to cope with the "Paradox of Automation"	Are black box technologies appropriate in areas of sensitivity?
How can we ensure that algorithms and data are used ethically?	What might be the impact on equality/ human rights?	Can humans adequately supervise technology, including self-learning systems?	What is the impact of cyber risk and cyber fraud?	What new commercial risks might arise, and how can these be managed through better contract management?
Traditional vs. "Born Digital" services, that is, new services based on technology	What is the impact on interruption to business?	How will governance be managed? For example will it be "Open" vs. "Closed"?	What democratic oversight will be needed?	What new risk management skill sets are necessary?

The topic of implementation is also a key issue, especially as the public sector has its own considerations when compared to the private sector. This is dealt with in detail, including issues likely to arise and mitigating actions that may be appropriate. The speed of change also needs to be considered, especially within the context of implementation. Key drivers of the rate of change include the:

- Degree of pressure on the public purse
- Impact of pressure groups, especially, for example, in matters of scrutiny, data privacy, and security
- Response of organizations representing public sector employees
- Attitude of citizens to perceived improvements or deterioration in public services
- Degree to which governments need to put in place safeguards and adequate regulation
- Support or otherwise by the media and other social influencers
- Rate at which public services organizations accept and endorse advanced technologies into their strategy

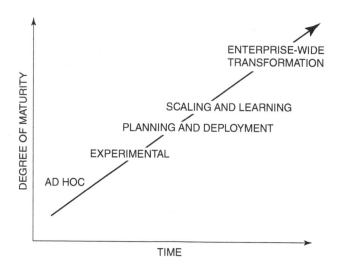

FIGURE I.1   Phases of Change of Maturity of AI in the Public Sector
Source: Adapted from "Artificial Intelligence in the Public Sector," IBM, 2021, https://www
.businessofgovernment.org/sites/default/files/Artificial%20Intelligence%20in%20the%20
Public%20Sector_0.pdf.

Figure I.1 reflects the phases the public sector may need to pass through when related to the degree of uncertainty of the possible outcome. It suggests a timeline that extends from the near future, say to 2025, and extends that period to as far out as 2050. By that later date, our understanding of the nature of public services themselves is likely to have changed. The question is whether we will recognize public services as being similar to those we experience today or if that change will be dramatic and unrecognizable. After all, 2050 is a mere few decades ahead of us, and is only slightly further in the future when compared to how far the new millennium is behind us.

THE POLITICAL PERSPECTIVE

In considering the use of AI in public services, there is invariably a political aspect that needs to be considered as well. The impact of the pandemic has resulted in many governments making huge payouts and taking on massive debts. The premise of this book is that they might be able and willing to carry on doing so for the moment, and may even continue in the short term to put their hands deeper into their proverbial pockets and provide more money. But there will be a point at which the ultimate bill will need to be paid. Financial engineering by governments may be useful in the relatively short term but cannot go on indefinitely. Some of this burden of repayment will fall on the taxpayer, either at a personal or business level, or will be reflected in savings through reductions in services, or perhaps both.

Neither of these is likely to be particularly attractive at the ballot box. The challenge for governments is not only how to settle the debts but how to implement the essential savings needed in the public sector while at the same time maintaining both public services and public confidence.

In his May 2021 *New Statesman* essay, former UK Prime Minister Tony Blair reflected on the many particular challenges that faced his own party. He referred to the need for political change against the "backdrop of a real-world transformation," which he describes as the "central political challenge of our time." Specifically considering public services, Blair says:

> *The way we teach and provide medical care and education will change dramatically, and therefore old ways of working will decline. New forms of social ownership will be needed to tackle the housing crisis. Solutions will often be practical, some more associated with traditional left thinking but some more with modern centre-right thinking. It will require steadfast adherence to values but complete agnosticism as to the means of implementing them.*[6]

Beyond this, Blair also considered the impact of technology on infrastructure, transportation, crime, and defense, and reminds the reader that "nations which are first-movers will get a disproportionate advantage." Blair is not the only political leader who has his eye on AI. In 2018, following an announcement that the French Government was to invest US$1.85 billion over a five-year program, French President Macron commented that "AI will raise a lot of issues in ethics, in politics, it will question our democracy and our collective preferences. . . . This leads me [sic] to the conclusion that this huge technological revolution is in fact a political revolution."[7]

In Germany, former Chancellor Angela Merkel compared the country's reputation for building prestige cars with their own country's developments in AI, saying, "the same brand 'Made in Germany' claim must also be a trademark in artificial intelligence," adding also that "people must be at the center of Germany's understanding of digitalization." There, as in many other countries, is skepticism about a digital future, especially misuse of personal data as well as fears regarding job losses. German Labor Minister Hubertus Heil aimed to reassure the electorate, saying in 2018, "Concerns over job losses . . . are very much real. By 2025, some 1.3 million jobs will have been replaced with artificial intelligence but . . . another 2.1 million jobs will have been created."[8]

The picture seems to be the same everywhere you look. Countries politically recognize the importance both of AI and in establishing some form of digital leadership. For many, this is mainly in order to challenge both the United States and China. However, these countries also recognize complex issues of data security, privacy, and intention. Adopting and implementing an AI strategy, while important at a national level, is unlikely in itself to be a vote winner, especially where job losses might be involved.

In conclusion, this book seeks to recognize the impact of data, analytics, and advanced systems in current and future public services. Beyond this, it aims to reflect the differences in nature between varying types of public service, as well as the variation of usage across different geographies. It argues for data-driven transformation as a panacea for the financial pressures brought on by the recent pandemic, but suggests that in any case there is a degree of inevitability that public services will become data and AI driven, and that many if not all of these changes would happen regardless.

In the next chapter, it is recognized that there is likely to be a varying degree of knowledge and understanding of readers of technology matters, so a level-set is initially provided for those with a more basic understanding. Those with greater technical knowledge may choose to pass over this section. It also is an appropriate time to provide some basic insights into the more modern areas of 5G and quantum computing. The concept of "Public Sector 4.0" is also introduced.

NOTES

1. Dsouza, R. (2021). "Global: More People Worried Than Not About Artificial Intelligence," YouGov, November 18. today.yougov.com/content/39497-global-more-people-worried-not-about-artificial-in.
2. Zurich Marketing. (2019). "Artificial Intelligence in the Public Sector." Zurich, September 26. https://www.zurich.co.uk/news-and-insight/artificial-intelligence-in-the-public-sector-the-future-is-here.
3. Adams, T. (2021). "Daniel Kahneman: 'Clearly AI Is Going to Win. How People Are Going to Adjust Is a Fascinating Problem.'" *The Guardian*, May 16. https://www.theguardian.com/books/2021/may/16/daniel-kahneman-clearly-ai-is-going-to-win-how-people-are-going-to-adjust-is-a-fascinating-problem-thinking-fast-and-slow.
4. Rubenstein, M. (2019). "Air France Flight 447: Ten Years On." *Degrees of Certainty* (blog), May 8. https://degreesofcertainty.blog/2019/05/08/air-france-flight-447-ten-years-on/.
5. Harford, T. (2016). *Messy: The Power of Disorder to Transform Our Lives*. Riverhead Books.
6 Blair, T. (2021). "Tony Blair: Without Total Change Labour Will Die." *New Statesman*, May 11. https://www.newstatesman.com/labour-in-crisis/2021/05/tony-blair-without-total-change-labour-will-die.
7. Thompson, N. (2018). "Emmanuel Macron Talks to WIRED about France's AI Strategy." *WIRED*, March 31. https://www.wired.com/story/emmanuel-macron-talks-to-wired-about-frances-ai-strategy.
8. Brady, K. (2018). "Germany Launches Digital Strategy to Become Artificial Intelligence Leader." DW, November 15. https://www.dw.com/en/germany-launches-digital-strategy-to-become-artificial-intelligence-leader/a-46298494.

CHAPTER 1

Understanding the Key Building Blocks of Progress

1.1 INTRODUCTION

This chapter provides a limited introduction to AI and its various subcomponents, recognizing that there will be some people for whom the entire topic is new. It also covers the different elements of the AI agenda and seeks to provide a simple explanation. Those readers with greater technical knowledge may choose to pass quickly through this section.

The idea expressed by many is that a new fourth age, often known as one of advanced technologies, has started, which is a natural progression from the previous eras of steam, hydrocarbons, and basic digitalization. The term *Industry 4.0* is often heard in that context and this book might now reasonably be called *Public Sectors 4.0*. Those involved in public services as leaders, practitioners, or recipients are unlikely to recognize a step change overnight, but the reality is that this is a concept that is likely to move relatively quickly, especially in the context of current and near-time future financial pressures.

For many, the starting point is the expression *Big Data*, which reflects the increasing amount of digitalized information becoming available. The growth of the amount of data means that we are being swamped with information, and increasingly need expert systems to help us make sense of the data collected. AI is viewed not only as being one of the ways in which insight can be obtained from this mass of information, but also as a way in which this information is best put to use.

While many people discuss AI and its impact, the reality is that the topic is still surrounded by a degree of hype. What many think of as AI would be described by more experienced users as being advanced analytics. Nevertheless, there is active progress being made in the area. When once there was excitement about an autonomous computer playing Kasparov at chess, nowadays systems exist that competitively play the board game *Go*, which is considered one of the more complex of traditional human games. Computers already play and beat humans at poker, which for many is thought to be a card game that exercises the innate cunning of the human brain.

At a national level, countries are actively encouraging AI-centered strategies. In Germany, the Federal Ministry of Education and Research, also known as BMER, exists to support research, identify potential areas of development, and avert danger,[1] while in the UK, the UK Government has also published an AI roadmap.[2]

One area of concern relates to control and ethics, and overwhelmingly the introduction of AI seems to lend itself more to private enterprise rather than to the public sector. Later in this book we particularly consider some of those issues and contrast the associated opportunities and risks, as well as implementation strategies.

It's helpful to understand what is meant by AI. In his 1990 book *The Age of Intelligent Machines*,[3] Ray Kurzweil provides one (perhaps tongue in cheek) definition: "The art of creating machines that perform functions that require intelligence when performed by people." The famous Turing Test also aimed to provide a methodology for demonstrating AI, in that a system was asked a series of questions by a human, with the test being whether the human could detect if the answer was being given by a machine.

1.2 KEY BUILDING BLOCKS OF DATA SCIENCE AND AI

The core element of AI is data science, which, according to the UC Berkeley School of Information, comprises the four key phases of data acquisition, data maintenance, analysis, and communication.[4] Beyond these, we will briefly consider machine learning and hard and soft AI, and review some of the risks and advantages involved.

1.2.1 Data Acquisition

This comprises capturing data from multiple sources, including its conversion from raw signals (as in the case of audio or visual data) or multiple devices into useful data input. A data acquisition system is one which converts this raw information using a combination of specialized software and hardware.

1.2.2 Data Maintenance

This usually comprises data cleaning, which removes errors, de-duplicating, transforming the data (through processes known as normalization and standardization), feature selection (to ensure that only relevant data is used), and ultimately storage, which comprises keeping it in a secure location.

As part of data maintenance, but also at the earlier stage of acquisition and maintenance, data may be removed, replaced, or even added to. Data is sometimes described as being "noisy," which is usually considered to contain too many outliers of information. As a result, data can be modified or "tidied up" by replacing the outliers with data taken perhaps from the median or mode of the data set.

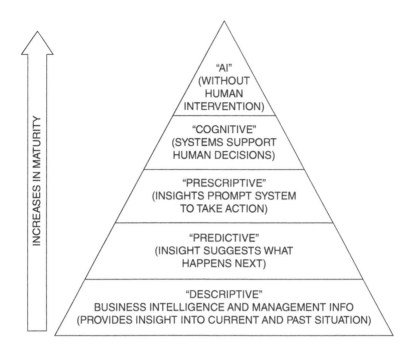

FIGURE 1.1 Pyramid of Analytical Maturity
Source: From Tony Boobier, *AI and the Future of Banking* (Wiley, 2020).

1.2.3 Analysis

This is commonly considered as the stage at which useful information is drawn from the data. Analysis will help understand the characteristics of the data, including its mean, mode, median, and what might be the standard variation, as well as the skewness of the data (which characterizes whether the tail of the data is heavy or light relative to its normal distribution).

Analysis may comprise two key approaches: univariable, where the analysis explores the relationship of other information relative to one variable, or bivariable, where the analysis explores the relationship relative to two variables, often visualized through some sort of scatter plot or bar plot. Analysis (or analytics) typically has three forms: descriptive, predictive, and prescriptive. Collectively they create a hierarchy or pyramid of analytical maturity, leading to AI at the pinnacle of the pyramid (Figure 1.1). Machine learning systems also help to create appropriate analysis. In essence, the overreaching aim of analytics is to provide actionable insight from which improved operational decisions can be made.

1.2.4 Communication

This relates to how the insights taken from the analysis of the data are transmitted, usually in the case of visualizations. These are often in the form of dashboards, which provide a graphical representation of the data that is easier for the layperson to understand.

1.2.5 Machine Learning

The concept of machine learning is one of switching the graphical axes between the investigatory and analytical process.

- Traditionally, the model comprises "Data + Logical rules = Answer." This customary approach requires the user to understand what the logical rules are and then to program them into the process.
- With machine learning, the problem is viewed through the other end of the proverbial telescope, typically "Data + Answers = Logical rules."

It follows that if the behavior of a system or relationship between sets of data can be identified and the process can be coded, then there is no need for machine learning. However, in many cases, the relationship between data and information is not obvious, and the machine system is required to discover it.

1.2.6 Artificial Intelligence

AI generally falls into two categories:

1. Soft AI, whereby the system works alongside a human decision maker.
2. Hard AI, whereby the system replaces the human decision maker.

We generally currently consider AI to be the combination of the series of technical capabilities. These comprise machine learning but also extend to facial analytics, voice analytics, palm analysis, and others. At a basic level, AI comprises a combination of advantages and risks, which are summarized in Tables 1.1 and 1.2, and are considered in more detail later in the book

1.2.7 Advantages and Disadvantages

TABLE 1.1   Advantages of AI

Superhuman capability	There are many situations where computers outperform human capability in terms of accuracy. This occurs in medicine (e.g., in the detection of cancer), but also in routine administrative tasks.[5]
Speed	Speed of execution is much higher than in human-based systems, with some tasks taking only split seconds. As a result, there are opportunities for improvements in operational efficiency and productivity.
Scalability	Changing the scale of a human-based system, either by way of increase or reduction in scale, involves training, physical property or asset management, and human resources (HR) contract management. Computerized systems, especially those supported by the cloud, are much more flexible.
Reliability	AI systems are more reliable, don't need days off or holidays, and the quality of work output is not affected by tiredness or illness.
Low unit cost	Once an automated system is in place, the cost per additional unit of work such as an action or decision is extremely low.
Flexibility	Algorithm-based models can be relatively easily changed, and in some cases the machine can make the changes itself. Additional training for operators and creation of new processes are not needed.

TABLE 1.2 Disadvantages of AI[6]

Data protection	Personal and medical data is highly sensitive and its loss can have serious and important consequences. The risk can be increased where data comes from different sources or where there are extended supply chains that rely on the information. Therefore, data security is a critical part of system design.
Data poverty	In the public sector, it is important to have a full spectrum of data. However, not all citizens or social groups have access to appropriate technology through which to provide this information.
Bias and discrimination	Although one of the advantages of AI is greater reliability, there are risks of bias and discrimination, especially if data models are skewed or there are inherent biases in the data sample collected. Also, computer systems cannot distinguish between ethical and nonethical decisions.
Transparency	The complexity of some of the more advanced models used in analysis makes them difficult for humans to understand, when compared to traditional statistics-based approaches. Proprietary "black box" systems make it impossible to understand the models that sit within them.
Overfitting and spurious correlation	Overfitting is a phenomenon where a model is suitable for a specific set of data, but is not valid for more general data sets. Spurious correlation occurs when a system detects a relationship between variables but it is either coincidental or fails to recognize the impact of another unidentified variable.
Deception and fraud	The creation of deception and fraud in expert systems usually requires expert skill, but may be more easily implemented where there is no human oversight to detect abuse of the system.
Setup costs	Building an advanced system from scratch is often difficult and costly. Return on investment calculations may be optimistic, and implementation may fail to adequately consider execution risks such as lateness of delivery and unsuitability for a system's purpose.

1.2.8 Four Key Focuses for Future AI

In her April 2021 article "The Future of AI in Insurance," Karin Golde invited readers to consider the future of AI, suggesting that there are likely to be the following four key fundamentals going forward.[7]

1. *Improved Management of Bias*

Models will need to be continuously monitored to prevent bias. Golde says that two key elements will need to form part of the solution to this particular problem. First, organizations will need to develop new ways of constantly monitoring and measuring bias. Second, humans will become more aware of issues of bias and will expect organizations to be able to explain outcomes, especially if decisions have been artificially generated. Relating this specifically to the public sector, those receiving public sector support will be even more critical of results if they appear to result in a disadvantage or the situation does not improve for those groups that the public sector is aimed at supporting.

2.   The Importance of Domain Expertise

Domain experts will matter even more. In this context, Golde provides a reminder that technical knowledge by itself is not enough and that technologists need to have some understanding of the domain or sector that they are working in. (This is a point that was also made in the author's own 2016 book *Analytics for Insurance*, which provided technologists with an understanding of the insurance market, and provided insurance practitioners with an understanding of the technology sector specifically related to data and advanced analytics.)

Currently the commonly accepted approach is that technologists and subject matter experts work together in a single team, usually coordinated by some sort of project leader. In this way, a rounded solution can be obtained that supports the interests of all key stakeholders. In the future, there is likely to be a coming together of technology and subject matter expertise into a new sort of hybrid role. In the private sector, there is already evidence of this happening, for example, in online investment banking.

Meeting this requirement in the context of public services is more difficult. The need for a convergence of technology and subject matter expertise is understood, but the public sector is not homogeneous in terms of its needs. Different domain expertise will arise in policing compared to, say, in health services. Even so, there are likely to be some horizontal capabilities that arise, such as the development and use of virtual advisors or chatbots. Providers of emerging technologies will also need to be sensitive to the special nature of public services, which has particular characteristics such as duty and public service, even if what seem to be common traits manifest themselves in different forms. By way of example, the organizational drivers (or organizational imperatives) of an effective policing service are different from those of effective healthcare or of education, even if the underlying spirit of duty remains more or less the same.

While it's doubtful that police officers or those serving in the military truly consider themselves in the same peer group as those working in the care of the elderly, they are all in effect under the same public service umbrella, and their public service values and true colors are almost always revealed in times of emergency.

3.   Increasing Importance of Unstructured Data

Data can be described as structured (i.e., originating from databases and already in an organized form) or unstructured (i.e., data that originates in many forms from many different devices). Unstructured data typically might include video or voice information. In the public sector, unstructured information might specifically come, for example, from greater analysis of MRI images in healthcare, or through facial recognition in policing or immigration services. The particular challenge of unstructured data is that it is likely to grow much more quickly than structured data. Expert systems will be essential to help manage both its extent and variety and to ensure that appropriate actionable insight is obtained.

4. The Need for Feedback Loops to Improve

This relates to the constant monitoring and testing of machine-driven outcomes to ensure that they match what is reasonably expected. This implies that there may still need to be some sort of manual process against which automated outcomes can be effectively benchmarked. One particular downside of automatic feedback loops is that while they are effectively improving the machine learning capabilities of the system, they do so by exploiting existing weaknesses in the system.

In other words, these existing weaknesses show themselves through poor service provided to individual members of the public, or perhaps to entire groups. This type of problem has to be of particular concern to the public sector, especially when the flaws are discovered in automated systems that are already in the process of development. These can relate to ethical decisions or even of bias. Individuals (or groups) cannot be allowed to suffer or be disadvantaged as a result of a faulty machine learning process in the early stages of implementation or in some sort of pilot scheme, even if the end result ultimately leads to an overall improvement in the service.

1.3 QUANTUM COMPUTING

In 2011, *TIME* magazine's article "The Year Man Becomes Immortal"[8] suggested that if processing power doubled at its current rate of every three years, then by 2023, some computers would have the processing power of the human brain, and by 2045 they could be 100,000 times more powerful, as illustrated by Figure 1.2. Ten years after that original article, perhaps it is for the reader to judge the accuracy of that statement.

Although advances in computing power as well as how data is stored and analyzed remain relatively linear, all the signs indicate that there will be some form of step change in these capabilities going forward. The scale of change could be to such a degree and at such a speed that few are truly ready for it. The ongoing development of quantum computing systems is likely to make this happen even more quickly and will be a key feature of a transformed society – and transformed public sector. One report suggests that a new quantum computer has already been created that can carry out calculations that are "one hundred trillion times faster than a classic supercomputer."[9] While some might suggest that this is still theoretical, the first use cases may be available in three to five years.

1.3.1 What Is Quantum Computing?

Many will be familiar with the concept of modern computing, which operates in a binary way – that is, in a series of 1s and 0s. In practical terms, computing systems are not concerned with actual numbers but rather with "states of existence" that represent 1 and 0. These binary states might, for example, comprise the voltage in a circuit, with

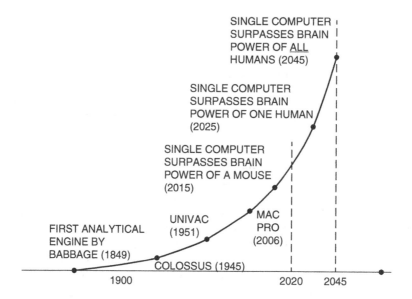

FIGURE 1.2   Singularity and Immortality
Source: Adapted from *TIME*, "The Year Man Becomes Immortal," 2019, http://content.time
.com/time/interactive/0%2C31813%2C2048601%2C00.html.

say 5V representing 1 and 0V representing 0. Alternatively, 1 and 0 could relate to the specific direction of magnetism in a magnetic drive. Quantum computing in theory allows both 1 and 0 to exist at the same time.

Using the analogy of a spinning coin for a binary-based approach in a traditional computer, the coin physically might land on a head or on a tail, with either representing the 1 or 0. On the other hand, quantum computing is a concept that reflects the state of the coin while it is actually spinning. It's a complex notion and there are many more detailed books already written about this. Invariably there will be more to come.

Some suggest that quantum computing could lack the flexibility of conventional computers and might not be able to perform specialist tasks. The reality is that how these new technologies will be used is probably not yet known. What needs to be taken into account is that preparations might soon need to start for a step change in technology, and that just as the public sector might be increasingly coming to terms with advanced analytics and AI, there could well be a tsunami of yet newer and more advanced capabilities around the corner.

According to experts, the ability of these supercomputers to network or work together might also lead to significant advances by making more accurate predictions on critical issues such as population, climate, and economic models. These estimates could be of a super-sized scale, macro in nature, and capable of quick analysis of hugely complex data sets.[10]

1.3.2 Impact on Cybersecurity

One of quantum computing's key areas of simultaneous threat and benefit is that of encryption. Traditional security methods are based on encryption and decryption keys. Once someone has access to the decryption key then they have access to all the information available. The concept of quantum computing suggests that there will be greater security. However, at the same time, the worry is that quantum will make all codes capable of being cracked, as a quantum system could try every combination of codes simultaneously. As a result complete security might prove to be impossible, which may have a particular impact on the safety and security of remote devices.

1.4 PROLIFERATION OF DEVICES

It's already possible to recognize the sharp rise in the number of connected devices, brought about by the relative ease that microchips can be incorporated into household devices, personal devices, vehicles, and what seems to be almost everything else (Table 1.3).

The massive proliferation of devices will result in them being almost everywhere. There appears to be potential for massive impact on the public sector, typically:

- Monitoring of climate and management of pollution
- Monitoring of drinking water, to measure purity and available quantity
- Monitoring of wastewater, to detect disease
- Predictive maintenance of machines and vehicles that support the public sector ecosystem
- Increased defense, through continuous checking of vital national infrastructure
- Improved transportation, through reduced congestion and control
- Population management and greater surveillance, which is more controversial and is considered in more detail in Chapter 11

TABLE 1.3 Number of Connected Devices[11]

Year	Connected Devices (billions)	Per person
2003	0.5	0.08
2010	12.5	1.81
2013	20	2.79
2015	25	3.41
2020	40	5.18
2040	95+	10.22

As these devices collect data, there has also been a massive rise in digitally stored information, and few would argue against this trend continuing (Table 1.4). The growth in the amount of data collected will also have a significant impact on the future of the public sector.

Key issues that may emerge from this proliferation of devices and stored data are considered in Table 1.5.

TABLE 1.4   Growth in Volume of Digitally Stored Information[12]

Year	Exabytes of Data*
2005	132
2015	8,251
2025	213,381
2035	6,172,127
2045	178,531,657

* An exabyte is a billion gigabytes.

TABLE 1.5   Issues That Emerge from Data Proliferation

Key Issue	Interpretation
Interpretation	The challenge of interpreting the vast amount of information and of obtaining sensible insights when faced with amounts of data that are already beyond human interpretation
Dependence	The degree to which industries and sectors are dependent on the information, including within the public sector
Personal freedom	The increased challenge of going offline, and whether this will ever be possible for those who wish to opt out.
Communication	The need for an improved communications infrastructure, which provides adequate bandwidth and coverage everywhere, without there being data holes
Social parity	The disparity between the "haves" and the "have nots," linked perhaps to the accessibility and quality of mobile personal devices, and the risk that the information explosion will reveal and exacerbate inequalities rather than flatten them.
Greater vulnerability	Greater vulnerability to cyberattack, as a greater number of devices create a greater number of points of entry for cyber criminals.
Increased cybercrime	Increased impact of the consequences of cybercrime, leading to a probable growth in ransomware.
Risk of misinformation	Disproportionate impact of social media groups, which disrupt traditional communication channels, and an increase in the potential for fake news.
Leveling out	A leveling out of an information advantage between large- and small-scale players (i.e., the larger-scale players were once able to leverage their data advantage but this disparity might diminish in the future)

Observers also point to the trade-off between retailers and consumers, for example, where consumers are often willing to share personal information provided there is an accrued benefit. This is not a universally held position and there are some contradictions. Younger people appear in general to be more prepared to trade information than older people, although paradoxically the younger are also more suspicious of information being collected from them.

Viewing this issue from a public sector point of view, citizens may ultimately need to balance the aspects of sharing information against the benefit accrued by them at a personal level. The implication of opting out might lead to fewer benefits or less care. Ethically and morally, governments might find it problematic to provide less care to those who opt out of data participation for personal reasons, which might include both suspicion and fear.

1.5 5G AND THE IMPACT OF ADVANCED COMMUNICATIONS

The continuous development of advanced communications through 5G systems will also be a catalyst for change. As this technology progresses, the number and development of devices is likely to proliferate. The cost and technical issues involved in the rollout of 5G, especially for developing countries, is likely to result in some global disparity in the short to medium term, but the leveling out process is only a matter of time, especially as nearly two–thirds of the world currently is connected by the internet. According to Statista, "As of January 2021 there were 4.66 billion active internet users worldwide – 59.5 percent of the total global population. Of this total, 92.6 percent (4.32 billion) accessed the internet via mobile devices."[13]

5G is the term used to represent the next (fifth) generation of wireless communication technology. A new generation seems to come along about every decade and it is only a matter of time before 6G and 7G emerge. Overall, 5G facilitates a world that has traditionally only been imagined in science fiction, such as autonomous cars, drones, smart homes, and the development of precise, customized medicines. This new infrastructure is extremely high performance, and data flows through the system that is perhaps 100 times greater in volume than is experienced today. These new communication systems will transmit over much higher frequency signals than before; the downside is that they use wavelengths that are more prone to interruption. The impact of a reduced wavelength is that there will be a need to have a greater number of transmitting sites than is presently the case, perhaps as many as 10 times more, but it is thought that they will be smaller in size.

Countries that are users of 5G technologies are almost certainly likely to have a technological, commercial, and perhaps even military advantage. China is the current global leader in 5G, which in 2020 was thought to already have 1.9 million wireless stations in contrast to only 200,000 in the United States.[14] In his 2020 report "China's Challenge to the US Is for . . . the Future," US politician Shay Stautz refers to China's need to develop 5G particularly as a response to the problem of its aging population. He suggests that with AI solutions and other advanced technologies, new solutions will be created for China's health challenges, and it will be better at managing health-related costs. These issues are not unique to China, as there are global issues of skewed demographics with a greater proportion of an aged population. We go into this in more detail in Chapters 4 and 5.

1.5.1 Global Transformation

Most countries in the world have already started to pursue a 5G strategy. *The Economist* reviewed the rate of progress of the development of 5G at a continental level,[15] making the points that:

- The effect of the pandemic has been a major factor in the rate of development of 5G, with those countries (especially Asia) that took an early grip of the epidemic having made the best start.
- South Korea, Taiwan, and China are viewed as being among the leaders in the rollout of 5G technology. Progress has been assisted by a combination of factors that include government support, low-cost loans, and a strategic decision to focus on geographical coverage rather than speed. Regulatory support has also been an important consideration.
- In Europe, despite slower early progress, the pace for the use of 5G will likely pick up in 2021–2022, especially because a higher number of base stations have been deployed that will support industrial usage.
- In the Middle East and Africa, although the UAE, Saudi Arabia, and Kuwait were among the early movers globally (with systems up and running in 2019), progress elsewhere in Africa has been relatively slow. According to the report, only 45% of the population in sub-Saharan Africa had a mobile device in 2019.
- In North America, although there are some limitations in capability (at the time of this writing, the United States and Canada do not feature among the top 10 countries in terms of 5G speed), sufficient progress has been made to facilitate early commercial development.

Overall, the impact of the pandemic has increased the need for digitalization, as evidenced by the increase in online sales and services, automation, and the development of supply chains. This has accelerated the use of advanced analytics and AI, especially in sectors such as healthcare, which in many ways has become the "tip of the spear." For the wider public sector, the pandemic has provided a loud call to action for rapid digital transformation as the main way of reducing costs while maintaining service to the public.

1.6   PUBLIC SECTORS 4.0

The subtitle of this book is *The Creation of Public Sectors 4.0*; and it would be useful for readers to understand what is meant by that expression. The term Public Sectors 4.0

aligns itself to the notion of Industry 4.0; that is to say, that we are now widely thought to be in the Fourth Industrial Revolution. By way of context:

1. The First Industrial Revolution (Industry 1.0, although that term is seldom used) spanned the end of the eighteenth century and extended into the beginning of the nineteenth century. It represents the industrialization of industry through more widespread mechanization and the use of coal to provide power for steam engines. To some degree, the First Industrial Revolution was defined by the increased use of coal.
2. The Second Industrial Revolution (Industry 2.0) started at the end of the nineteenth century when there was massive improvement in industrial capabilities as a result of the impact of oil and gas, followed by the use of electricity.
3. The Third Industrial Revolution (Industry 3.0), which was in the second half of the twentieth century, is defined by the introduction of electronics, telecommunications, and computing, which were subsequently used to automate production. If this revolution were to be additionally defined by a particular source of energy or fuel, it would be nuclear energy.

What is now thought to be the Fourth Industrial Revolution (Industry 4.0) is now actively happening. The Fourth Industrial Revolution builds on the Third, in that it represents a convergence of technologies and capabilities such as data management, analytics, cloud, and AI. These together are leading to massive growth in the speed of innovation. As a phenomenon, the revolution is proving to be both expansive and disruptive, affecting almost all industries and professions in every country, and at a speed that far exceeds the impact of earlier transformations.

In what we might call Public Sectors 4.0, the collective impact of these new technologies on governments and the public sector cannot be overlooked. Whereas earlier revolutions were relatively linear in their progress, the exponential growth of ideas in this new revolution is placing significant challenges on the ability of all parts of industry and the public sector to cope. Governments' particular challenges are to ensure that there is appropriate leadership and to provide a governance framework to accommodate this progress. In addition, Public Sectors 4.0 will also affect people, both within the individual parts of the public sector and those citizens who look to the sector for safety, security, and the provision of adequate benefits.

There are some overlaps in terminology. Government 4.0 is another term that similarly describes the digitalization of the public sector, digitalization of the administration, and automation of public works. Bureaucratic processes such as those in this sector lend themselves especially to automation. All these changes also need to be made within the context of additional scrutiny and against a continuous threat of cybersecurity. With public sector expenditure in most countries representing 35–60% of GDP, digital transformation of the state is likely to represent one of the largest and most challenging areas.[16] This change forms what is a three-stage process, comprising:

1. Analog government, in which the government is mainly inward-looking and views itself as a provider of services.

2. E-government, which uses information and communication technology (ICT) but remains analog and one-directional in nature.
3. Digital government or Government 4.0, which is digital by design, all embracing and adopting the concept of government as a platform (GaaP), and principally data driven.

At the frontier of digital government, or Government 4.0, is an approach known as GovTech. Implicit in this idea are bidirectional information flow, transparency, and an inclusive approach to change across all parts of the public sector. The World Bank set out three key themes for GovTech:

1. Citizen-centric public services that are universally accessible
2. Simple, efficient, and transparent government systems
3. A whole-of-government approach to digital government transformation.[17]

1.7   CONCLUSION

In summary, this chapter not only sets the scene by describing advanced analytics and AI but also goes into more depth regarding more forward-thinking issues such as quantum computing and 5G/6G communications. There are plenty of other sources available on all these topics but they may be more highly technical than we require for our discussion.

The reality is that as technology marches forward, so does the challenge of complexity. Those experts at the heart of progress will by necessity be both very experienced and knowledgeable in these fields. There is a risk that these technical specialists (and perhaps tech-savvy management) will leave many other traditional practitioners behind as a new cadre of public sector professions emerges.

This does not, however, mean that the majority of the population or workforce need not be engaged in some way in the discussion about the use of data and AI, especially as almost all are likely to be stakeholders in this brave new world, which we describe as Public Sector 4.0. In this future place, there will be important ethical and moralistic issues to contend with, as well as technical considerations and their impact on the way that work in the public sector is done. To be able to engage in those discussions does not necessarily require that an individual is qualified in data science or is even a subject matter expert, but rather that they know enough about the topic to be able to take part in the debate and make an active contribution. While the private sector has been an early mover in terms of the adoption of technology, there is no doubt that public services will be impacted by these new data-driven approaches. The next chapters start to look at where these capabilities have already been deployed and what might be the next steps in their development.

1.8 NOTES

1. Federal Ministry of Education and Research. "Artificial Intelligence." https://www.bmbf .de/bmbf/de/forschung/digitale-wirtschaft-und-gesellschaft/kuenstliche-intelligenz/ kuenstliche-intelligenz_node (accessed November 16, 2021).
2. UK AI Council. (2021). "AI Roadmap." Crown copyright. https://www.gov.uk/government/ publications/ai-roadmap (accessed November 16, 2021).
3. Kurzweil, R. (1990). *The Age of Intelligent Machines*. MIT Press.
4. UC Berkeley School of Information. (2022). "What Is Data Science?" https://ischoolonline .berkeley.edu/data-science/what-is-data-science/.
5. Thorbecke, C. (2020). "AI-Powered Computer 'Outperformed' Humans Spotting Breast Cancer in Mammograms: Study."ABC News, January 2. https://abcnews.go.com/Technology/ai-powered-computer-outperformed-humans-spotting-breast-cancer/story?id=68031128.
6. Adapted from Ohlenburg, T. (2020). "AI in Social Protection – Exploring Opportunities and Mitigating Risks." Bonn: Deutsche Gesellschaft für Internationale Zusammenarbeit (GIZ) GmbH, April. https://socialprotection.org/sites/default/files/publications_files/ GIZ_ADB_AI%20in%20social%20protection.pdf.
7. Golde, K. (2021). "The Future of AI in Insurance." Insurance Thought Leadership, April 9. https://www.insurancethoughtleadership.com/emerging-technologies/future-ai-insurance.
8. *TIME*. (2019). "The Year Man Becomes Immortal." http://content.time.com/time/interactive/ 0%2C31813%2C2048601%2C00.html (accessed November 16, 2021).
9. Letzrer, R. (2020). "China Claims Fastest Quantum Computer in the World." *Live Science*, December 7. https://www.livescience.com/china-quantum-supremacy.html.
10. Ministry of Defence (MOD). (2014). "Strategic Trends Programme Global Strategic Trends – Out to 2045." Crown copyright. https://www.defencesynergia.co.uk/wp-content/ uploads/2018/03/20140821_DCDC_GST_5_Web_Secured.pdf.
11. EMC². (2014). "The Digital Universe of Opportunities: Rich Data and the Increasing Value of the Internet of Things." https://www.iotjournaal.nl/wp-content/uploads/2017/01/idc-digital-universe-2014.pdf.
12. Gantz, J., and E. Reinsel. (2011). "Extracting Value from Chaos." IDC's Digital Universe Study, sponsored by EMC.
13. Johnson, J. (2021). "Worldwide Digital Population as of January 2021." Statista, September 10. https://www.statista.com/statistics/617136/digital-population-worldwide.
14. Stautz, S. (2020). "China's 5G Challenge to the U.S. Is for . . . the Future." Foreign Policy Research Institute, November 24. www.fpri.org/article/2020/11/chinas-5g-challenge-to-the-us-is-for-the-future/.
15. The Economist Intelligence Unit. (2021). "The 5G Readiness Guide: Deployment Strategies, Opportunities and Challenges Across the Globe." Economist Intelligence, July 7. https:// www.eiu.com/n/the-5g-readiness-guide/.
16. McKinsey & Company. (2018). "Government 4.0 – The Public Sector in the Digital Age." https://www.mckinsey.de/publikationen/leading-in-a-disruptive-world/government-40-the-public-sector-in-the-digital-age.
17. "About GovTech." The World Bank. https://www.worldbank.org/en/programs/govtech/ priority-themes.

2

Office of Finance

2.1 INTRODUCTION

Although this book aims to consider public services' mitigating strategies, principally infused with analytics and AI, the reality is that the public sector has needed to deal with the challenge of austerity for some while. There is political pressure on all elements of government administration to not only control costs, but increasingly to reduce them without necessarily reducing services – or, if services do need to be cut back, then to a degree that is acceptable to the citizen. The natural tendency is to focus on the short term and apply short-term controls that manage the public purse, even though this may be detrimental to the longer-term picture.

Additionally, there is pressure due to reallocation of responsibilities. What was once a service being provided by central government is now becoming more and more devolved to local government, in many cases with only limited extra funding being made available, while at the same time remaining true to their agreed mission.

Because of this, local governments are being required to:

- Understand the true cost of services
- Implement improvements and efficiently track the financial benefit of those improvements
- Have a greater understanding of the issues of insourcing versus outsourcing

Funding services is not simply a matter of raising taxes or identifying new revenue streams, some of which may not be sustainable in the long term in any event. Rather, governments must both get a firm grip on cost control and have a clear view of the benefits of change. These elements are already firmly understood in the private sector, where there is greater understanding of cost control. Financial performance management (FPM) processes are relatively well-established capabilities, although there are many organizations that still use spreadsheet-based systems. Even so, these FPM systems in the private sector are themselves under threat as they increasingly blend with enterprise resource planning (ERP) systems.

Matters are often made more difficult as a result of the annual budget cycle, which usually requires a degree of negotiation and prioritization. There are few managers who will readily accept a reduction in their budget allocation and consequently the amount of projects undertaken may even increase toward the end of the financial year to ensure that there is no surplus of funds.

There is a direct link between cost control and demand management. Greater road traffic leads to increased pressure on the road maintenance budget. Pressure to provide more housing places creates more pressure on the infrastructure budget. Forecasting of demand, and therefore forecasting of future expenditure, is a key issue. Without adequate controls in place, new and sometimes politically-motivated pressures are placed on the systems. This invariably leads to reprioritization and ultimately can even affect broader strategies. Forecasting is a key part of effective decision making. Poor forecasting results in services being delayed or needing to be rescoped and, as a result, the benefits – hard or soft – may not be realized in a timely manner.

In the UK, the track record of accurate forecasting has been called into question. Poor estimating for the West Coast rail franchise in 2012, for example, created unforeseen costs to the taxpayer of £54 million, and this resulted in authorities placing greater focus on the forecasting process. Because of this, the UK Treasury commissioned the McPherson report,[1] which examined the quality of forecasting, and suggested greater emphasis on having both the right processes and culture.

In effect there are two elements to the forecasting process – qualitative forecasting and quantitative forecasting. Forecasting, especially of benefits, cannot be put to one side as being too difficult, as it is an integral part of the service delivery process. Effective forecasting also forms part of the signoff process by which major initiatives are processed.[2]

2.2   FORECASTING AND PUBLIC FINANCE MANAGEMENT

The need for effective forecasting is critical, as it:

- Ensures value for money
- Prevents overspending
- Means that other worthy projects are not missed

In their 2014 report, the UK National Audit Office also identified a number of root causes[3] of the poor production of accurate forecasts, including:

- Lack of understanding of forecasts by decision makers, so that they can accurately challenge the assumptions made and manage the risks
- Poor anticipation of new risks that might occur when there are new interventions or changes of decision
- Optimism bias, which needs to be removed to ensure that forecasts are realistic rather than optimistic. (In 2012, the UK Committee of Public Accounts noted that only one-third of government projects were delivered on time and on budget.)

- Budgeting being considered a "black box," in that the function was not adequately transparent and there were communication breakdowns between the finance function and departmental heads.
- Cultural issues relative to financial management were recognized, and that a failure of trust and transparency had meant that departmental heads failed to make the best use of the forecasting process.
- Finally, the masking of errors as a result of the practice of a department being able to draw down on previous underspending and to obtain late shifts in funding.

Improved forecasting improves the accuracy not only of individual projects but also of aggregate forecasts. In terms of the implementation of analytics, AI, and other technologically infused systems into public services, poor forecasting and weak financial control provide those who have vested interests in maintaining the status quo with ample ammunition to resist change.

2.3 FORECASTING

There are a number of ways that forecasting can be carried out. These normally fall into two categories, *qualitative* and *quantitative* forecasting.

2.3.1 Qualitative Forecasting

Qualitative forecasting is based on the advice of experts who are using their judgment, as opposed to the application of numerical analysis. In other words, it is forecasting that is based on individuals or teams applying their experience to anticipate future conditions. It's an approach that is very different from quantitative forecasting, which relies on historical data and trends to anticipate future states. Qualitative forecasting is best used when there is a possibility that the future outcome will be different from historic trends so that it becomes highly difficult or even impossible to extrapolate the future condition from what has gone before.

The approach also applies where:

- There is existing data, but that data is highly concentrated and may not apply to the wider spectrum of conditions.
- There is insufficient data, or perhaps data in a different field, that needs to be applied to a particular situation. In this case, forecasting may also be combined with intuition or, as some might less kindly describe it, with guesswork.

Examples of qualitative forecasting may include:

- Market research, where information is collected for example by user groups in a formatted approach.
- Opinions of knowledgeable people, although it is important to recognize the impact of bias – typically the over-optimism of sales staff.
- The Delphi method, a structured and facilitated approach that aims to gain an agreed consensus from a group of experts.

Qualitative forecasting may also comprise a two-stage approach. This is where initial intuitive forecasts are reviewed after there is some real experience, perhaps of the outcome of changes, and then the quantitative forecast might be updated.[4]

2.3.2 Quantitative Forecasting

Quantitative forecasting is based on data that can then be used to apply statistical methods, typically:

- **Causal Methods:** These are methods that link cause and effect based on one or more variables. The primary causal method is regression analysis, which is a statistical approach to forecasting change in a dependent variable based on changes in one or more other variables. It is also often known as curve fitting or line fitting.[5]
- **Time Series Forecasts:** These are forecasts based on historical patterns over regular time periods, and that assume that the same pattern will occur in the future. There are three key types of time series forecasts:
  1. Rule of thumb, which infers that any pattern of change will simply repeat itself into the future without alteration.
  2. Smoothing, where data removes outliers and uses averages rather than exact figures. As a result, historical trends are "smoothed."
  3. Decomposition, where historical trends are broken down into their key elements, perhaps considering cyclical or seasonal change, and predicts the impact of each of the elements.
- **Financial Performance Management Tools:** These systems originated in the private sector and are gaining greater acceptance in the public sector. Effective use of these systems allow users to:
  - Optimize operational expenses
  - Maximize long-term asset returns
  - Deliver sustainable services at competitive costs

Traditionally, experts would be adept at slicing and dicing tables of information so as to understand issues such as who, how, where, what, and when. Their ability to gain insight was critical in being able to make decisions, but the landscape changed so that there was a greater need for improved collaboration and interaction between a wider group than just analysts. This wider group included executives, professionals, and administrators who, between them, required what is generally now considered a "single version of the truth."

Work responsibilities also became more stratified with regard to the need to access information, and now there are generally considered to be three levels of involvement:

1. Primary, where individuals need access to correct and timely data so that they can make informed decisions.
2. Contributory, where individuals need information to support decisions elsewhere within the organization.
3. Status, which relates to individuals who need to know the status of any situation, and may only become aware of an issue when it falls outside accepted norms.

The impact of this stratification is that information has increasingly needed to be customized to meet the needs of individuals, albeit from the same core of data. In other words, it needs to relate to the individual's use and their responsibilities. As a result, the concept of integrated business intelligence emerged and has evolved to such a degree that:

- Data is now effectively integrated from a number of sources.
- It is provided consistently to a wider group through the use of a single data platform or query engine.
- It provides information to the right people, but also restricts information from others on a need-to-know basis.

Beyond this, new capabilities not only provide self-service options, but can set up automated delivery of defined information, which also provides for management by exception. While these capabilities might be used in many parts of an organization, the Office of Finance is unique in that it processes more information than others and thus is able to act not as a gatekeeper as it aligns expenditure against anticipated forecasts, but rather can advise key parts of the organization on future directions. Its role is also one of balancing short- and long-term management, as well as being able to provide detailed focus and convey the big picture.

2.3.3 Forecasting for Public Sector Transformation

Effective forecasting is critical not only in respect to new investments but also in identifying whether existing initiatives need to be expended, contracted, or re-scoped in some way. Forecasting needs to provide an accurate assessment of:

- Future demand
- Future cost
- Future manpower requirement
- Future revenues, where appropriate

In the public sector, poor forecasting can lead to poor decision making, potential reductions in service, and even the citizen as taxpayer needing to foot the bill of any error in prediction. Underspending can mean that opportunities are missed, whereas overspending can mean that important projects in other departments might need to be either reduced in scope or abandoned altogether.

In their 2015 report, the UK National Audit Office identified the four key issues of poor forecasting as being:

1. Poor or inadequate data
2. Over-optimism and lack of realism regarding assumptions
3. Lack of adequate modeling
4. Inadequate sensitivity and scenario planning

As a result, it recommended the use of high-quality data, skilled staff, well-reasoned assumptions and clear presentation of uncertainty, and decision makers' need to understand the nature and level of risk and the reasoning behind it. Their report calls for:

- Clarity regarding the aims of the forecast, including the required outputs
- Sufficient skills, including the need for analysts to be capable and experienced in the process of forecasting
- Use of accurate and timely data that is "fit for purpose"
- Adequate sensitivity analysis, recognizing that the process is that of testing how the outcome changes relative to variation in assumptions made
- Quality control, for example, in the use of a model used in one area and then reused in another where it is less suitable
- The need for clear presentation, including the use of effective visualizations, especially when communicating any uncertainty regarding estimates

Additionally, the National Audit Office suggested there were other, perhaps less technical, elements that are important in effective forecasting. These included a supportive department, an absence of time pressure, and an environment of "informed challenge."

2.3.4 Managing Risk and Uncertainty

The financial meltdown of 2007/2008 gave rise to increased attention on the management of risk and uncertainty, including the way these elements are communicated to key decision makers. The predominant aim is to give some degree of measurement of the risk and uncertainty of a forecast, usually in numerical form. At the outset, it is important to recognize the language involved, as "risk" and "uncertainty" are not the same thing. The aim of forecasters is to measure uncertainty, and then to quantify the underlying risk that attaches as a result.

At the end of the day, the forecaster needs to give some indication of the most likely outcome of a set of decisions[6] either by:

- Creating an envelope of possibilities, that is, a "confidence interval," with the likelihood that 90% of the outcome will fall within that envelope. This is often done using a Monte Carlo simulation, which is a way of combining uncertainties. As an alternative, statistical models such as the Black–Scholes model or decision trees might also be used. Black–Scholes is usually used for investment decisions, whereas the use of decision trees is a logically based approach that links decision choices with judgmental probabilities.
- Alternatively a scenario-based forecast might be used. This is where one or a small number of key assumptions or variables are changed. In this way, forecasters can incorporate assumptions, trends, knowns, and unknowns into a number of alternative outcomes and scenarios. In such a process, analysts might want to make

particular assumptions about key variables (e.g., technology changes, political impact, or demographic changes) and then reduce a wide range of scenarios to perhaps only two or three that can be evaluated in more detail.

Increasingly the mood is moving toward the "rolling forecast," which moves away from a single annual planning process to one that is more agile and continuous based on the most up-to-date information available. This allows better management of the process, including the management of risks, and allows resources to be more effectively applied on a more dynamic basis.[7]

2.3.5   Forecasting in IT Projects

As this section is fundamentally concerned with IT transformation, it might be helpful to spend a few moments on the matter of IT project forecasting. This seems at face value to be a particularly problematic area, especially in the public sector. This may be due to a number of key reasons, including:

- Overoptimistic expectation of the likely outcomes of IT transformation, especially where they attach to new initiatives
- Lack of critical analysis of a project as a result of "groupthink"
- Lack of understanding of risks and uncertainties, especially in a new area
- Overpromising by technology vendors of the value of their solutions
- In the early stages, an absence of knowledge
- Unrepresentative case studies and proof points that support the business benefit
- Poor benefit tracking and measurement

The road to technological change of public services is littered with disaster stories,[8] such as:

- One of the largest failed IT projects of all time is the UK's NHS attempt to create a national health record system with a price tag of £6.0 billion. It began in 2004 and its completion was planned to be by 2010 but it was canceled in 2011 at a cost of £9.8 billion, having realized only 2% of its expected benefits.
- The UK "FiReControl" project, which aimed at integrating 46 standalone fire control departments into nine regional centers. The planned £100 million project was started in March 2004, was scheduled to be finished in November 2007, and was canceled in December 2010 after £467 million had been spent on it.
- The planned six-year, $208 million California Department of Motor Vehicles modernization project to replace a 40-year-old legacy system that was the cause of delay, incorrect registrations, and other problems, was canceled in February 2013 after seven years and $134 million was spent.
- Pennsylvania canceled the modernization of its 40-year-old unemployment compensation system in August 2013 after it had fallen 42 months behind and had cost $60 million over its planned $106.9 million budget.

In more recent times, following criticism of misspending of the public purse leading in some cases to technology projects being abandoned, scrutiny is being increased. In 2021 the US Department of Justice (DOJ) Antitrust Division created the Procurement Collusion Strike Force, in reaction to anti-trust crimes, such as collusion, bid rigging, and price fixing, in public sector procurement. The government in Australia adopted what was called the High Value High Risk (HVHR) process in 2010 because of past cost overruns of more than AU\$2 billion "attributed to inadequate management of project business cases and procurements."[9]

As the public sector increasingly moves toward automation and AI, it is essential that this type of scrutiny be not only maintained but also solidified.

2.3.6   The Move Toward Activity-Based Costing

Activity-based costing (ABC) and activity-based management are seen by many as a route to improved control of the public sector purse.[10] At its most simple level, ABC is a way of translating input into output. To put it differently, by way of example, it identifies the individual costs of labor, plant, and materials to establish the cost of filling a hole in the road.

ABC is not always a straightforward calculation. Often, the cost of individual work activities is unknown, or is distorted in some way by unfair allocation of costs to the unit rate. As a result, the true cost of an output can be both wrong and, in many cases, unrealistic. The essence of ABC is to accurately track the elements of cost that apply to a particular function. Here is a good example by way of illustration of ABC: You (the reader) and three other people go into a restaurant. You order a cheap salad and the three others order expensive steak. When the meal is finished, the waitress presents the total bill and suggests that it be split equally into four. Alternatively, using an ABC approach, each diner would be presented with their individual bill for what they had consumed.

This chapter is not aimed at providing a detailed insight into the management of government budgets but rather at highlighting the challenges in being able to accurately measure financial benefit through the future use of AI and automation. The challenge is that traditionally there is usually only limited information on which to make decisions, and this is dependent on good-quality and accurate input. In addition, a government must also comply with standardized government accounting procedures that are in place not only to control costs but also to mitigate fraud and overspending.

2.3.7   Hard Benefits and Soft Benefits

An understanding of the likely and actual impact of change is a critical part of the transformation process. Roughly speaking, benefits fall into two categories:

1. **Hard Benefits:** These relate to calculating financial improvement when everything has been taken into account. It is likely that this part of benefit forecasting and management, as well as the calculation of financial risk and uncertainty, will be dealt with by the Office of Finance.

TABLE 2.1   Share of Transformation Effort That Includes Objectives

Type of Transformation	Degree of Effort % (of total effort)
Improve outcomes	47
Reduce cost	43
Improve speed and quality of services	42
Improve citizen opinion of public service	29
Increase revenue/income	20
Make economy more resilient	17
Deliver election promises	12

2. **Soft Benefits:** These relate to understanding and managing of nonfinancial improvements. These include not only the quality of the delivery process of a public service to the citizen but also citizens' perception of that service. These are areas that are most likely to rest in the domain of operational management. Although traditionally these may have been measured through survey, increased use of technology opens the door to more sophisticated methods. Additionally, social media analytics also provide a useful insight into how citizens feel about a public service, usually expressed in an informal and spontaneous way.

In their 2018 article "A Smarter Approach to Cost Reduction in the Public Services,"[11] consultants McKinsey & Company carried out a survey of 3,000 public servants across 18 countries on the topic of public sector transformation (see Table 2.1). This group comprised national, regional, and local governments as well as state owned enterprises. Their survey indicated that cost cutting was among the highest desired outcome of cost reduction, although improvements in service to citizens were also ranked highly (Table 2.1).

Focusing specifically on the cost-cutting objective, only 19% of those surveyed thought they were "completely or very successful" in achieving their objective. McKinsey's view is that the relatively low success rate principally arises because budget cutting was viewed by those participants as being the primary objective, as opposed to taking a wider transformational approach to their business. In most situations, budget cutting, which usually takes the form of headcount reduction, is the easiest element to measure.

McKinsey identified three key elements that lead to greater success:

1. More effective use of resources, especially those involved in implementing the change. 92% of "completely or very successful" transformations had adequate staffing to undertake the work needed during the transition.
2. The use of accrued savings to fund other citizen-focused initiatives, which resulted in a more meaningful purpose to any transition program and to greater motivation on the part of those involved.
3. Using data and analytics to transform the operation, with those organizations using a data-driven approach being twice as likely to succeed.

When considering these three elements, placing them into some order of importance is desirable. As this book considers the use of advanced analytics and AI as key components in a transformation program, it is tempting to place these at the top of the list, yet it is clear from the survey that the issue of staffing and motivation for change remain extremely important. That being the case, there are concerns that there are not enough skilled people currently available to successfully implement public sector change on such a wide scale; concerns about the speed at which new people are being trained and gaining adequate experience; and, perhaps most importantly, concerns about the inability of public services to attract these skills from the private sector.

Also, with transformational change likely to be imposed sooner or later as a result of the need for greater austerity, the possible inability to successfully carry it out in a "burning platform" could be more likely to constitute a disincentive to change, rather than an encouragement to do so.

2.3.8 Enterprise Resource Planning

In the 1980s, governments started to explore systems that were available in the private sector as part of what was described as "New Public Management" (NPM). One of the areas that gained traction was the concept of enterprise resource planning, or ERP. In 2020, the ERP market was estimated to be a massive $94.7 billion, and is predicted to reach $97 billion by 2024. The top users of ERP are the manufacturing sector, representing about one-third, whereas the public sector comes in at a more modest 6.93%, or about $6 billion (see Table 2.2). Two-thirds of implementations are cloud based (Table 2.2).[12]

Enterprise resource planning is recognized as providing one of the most significant ways of improving the operational efficiency of an organization, usually by combining multiple business procedures, applications, and departments in a single database. As a result, it provides real-time information to the user and gives a single holistic view of the enterprise.

TABLE 2.2   Top Consumers of ERP Software

% of Usage	Sector
33.66%	Manufacturing
14.85%	Information technology (IT)
13.86%	Professional or financial services
9.90%	Distribution and/or wholesale
6.93%	**Public sector and nonprofit**
4.95%	Healthcare
3.96%	Retail
3.96%	Utilities (oil, gas, electric, etc.)
1.98%	Construction
1.98%	Mining
0.99%	Education
0.99%	Transportation

Source: Panorama Consulting.[13]

A 2016 paper, "The Impacts of ERP Systems on Public Sector Organizations," identified no significant reduction in the cost of sales (in a private sector situation), general costs, and administration by revenue, although there was a significant reduction in the number of employees by revenue, suggesting that ERP is a proven methodology when organizations want to reduce headcount.[14] The report also identified improvements in productivity, inventory management, customer responsiveness, and implementation processes.

Looking specifically at that paper in terms of the public sector, a survey of 23 public service executives identified high satisfaction in the use of ERPs, particularly citing productivity improvements. According to their report:

> *Study in public healthcare in Greece found that there are many improvements caused by the implementation of ERP such as better data integrity, procedures and information quality, higher visibility and information timeliness, healthier communication among the nurses and the storage locations' personnel, automated generation of the clinic orders, lower transaction costs, standardized data definitions and procedures across departments, higher accuracy of billing procedures.*[15]

Additional studies conducted in India on the impact of ERP systems in small and mid-sized public services organizations found the main tangible benefits of implementing ERP systems to be productivity enhancement, inventory management, decreases in operating and maintenance costs, and cash management. On the other hand, nontangible or "soft" benefits were identified as being improvements in business processes, improved standardization of processes, and better visibility of information.

The relationship between ERP and AI should not be overlooked, especially in respect to the business case for change. Increasingly, AI allows ERP users to improve their systems using data-driven insights. In their 2019 report, Panorama Consultants suggested a series of key ways that AI might improve ERP systems:[16]

- Use of advanced analytics in order to identify customer trends
- Warehouse and demand management
- Improved forecasting
- Better financial management
- Improved interdepartmental processes, moving away from a silo approach
- Enhancement to field service, for example in the evaluation of service
- Process enhancement, including removal of frictional or non-added-value operations
- Improvement in the management of human resource, including individual performance management
- Sales automation

This book is not specifically about ERP, but recognizes the overlap between ERP, advanced analytics, and AI. This overlap implies that until public service organizations are more willing to embrace ERP, there will be a struggle to effectively use data and analytics within their organization. From an Office of Finance point of view, the ability of a public service organization to have a single view of the truth ultimately will contribute to greater clarity not only around the business case for change, but also around the benefits that have been accrued through transformation.

2.3.9   AI and Governmental Administration

The "administration," when used in the general context of government, is a term generally adopted to describe the managerial function of the control of both public services and, to some degree, its citizens, and that might also include local government. It is also taken to mean "public administration," which is the process by which the government manages public policy. It is usually synonymous with "government" but can also be "ministerial departments."

Looking specifically at the United States, "administration" refers to the executive part of the US government which relates to the ability of the President, as head of state and chief executive, to ensure that the "laws are faithfully executed" and that includes judicial and legislative powers. While AI may not have a direct role in government and the administration per se, both are extremely instrumental in the implementation of AI, especially in respect of its governance. Increasingly, there is also a move toward "government by algorithm," which is an expression used to reflect the use of algorithms, AI, and blockchain in regulation, law enforcement, and almost all parts of everyday life. It is considered by some to be relatively controversial, going beyond e-government and forming some sort of wider social machine where humans and technology converge into a single, interconnected system. In many ways, this relates to the AI transformation of public services into Public Sectors 4.0.

It is not surprising that some governments are taking a structured approach to the matter. For example, the US Congress tasked a new national AI office with orchestrating and administering additional AI research funding as well as formalizing AI practices. According to the Brookings Institute,[17] which is a not-for-profit public policy organization based in Washington, DC, there is expectation that a number of significant developments will emerge that will provide greater definition to the use of AI, including that the Office of Management and Budget (OMB) will give final guidance to federal agencies on when and how to regulate the use of AI. In its framing document, OMB recognizes that "the regulation of private sector AI is fundamentally different than the government's deployment of AI systems, leaving the latter for a separate document."[18]

The White House has also issued an executive order setting out the timelines for the use of trustworthy AI in federal government, and has also laid out requirements for an inventory of AI applications. This extends the work of the "government by algorithm" report that had determined that 45% of US government agencies have already looked into the use of AI and machine learning tools. Of these, only 12% at the time were described as being high in sophistication.[19]

Additional initiatives comprise:

1. The formation of the White House National AI Initiative Office to provide federal AI coordination as part of the National Defense Authorization Act.

2. The expansion of research through the development and funding of new AI research institutes at domestic universities.

Elsewhere (e.g., in Europe), the EU's new legislation on AI proposes new oversight for the use of AI in what the EU describes as high-risk situations such as the use of recognition technologies. In addition, (at time of writing) it is considering the issue of digital boundaries, which takes into account that the use of high-risk systems will operate across borders and may have a particular bearing on processes such as immigration.

Even so, concerns are being expressed about there being regulatory differences in the use of AI has the potential to dampen trade. European Union President Ursula von der Leyen has called for the need to act together.[20]

The European Commission has also put forward two other important acts[21] that are perhaps less important in the context of public services but are included here for the sake of completeness:

1. The Digital Markets Act, which is primarily about how larger-platform companies increasingly act as gateways or gatekeepers between business users and end users and enjoy an entrenched and durable position. This looks at the issue of unfair practices and weak contestability.
2. The Digital Services Act, which looks at issues such as responsibilities and accountability for providers of intermediary services, and in particular online platforms such as social media and marketplaces. Although the Act doesn't require detail of the algorithms used, it nevertheless aims to provide greater transparency. One particular issue of interest is that this Act requires a platform provider such as Facebook, Twitter, YouTube, TikTok, or Amazon to set out the parameters as to why an advertisement has been targeted at an individual.

These two guidelines overall could result in a reduced dependence on some AI-infused functions (e.g., facial recognition) where there might be concerns regarding bias. On the other hand, together with the work being done by the Global Partnership on AI (below), they may assist in providing a further catalyst for the democratic and ethical use of AI.

2.3.10 Global Partnership on AI

The Global Partnership on AI (GPAI) "aims to bridge the gap between theory and practice on AI by supporting cutting-edge research and applied activities on AI-related priorities." GPAI was launched in June 2020 as an idea brought to fruition by France and Canada during their G7 presidencies. GPAI's 15 founding members are Australia, Canada, France, Germany, India, Italy, Japan, Mexico, New Zealand, The Republic of Korea, Singapore, Slovenia, the UK, and the United States. They were joined by Brazil, the Netherlands, Poland, and Spain in December 2020.[22]

Bearing in mind that the background of this book partly has arisen through the Covid pandemic's impact on public services, it is worth mentioning that a subgroup of the GPAI also worked on the responsible development of AI technology. This included the use of AI solutions to ensure "that methods, algorithms, code, and validated data are shared rapidly, openly, securely, and in a rights and privacy preserving way, in order to inform public health responses and help save lives."[23]

2.4 CONCLUSION

This chapter, together with the previous one, has provided information not only about some of the key components of AI, including more advanced technologies, but also of the importance of the Office of Finance within the process generally. In most cases, the Office of Finance is the effective gatekeeper of the process, although the public sector needs to be recognized as a complex and interconnected stakeholder landscape.

Most importantly, it needs to be understood that the increased use of advanced technology and AI is not simply a matter of incrementally improving public services but rather one of transforming the sector. The Office of Finance can prove to be either the inhibitor or the facilitator of change. To undertake effective transformation requires that the finance department and its officers take the latter role of being facilitators. Finance controllers of the future need to be increasingly transformative, rather than conservative. Their role is not only to assist in the accurate estimation of the benefit case but also to track improvements. In reality it is a difficult task for public sector organizations to chart the relatively unknown territories of AI, especially where there is a degree of uncertainty and therefore risk in the wider outcome. We consider this area in more detail under the Implementation section (see Chapters 13 and 14).

Earlier in this chapter, we briefly discussed IT failures, some of which were both dramatic and potentially traumatic to those more personally involved. In some cases, there were even political consequences, such as when, for example, the failure of the California Department of Motor Vehicles turned into a campaign issue. There are always some people who will plead a case for retaining the status quo "as it wasn't successful last time" but the public sector – and its officers – need to rise above that stance, especially in current times. There is no shortage of constructive advice.[24] Importantly, the sector needs to take the learning from those earlier episodes which themselves, like the use of data and analytics, provide actionable insights.

In the next chapters, we start to look at some specific public sector areas to help gain greater understanding of the issues and advantages of a transformative program. It should not be forgotten that behind every program of planned improvement almost certainly sat someone from the Office of Finance who signed off a "return on investment" case, and who tracked progress.

2.5 NOTES

1. HM Treasury. (2013). "Review of Quality Assurance of Government Analytical Models: Final Report." Gov.UK, March. https://www.gov.uk/government/publications/review-of-quality-assurance-of-government-models.
2. Chartered Institute of Public Finance and Accountancy. (2021). *A Guide to Forecasting Methods in Public Services.*" https://www.cipfa.org/policy-and-guidance/publications/a/a-guide-to-forecasting-methods-in-public-services-book.

3. National Audit Office. (2014). "Forecasting in Government to Achieve Value for Money." Report by the Comptroller and Auditor General, HC 969 Session 2013-14, January 31. https://www.nao.org.uk/wp-content/uploads/2015/01/Forecasting-in-government-to-achieve-value-for-money.pdf.

4. AccountingTools. (2021). "Qualitative Forecasting Definition," February 9. https://www.accountingtools.com/articles/what-is-qualitative-forecasting.html.

5. Market Business News. "What Is Regression Analysis? Definition and Examples." https://marketbusinessnews.com/financial-glossary/regression-analysis/ (accessed November 5, 2021).

6. Finney, A. (2011). "Understanding Uncertainty and Risk in Pharma Forecasting." Reuters Events, May 5. www.reutersevents.com/pharma/commercial/understanding-uncertainty-and-risk-pharma-forecasting.

7. Stretch, J. (2018). "How to Manage Forecasting Risk?" FP&A Trends, March 4. fpa-trends.com/article/how-manage-forecasting-risk.

8. Charette, R.N. (2019). "Five Enduring Government IT Failures: Costly Consequences Go On and On." *IEEE Spectrum*, February 5. https://spectrum.ieee.org/five-enduring-government-it-failures.

9. Victorian Audit Generals Office (VAGO). (2014). "Impact of Increased Scrutiny of High Value High Risk Projects." June. https://www.audit.vic.gov.au/report/impact-increased-scrutiny-high-value-high-risk-projects?section=.

10. SAS. (2012). "Activity-Based Cost Management in the Public Sector." From Cokins, G. (2006). *Activity-Based Cost Management in Government*, 2nd ed. Management Concepts.

11. Allas, T., Dillon, R., and Gupta, V. (2018). "A Smarter Approach to Cost Reduction in the Public Sector." McKinsey & Company, June 8. www.mckinsey.com/industries/public-and-social-sector/our-insights/a-smarter-approach-to-cost-reduction-in-the-public-sector.

12. Chang, J. (2021). "144 Key ERP Statistics 2020/2021: Analysis of Trends, Data, and Market Share." Finances Online. financesonline.com/erp-statistics.

13. Panorama Consulting Group. (2020). "The 2020 ERP Report." https://cdn2.hubspot.net/hubfs/4439340/Panorama-Consulting-Group-The-2020-ERP-Report.pdf.

14. Fernandez, D., Zaino, Z., and Ahmad, H. (2017). "The Impacts of ERP Systems on Public Sector Organizations." *Procedia Computer Science* 111: 31–36.

15. Ibid.

16. Panorama Consulting Group. (2019). "How Artificial Intelligence Improves ERP Software." https://www.panorama-consulting.com/how-artificial-intelligence-improves-erp-software/.

17. Engler, A. (2021). "6 Developments That Will Define AI Governance in 2021." Brookings Institution, January 21. https://www.brookings.edu/research/6-developments-that-will-define-ai-governance-in-2021/.

18. Engler, A. (2020). "New White House Guidance Downplays Important AI Harms." Brookings Institution, December 8. www.brookings.edu/blog/techtank/2020/12/08/new-white-house-guidance-downplays-important-ai-harms/.

19. Engstrom, D.F., Ho, D.E., Sharkey, C.M., and Cuéllar, M. (2020). "Government by Algorithm: Artificial Intelligence in Federal Administrative Agencies." Report Submitted to the Administrative Conference of the United States, February. https://www-cdn.law.stanford.edu/wp-content/uploads/2020/02/ACUS-AI-Report.pdf.

20. Council on Foreign Relations. (2021). "A Conversation with President Ursula von der Leyen of the European Commission," November 20. www.cfr.org/event/conversation-president-ursula-von-der-leyen-european-commission.

21. Proposal for a Regulation of the European Parliament and of the Council on a Single Market for Digital Services (Digital Services Act) and Amending Directive 2000/31/EC. European Commission, December 15. https://ec.europa.eu/info/sites/default/files/proposal_for_a_regulation_on_a_single_market_for_digital_services.pdf.

22. The Global Partnership on Artificial Intelligence (GPAI). https://gpai.ai (accessed November 5, 2021).

23. The Global Partnership on Artificial Intelligence (GPAI). (2020). "AI and Pandemic Response Working Group Report." GPAI – Montreal Summit 2020. https://gpai.ai/projects/ai-and-pandemic-response/gpai-ai-pandemic-response-wg-report-november-2020-summary.pdf.

24. Ioryer, O.S., Boniface, I.D., and Patrick, Z. (2017). "A Critical Appraisal of Budgeting and Budgetary Control in the Public Sector." *International Journal of Scientific & Engineering Research* 8, no. 1 (January). https://www.ijser.org/researchpaper/A-CRITICAL-APPRAISAL-OF-BUDGETING-AND-BUDGETARY-CONTROL-IN-THE-PUBLIC-SECTOR.pdf.

Public Order and Safety

3.1 INTRODUCTION

For many, one of the most important public services is that of public order and safety, which embraces not only policing but also immigration and border control (and within this section the fire service is also considered). These are all public services that carry the greatest burden of mainly positive public emotion, as there is a high degree of dependence on them. All of these services are likely to undergo some degree of transformation as finances are squeezed and the impact of technology increasingly takes effect. At the same time, they will continue to be under considerable public scrutiny and as they evolve technologically, it is both hoped and expected that this happens with an enhanced rather than deteriorated quality of service.

On the whole, public opinion remains relatively stable and reasonably positive toward policing. The exception is when sentiments rise as a result of a specific adverse and isolated action, which is an issue that is often shared and magnified through social media. Regarding border and immigration services, many view these as being a necessary requirement in order to maintain frontiers, although increasingly the manner in which these services are being delivered is coming into question as a result of illegal migration, especially as much of this involves people trafficking.

Beyond this, fire and emergency services are considered to not only being essential but also tending to have a broader mandate in terms of emergency support and overall existing predominantly for the public good in a nonpolitical way.

3.2 THE FUTURE OF POLICING IN AN AI ERA

The police are generally recognized as a body established by law, paid for by the taxpayer and whose responsibility is to uphold the law and ensure the safety, health, and possessions of citizens. It's a role with a long history, going back to ancient times.

The concept of law enforcement is several thousand years old, with evidence of its existence in ancient China, when the role was discharged by prefects; in ancient Greece, when publicly owned slaves were used to control crowds; and in ancient Egypt, where there are records of there being a police service at the same time the pyramids were being constructed in 2700–2200 BCE. Although the role of the police is different from that of the military, which focuses on defending the state, there can, however, be some overlap. For example, in France, the "gendarmerie" is a military force with law enforcement responsibilities. Similarly, the Carabinieri ("Arma dei Carabinieri") in Italy is one of the country's main law enforcement agencies, being a military force and coming under the control of the Ministry of Defence.

The longstanding nature of the police service inevitably means that it has gone through multiple iterations over its history. While in ancient Egypt officers were armed with wooden sticks, nowadays police are more likely to be equipped with firearms. As Robert Kennedy once stated,

> *Every society gets the kind of criminal it deserves. What is equally true is that every community gets the kind of law enforcement that it insists on.*

Continuing the trend of ongoing transformation as a result of digitalization, the nature of the police service is in continuous flux. Policemen are now seldom seen walking "the beat," which is a longstanding term that represents both the time and territory that a policeman might cover. Walking the beat is a tradition in the police service that not only acts as a deterrent but also reinforces the relationship of the police with the community. Nowadays there is less regular visibility of patrol cars except in trouble hotspots.

The traditional policeman has been partly replaced by community officers who share some but not all the powers of police, such as maintaining public contact and managing public social conduct. In the UK, for example, community officers (otherwise known as police community support officers) do not have powers of arrest. There and elsewhere, the public's impression of the police service is often influenced by the mainstream press and by social media. Many police officers who are seen on our screens are black-suited, often behind a shield, sometimes armored, and overall appearing to be rather threatening individuals.

Despite being in this spotlight, there is a constant demand on the police service for speed and early action. This especially places police officers at risk of making an incorrect decision or taking the wrong action. Not only has society become more impatient, but the impact of social media means that events can either happen or become out of control more quickly. In addition, police also have the burden of regulation on their proverbial shoulders. Incorrect prosecutions not only place decision makers under the microscope but also undermine their credibility and public respect.

3.2.1 Transformation of Police Work

Policing as we know it has necessarily changed as a result of the greater breadth of service that is expected of it. In addition to the "normal" work in areas ranging from crime and incident management to finding missing persons, the pandemic originating in 2020 accelerated the need to provide protection against new areas of concern, typically:

- An increase in online crime, which resulted in police forces needing to develop new policing methods.
- Public order events such as mass demonstrations, not only against vaccinations and the wearing of PPE but also about environmental issues.
- Police being, in many cases, the first port of call for mental health issues as the pandemic led to an increase in the number of those diagnosed with depression against a background of an already increasing trend.[1]

Although pandemic-induced restrictions on traveling as well as the closure of many public places might at face value have reduced the potential for terrorist activities, the risk of terrorism has remained real and police have been heavily involved in supporting anti-terrorist activities. Issues of isolation and problems with mental health can result in increases in radicalization, especially against a backdrop of greater online activity. Similarly, the closure of public places has only served to shift the problem to other locations, often behind closed doors.[2]

The sophistication and complexity of modern crimes and the inventiveness of modern criminals are also placing massive and new demands on police forces. These issues create stresses not only on front-line officers but also on those leading them. Like many other professionals, police officers tend to suffer from four types of stress – organizational, external, personal, and operational – but for them the problem is in many ways more acute. The normal human response of the body when under a stressful situation is that of fight or flight but unlike in many other types of employment, the front-line police officer cannot run away as they have a duty to the public and citizens are dependent on them. The nature of this stress, which can also be exacerbated by other personal issues and organizational pressures, including new technologies, can lead to mistakes happening. While having an obligation to the citizen, the police force has, like all employers, a duty of care to its staff as well.[3]

Beyond all this, members of the police force are also continually faced with the challenge of austerity and budget management, and these are issues likely to be increasingly important going forward. The main challenge for the police service is not only that of fulfilling all their existing and new obligations but to do so with less funding. That they must turn, at least in part, to the use of advanced technologies is inevitable.

In their 2019 report "The Future of Policing," Deloitte points to 10 global megatrends that they consider to also affect the police force:[4]

1. A growing and aging demographic, which creates more vulnerable people
2. Globalization and its impact on fraudulent behavior, especially in the supply chain
3. Urbanization and increased segmentation between the "haves" and "have nots"
4. The increase in technology and abundance of data
5. New models of working and how they will impact the traditional approach to policing

6. The rise of individualism, which favors freedom over state control, and its impact on personal behaviors
7. Climate change and the effect of extreme weather on the services the police force needs to provide
8. Resource scarcity
9. Increases in nationalism and separatism
10. The market economy, especially the impact of private technology-infused policing

Deloitte describes the police as facing six new realities, which are:

1. Operating in a digital world
2. Being "outgunned" by the private sector, especially in terms of investment
3. Responding quickly enough to change
4. Managing the boundaries between the physical and cyber worlds
5. Using an increasing amount of data and technology
6. Operating transparently

While referenced specifically in respect of the police, it might be argued that these six new realities might also be relevant in part to many other parts of the public sector.

3.2.2 Criminal Use of AI

In the context of AI it should be recognized that criminals are capable of using advanced methods to commit crime, typically:

- The use of driverless vehicles to carry out terrorist activities.
- Greater cybercrime, where criminals use snooping devices to identify bank passwords and passcodes and where, according to cybersecurity experts, criminals are increasingly linking machine learning to AI in order to create more effective attacks.
- Identity theft.

It is generally accepted that police forces have no real option but to fight fire with fire and to develop appropriate capabilities to match those of criminals. As mentioned earlier, the proliferation of devices and the advent of quantum computing will potentially bring these threats to a new and higher level of concern. According to retired California police chief Jim Davis, comparing when he started his career to current times, "If we were 10 or 20 years behind in technology it really didn't matter that much. But now, if you are 10 to 20 days behind in your technology the bad guys are getting way ahead of you."[5]

3.2.3 Police Use of New Technologies

There is already considerable evidence of police using new technologies. One might not need to look much further than China where there is already considerable infusion of technical capabilities, but this is in fact a global phenomenon. A Deloitte UK survey

TABLE 3.1   Police Technology Focus

Heavy investment	Cybersecurity
	Cloud
	Data
	RPA
	Wearables
	AI
	Biometrics
	Drones
Somewhat heavy investment	Internet of Things
	3D printing
	Blockchain

of nine police forces showed that they had already invested "somewhat or heavily" in these areas (Table 3.1). Of those police organizations interviewed, only augmented reality and autonomous vehicles failed to make the list, although for all of them the use of augmented reality was on their radar.

3.2.4   Case Studies in Policing

There is no shortage of case studies and reference points for the use of technology in the policing sector. In their recent report, Deloitte identifies UK case studies, including, for example, the use of augmented reality for firearms training, AI for gun licensing, image recognition, and new forms of community outreach. Avon and Somerset Constabulary use a next-generation advanced analytics tool called Qlik Sense that connects internal databases with local authority databases. Using AI predictive modeling, this particular capability uses individual risk assessment and intelligent profiling to assist officers' decision making so that offenders can be handled according to their perceived risk level. The predictive models used are regularly validated on a quarterly basis to ensure quality and accuracy.[6] Other examples include:

- In the Netherlands, Dutch cyber capacities support the International Criminal Police Organisation (Interpol), while elsewhere there is citizen collaboration by rewarding citizens who find stolen cars.
- New Zealand has adopted a cultural change approach through their Prevention First model, which is the national operating model for New Zealand police.
- The Canadian police service is using chatbots.
- Spanish police departments are using drones for situational awareness.

In the United States, there is not a single national police force but instead policing is organized on a state or local basis. Overall there are estimated to be 500,000 police officers who operate in an estimated 42,000 police organizations, over half of which are one- or two-person sheriff's departments in small towns. Organizational features range from small informal structures comprising a small number of employees to very large and complex organizations employing thousands of staff; as a result, the use of technology varies considerably. In the case of the use of drones in New York, for example, it is recognized that there are issues of privacy but according to New York City police chief Terence Monahan, "NYPD drones will not be used for warrantless surveillances. NYPD drones will be used to save lives and enhance our response in emergency situations."[7]

Other additional technology use by police includes:

- In UAE, the use of robotic police/chatbots to provide advice to citizens.
- Automatic number plate recognition, which is used around the world not only to identify vehicles and check on licensing but also to provide vehicle location data.
- "ShotSpotter," which is a detection system that uses data to pinpoint where a gun has been fired from within 60 seconds of the shot being fired (according to company claims).
- Thermal imaging, which allows police forces to locate and capture criminals more efficiently in adverse weather conditions, dense foliage, woodland, or where there are various other factors that can contribute to a criminal being able to remain hidden.
- Smarter patrolling, which comprises police vehicles with WiFi-connected laptops and devices for instant access to vital information.
- The use of AI to detect counterfeit goods, a market worth over US$500 billion, through the use of machine learning and accurate imaging to detect anomalies.[8]

At the end of the day, smarter policing is not simply about the increased use of technology but about providing an effective service within the constraints of tighter budgets. According to one article:

> There are significant and tangible benefits available to forces that take this approach. One force has seen 14,000 hours saved by using automation to process over 75,000 cases across various processes.[9]

3.2.5 Policing in China

Paying attention to what is happening in China can provide an important insight in considering the future of policing. There, the Ministry of Public Security is the principal police authority, with functional departments carrying a broad remit such as internal security, intelligence, counterterrorism, police operations, prisons, and political, economic, and communications security. All these are undertaken by a combination of officers, including both armed police and community officers.

Technologies in use in China include:

- Robotic traffic police that are equipped with facial and number plate recognition, and integrated with Beijing's national surveillance system in order to identify vehicles and drivers involved in an incident.
- Traffic accident robots that can be deployed to manage accidents and keep order.[10]
- Deployment of AI and facial recognition in police stations to detect people's emotional states.[11]

- Sunglasses equipped with facial recognition technology to identify suspected criminals. The glasses are connected to an internal database of suspects, allowing officers to quickly scan crowds while looking for fugitives.[12]
- Police are also said to stop passers-by regularly, not only to check that their identity details correspond to the details kept on the national database, but also that mobile devices are not using banned apps and have appropriate web cleansing software.[13]

Of course, there are many potentially controversial issues in this approach and level of scrutiny. Some of these are considered later under the topic of surveillance and the role of the State, which takes into account matters of civil liberty, but it is difficult to argue that the combination of technologies does not seem to provide an effective policing solution. At the end of the day, a different question might be that of the *purpose* of policing – but that perhaps is the subject of a different book.

In the Chinese context, a facial recognition system used at a major 2017 festival in Qingdao (population 10 million) was used to identify and detain 25 criminal suspects who were wanted for drug-related crimes and other theft incidents. Some were found to have stolen items in their possession. Eighteen cameras had been installed at four entrances to the festival, and during the course of the event they had captured the images of 2.3 million faces. According to reports, the system is able not only to identify individuals within one second, but also to compare captured images with the national database. In this way the system was also able to identify an additional 190 people who were wanted for financial crimes and prostitution. These were not one-off successes. Earlier in 2017, police in Shenzhen (population 17 million) had also cracked a child abduction ring using facial recognition. Elsewhere, in Shenyang (population 9 million), police had arrested three wanted criminals two weeks after a facial recognition system was introduced into the city's subway system.[14]

Is this amount of scrutiny justifiable, and does the end justify the means? The OSAC (Overseas Security Advisory Council), department of the US Bureau of Diplomatic Security, seeks to ensure the safety of US businesses and citizens around the world. Their 2020 report on Shanghai described the risk level to US visitors as low compared to that of other cities of comparable size. The OSAC report states: "China's high conviction rate, use of modern technology in policing, and extensive law enforcement presence throughout the city serve to deter most criminal activity."[15]

At the end of the day, citizens may not necessarily get the police force that they want nor even that they deserve. Rather, in some cases police forces are provided and managed by governments that are themselves trying to meet a set of social, political, and legal obligations. Perhaps this is one of the keys to truly understanding the purpose and methodologies of policing, including the use of technology in the modern era. In discussing whether the end justifies the means, the purpose of policing also has to be considered.

3.2.6 Forward-Looking Policing

One of the principal issues that police need to address is their sense of purpose. In an environment that is typified by multiple demands for support from the citizen against a backdrop of increasing cyber criminality, not only must the police ask themselves what their purpose is, but also citizens must ask themselves what it is that they want from their police force. This may be a question that is unique to the public sector. Should citizens expect an inclusive service or would they be prepared to accept some sort of two-tier arrangement?

By way of example, in healthcare the use of private medical services appears to provide quicker and more personalized care, but would such a two-tier approach be tolerated in policing in modern society? If so, what are the very considerable practical issues that would attach to that sort of strategy? There is already widespread use of private policing, which are law enforcement organizations operated by nongovernmental organizations. In South Africa, for example, the private policing sector employs over 200,000 staff working for approximately 3,200 private companies.

In addressing the question of tolerance of a two-tier system of policing a single answer is unlikely to emerge. In the face of multiple demands it follows that there might be a need to prioritize, not only the function of police but also the services to individuals or groups. In respect to function, perhaps human safety naturally comes above protection of public possessions or cybercrime, although in many cases there can be synergy between them. Identifying the purpose of policing, and then somehow establishing a degree of prioritization, inevitably invites discussion on the skills and capabilities needed by future policing, especially in a digital age.

In an increasingly data-driven era, there is a more disproportionate focus on the need for improved data and analytical capabilities to enable better decisioning and to optimize operations, in comparison to traditional skills. The rationale for such change is that machine learning and AI can ultimately form part of a solution mix that automates some elements of decision making and is able to free up experts to deal with more complex issues or those requiring a greater human touch. Beneath the proverbial waterline, the real onus is on improvements in operational efficiency and greater cost reduction without detriment to service.

Like in many other industries, the temptation is to digitalize existing processes, but the reality is that forward-looking policing needs to do much more than this and start to reinvent policing business models. One of the key issues to consider is that of "build or buy" in terms of technological solutions, and many police forces already outsource large proportions of their IT capability. Most citizens assume that police use data in some way, but few are aware that these services are in fact being managed by third parties.

There is also the challenge of transitioning from an existing model of policing to a new one, without undue disruption to existing services. This implementation process inevitably places more pressure on front-line officers to operate two systems in parallel in what is already a stressful occupation. New policing business models will need to address the challenge of reduced staffing, especially as there is likely to be increased and continuous pressure on their budgets. In the UK, for example, according to Deloitte, police budgets have fallen in real terms by about 20% over the past decade, and while manpower levels are currently the same as that at the turn of the century, there are in the UK alone about 10% more people to police. Perhaps in what was once thought of as a job for life, policing in the future might start to mirror other professions in an approach that best reflects the gig economy.

3.3 AI IN POLICING

Ultimately, one of the big questions to consider is to what degree AI will supplement existing police services or replace them. The use of AI tooling in this most sensitive of areas invites a number of key concerns:

- Where automation is used in AI, how transparent are algorithms used? In other words, will black box systems prove to be acceptable in modern policing?
- Are there any conscious or unconscious biases that might exist in algorithms used in policing, as has been found to be the case in facial recognition?
- Would these advanced systems meet the appropriate levels of scrutiny and accountability, including ethical considerations?
- How comfortable is the general public in knowing not only that their expectations of policing are being satisfied by an automatic system, but are also being operated by an external vendor?
- How good has the procurement process been in identifying and choosing an appropriate third-party technology provider?
- Are there tangible hard and soft benefits as a result of this changed approach, and have they been independently verified?
- What is the limit to which data can be kept on citizens, including the nature of the data and how long it is kept?
- How will efficiency be improved without compromising operational service, and can workflow management processes effectively converge with intelligent AI systems?
- How does AI interact with the front-line officer in terms of providing situational data in real time, and how does the improved use of wearables feed into the AI overview, providing bidirectional insights?

Many of these issues are matters of process and technology. Perhaps the greatest hurdle to cross is that of the cultural change. The police function is longstanding in nature and has gone through continual new developments; only this time there may be a conflict between the speed of transformation and a "burning platform" of continued financial pressure and rapidly advancing technology.

The term *burning platform* was first coined in the 1988 book *Managing at the Speed of Change* by Daryl Conner. In it, he describes a fire on the North Sea oil platform *Piper Alpha*, which led to 167 lives being lost. Conner's book describes the experience of Andy Mochan, who was one of the superintendents on the platform. His personal choice was between remaining on the oil platform and suffering certain death or leaping into the cold North Sea and facing only probable death. He decided to jump, as staying on the platform and maintaining the status quo was not a realistic choice; he survived to tell the tale.[16]

"Burning platform" is a good metaphor to illustrate when maintaining the status quo is not an option due to cost constraints, resource shortages, greater demands from end users, or even external factors such as a pandemic.

3.3.1   Impact on Police Behavior

While the use of AI is often considered a way to improve efficiency and effectiveness, there are other aspects to consider. The issue of bias is of concern and has been mentioned already, although previous references elsewhere in this book have principally related to technical issues such as errors in facial recognition. There are other elements of bias to consider, such as that shown consciously or unconsciously by police officers in the normal course of carrying out their duty.

Stanford University's Fei-Fei Li is the co-leader of their Human-Centred Artificial Intelligence Institute, known as HAI. The Human Centre is a group of researchers whose aim is to turn AI from a niche lab science to a major driver of societal change by promoting human values and guidance in technology. They believe that human development and technological development can go hand in hand rather than create conflict, and they suggest that the human aspect of tech should not be an afterthought.

One area that researchers at Stanford have been working on is the analysis of body language taken from a body camera when suspects are stopped by front-line police officers. They discovered that there was significant variation in the way that people were spoken to, and that the skin color of the suspect was a major determinant. The use of natural language AI to analyze conversations with suspects also helped gain an insight into these areas of conduct.

Similarly, another Stanford professor, Sharad Goel, looked at the way in which police reports were constructed and found that certain information, such as ethnicity, inadvertently also creates bias in the reading of a police report.[17] One example given is an extract from a hypothetical report that might state, "there's an Asian female in the parking lot, driving a Toyota, (who) bumped into a car." Goel suggested that using natural language processing techniques, this report could be rewritten to anonymize the report and refer to "Female" or "Person A" instead of "Asian female." The argument being put forward is that these subtle signals influence our decision making and response. Of course, some might argue that this approach is being hypersensitive, but it is yet another example of the degree of scrutiny that police forces are increasingly finding themselves under.

3.4   THE CITIZEN AS A KEY COMPONENT OF FUTURE POLICING

One way in which police forces can effectively discharge their obligations might be through the use of the citizen as a key component of the policing function. That is to say, while the citizen will not have any statutory powers in terms of policing, they can nevertheless be involved in both the prevention and reporting of criminal activity. There is also a degree of self-service that seems to mirror what has happened in other sectors such as retail banking, and the likelihood that the number of police stations will be reduced in the same way that the number of high street banks has been reduced.

Citizen policing may at face value be an important revision to the existing business model for policing. Referring again to the Chinese model, in some areas where there is considered to be a need for additional policing, such as was the case during pandemic control, a form of social management emerged that involved local representatives as well as more formal police services.

In the UK, as part of a drive toward increased digitalization and self-service, the Government in conjunction with external partners has also created the model of Single Online Home, with the aim of providing citizens with a transformational approach to interacting with the police.[18] This is part of what is known as the Digital Policing Portfolio, or the DPP, a national UK delivery organization that was created to support the evolution of policing and to enable forces to respond and adapt to an increasingly digital world. It is responsible for delivering the Policing Vision 2025 by developing nationally consistent services and capabilities enabled by technology.[19]

The overall intention of the digital policing portfolio is principally reflected by their mission statement, which has its aim that "The experience of connecting with police through digital channels will be as helpful, personal, and reassuring as approaching an officer on the street." The project intends to involve all 43 UK police forces as well as other ancillary bodies with a view to free up time and budget, reduce administration, and invite citizens on a local basis to:

- Report
- Tell Us about
- Request
- Provide Feedback

This technological approach seems to relate especially well to a digital age, where citizens are more likely to act online than make a physical report at their local police station (if it still exists). It provides the potential for greater interaction between police and the community, opening the door to better productivity and the ability to provide a better service but in a less stressed working environment. An online solution to policing also seems to provide a possible platform for introducing a new "bot" capability that could support existing services by analyzing information and routing decisions to the most appropriate solution. Beyond this, policing bots could, when linked to appropriate systems, link new individuals or information to past or existing crimes.

3.5   POLICE AND LOCATION ANALYTICS

One key element of future policing is that of location analytics. The old mantra "everything and everyone is somewhere" also applies to crime, perhaps with the main exception being cybercrime, which notionally occurs in the ether even if the offenders still have a physical location. Location analytics and location intelligence are key elements of AI but are often overlooked. The challenge for many police services is the amount of locational data involved, the speed at which it is received, and the many different forms in which it is provided. The ability to quickly be able to translate the data into some form of location analysis becomes critical in terms of lines of inquiry, event management, and deployment of services.

The ability of active systems to share both active and historical events with a location perspective also allows complex and diverse information sets to be digested and valuable insights to be obtained. They provide vital enablers into how best to manage the balance between police supply and demand, as well as how to provide greater visibility for optimum effect. While during this transitional stage location intelligence might principally take the form of improved visualizations, location analytics will inevitably play a major part in an AI-infused police force of the future.[20]

A side discussion of the impact of technological change and the increased pressure on police budgets is the number and location of police stations. The pandemic has changed perspectives on the workplace in many ways, and it is natural to reflect on the impact on police stations as well.

First, the purpose of the traditional police station needs to be considered in the digital age. Between 2006 and 2016, the number of UK crimes reported at the desk of the police station was reduced by 20% in favor of online and call center notifications. It is perhaps a chicken-and-egg situation, as reductions in the number of police stations (mainly as a result of budget cuts) have forced citizens to report issues in a different way. Some even suggest that a reduced number of police stations has also undermined public confidence in police services. In 2019, the UK Government Minister for Policing and the Fire Service, Nick Hurd, made the point that decisions to close police stations were local issues, saying:

> *The Government believes in local policing accountable to local communities. This is why decisions on the number of police stations and their locations are for Chief Constables and directly elected Police and Crime Commissioners (PCCs) and Mayors with PCC functions. They are best placed to make these decisions based on their local knowledge and experience.*[21]

In an era in which finances are under pressure, important and difficult decisions will need to be made about the future of police stations. For an AI-infused police service, digitally driven and analytically operated, the concept of police stations must inevitably be under question, including whether they are likely to become a thing of the past. Are they to become no more valid than the traditional corner shop in an era of megastores and online retail?

3.6 POLICING SUMMARY

The police service is evolving in the same way technology is evolving, and in the same way crime is also evolving. It is a continuous cycle of change. Law enforcement is increasingly being asked to cross new criminal barriers, including broader and previously unimaginable topics such as fake news and the impact of doubtful communications, especially in the political arena.

The expectation of citizens and perhaps also their perception of future policing might also be unduly influenced by the movies (e.g., the idea of predictive policing that was adopted by Tom Cruise in *Minority Report*). The reality is that predictive policing has already been tried in the United States but only with limited success as a result of accusations of bias, but this may be an operational issue that can be resolved in the long term.

Outside of this, there seem to be many examples of the increasing use of AI and advanced analytics in the police service. It is a trend that is bound to continue. What we must recognize, and the citizen in the street must recognize, is that our traditional view of policing is now long gone, together with the tradition of walking the beat. It is a notion that is increasingly confined to history and perhaps a different type of movie, that of historical drama.

3.7 BORDER SECURITY AND AI

It appears to be in the nature of many countries to maintain and even strengthen their borders. Although the most visible sign of this might be the building of physical walls and fences, elsewhere it is often evidenced by long queues at passport control. Automation is being used where possible to streamline the passport process but, increasingly, consideration is being given to the use of AI-based solutions.

In the context of border control, areas of particular interest include the use of AI to monitor people's movements as well as the use of facial recognition. While some applaud the use of AI to undertake tasks that are normally beyond human capability, others are worried about the collection and control of data by automatic and robotic systems.

In many countries, including the United States and Europe, the use of the Visa Waiver Program has significantly increased the amount of cross-border traveling. For example, the Schengen Area (comprising 26 European countries) process allows Europeans to cross borders by simply showing a passport, resulting in more difficulty in identifying dangerous individuals. In addition, there are controls on individuals who enter the Schengen Area from third countries. To meet the ETIAS (EU Travel Information and Authorization System) waiver requirements, travelers need to have a biometric passport that contains all their biographical information as well as other biometrics in a machine-readable form. This data is part of the Entry/Exit System and prevents irregular migration, identifies overstayers, and prevents identity fraud – all ultimately aimed at protecting European citizens.

In Europe, the ETIAS process comprises a large-scale database in order to maintain a watchlist and to verify visitor information. ETIAS also uses a smart border approach to provide additional security, which the EU describes as being "an unbeatable mechanism in tackling the ongoing global challenges of terrorism and human and drug trafficking whilst abiding by its own guidelines for trustworthy AI (as) published by the (EU) Commission in April 2019."[22]

Part of the solution is the use of facial recognition, which is already used by many police forces, including Interpol, which facilitates global police cooperation. Used properly, facial recognition is considered to be a highly effective tool for border control. The EU has also launched the "iBorderCtrl" (Intelligent Portable Control System) project to detect illegal migrants at border controls by using analysis of facial expressions.

Current advanced capabilities include the use of self-service kiosks and automated passport controls.[23] Future capabilities might include the use of robotic AI-infused border guards that also incorporate lie detection capabilities. These border guard robots are expected to be more effective than humans because of:

- Their ability to pick up deceptive movements such as nonverbal communication
- Recognition of distortions in voice pattern or facial patterns
- Alignment of this information to detect unusual travel patterns, for example an individual traveling with different children or in the process of people trafficking.

The potential for these robot guards is to speed up entry but to reduce cost as well.[24] There are naturally some concerns, such as:

- Technical robustness
- Privacy and data protection
- Adequate human oversight
- Societal and environmental well-being

Above all, there is the impact of incorrect decision making. Mistakes in the immigration process can be devastating to an individual who might suffer delay, financial cost, and even detention or deportation. Incorrect automatic decision making as a result of incorrect algorithms, bias, or system failure can add to preexisting vulnerabilities on the part of immigrants. Canada has introduced automated decision making in its immigration and refugee system. According to a Government report, "Predictive analytic systems automate activities previously conducted by immigration officials and support the evaluation of some immigrant and visitor applications. This results in a more efficient service, but has life changing implications. The Canadian government has put in place a series of mitigations to reduce risk such as algorithmic impact assessments and bias testing."[25]

3.8 CUSTOMS REFORM

Distinct from immigration control, customs control focuses more on the effective collection of taxation revenue. In the case of import and export, although this book focuses on the use of AI in the public service, tax collection can be made much easier by importers and exporters (those who are predominantly in the public sector) by automating their tax processes. Advanced analytics and self-learning algorithms offer significant opportunities for the tax collection process to be automated with greater accuracy and at lower cost, as well as with less likelihood of fraud and with shorter goods clearance times.

In effect, AI-infused automation of imports and exports helps create a digitized tax department that includes the management of goods manifest documentation and declaration processing, through to accounting. A fully integrated system also includes goods tracking with predictive positioning on the journey. The most effective systems are also able to create lists of compliant and noncompliant entities, and to predict fraud.[26]

The use of AI by the Customs Office itself can play a large part in maintaining controls. In the UAE, the Ajman Department of Ports and Customs launched an integrated customs system in 2018 as part of the UAE Government's strategy of embedding AI into all of its operations. The system, called Enjaz, provides a suite of technology solutions, including AI, machine learning, and business intelligence. The system takes advantage of what is known as the Harmonized Commodity Description and Coding System, or HS. With the use of AI, traders and clearing agents can identify the code of a product more quickly, which increases accuracy and allows greater volumes to be managed. As a result, customs officers can focus on more important problems such as risk management and audit.

3.8.1 The Citizen and Taxation

Customs does not deal solely with imports and exports, although that is a significant proportion of their efforts. The role of the Customs Service is also to ensure that citizens pay their personal taxes, as well as collecting taxes from businesses. Issues of improving taxation are not confined only to large and rich countries but are of interest to almost all of them, and some countries attach very considerable seniority to the role. For example, the National Agency for the Information Society is the government body in Niger that designs and supervises new technologies for public and parapublic administration, including taxation, and has a director whose rank is at the ministerial level.

The most used applications of AI by Customs are for security and fraud detection, as these have already been developed for the intelligence services, police, and the military. Chatbots are already used in the UK and Australia to help citizens with their tax enquiries.

In their report "If algorithms dream of Customs, do customs officials dream of algorithms? A manifesto for data mobilization in Customs," authors Kunio Mikuriya and Thomas Cantens set out in some detail not only the background but also the opportunities of an AI-infused Customs Service.[27] They identify three key issues applying to customs and taxation (themes that also appear to resonate in all areas of AI in the public sector), principally:

1. **Bias:** Particularly in customs operations, the problem of incompleteness of data sets or the creation of deliberate fraud.
2. **Interpretability:** This relates to the issue of transparency, in that the payment of taxes and the operations of algorithms need to be understandable by the public as a general ethical consideration. For many, taxation is already a challenging subject and automation may make it less clear.
3. **Inability to measure errors:** The identification of mistakes in the tax collection process is an important consideration. In a system that is already opaque and difficult for the public to understand, the authors point to a scenario where different algorithms used on the same data might come up with different answers for the amount of tax to be paid. If so, which one is correct?

Additionally, it is suggested that although there are some similarities between predicting a crime and predicting a tax evasion, there is one significant difference. This is that the police use different indicators with which to teach the machine that are arguably clearer and more numerous, whereas the customs officer has more limited experience and therefore a reduced ability to accurately make predictions, as their algorithms are based on a smaller data set of fraud.

Finally, the Customs function might have particular service characteristics that could make it more difficult for them to implement effective AI systems for tax collection. These are:

- **Ethnicity and surveillance:** Currently, the onus is mainly on the citizen or corporation to provide information, but it is becoming more usual for Customs organizations to look into other data sets. As the amount of data sharing increases, there is a risk that citizen confidence could fall as a consequence of perceived intrusion into private financial matters. Local issues might also impact on cross-border sharing of data, which will add to the problem.
- **The concept of equality:** The basis of this concept is that all are equal before the tax man. One particular concern is that certain industries or sizes of supplier, or types of citizen, could be expressly targeted by an automatic system, which is a variation of bias. Beyond this, there is the matter of the connection between surveillance of individuals that provides them with greater protection and public safety, and surveillance to obtain greater insight into their financial affairs. Putting it another way, the safety and security of citizens is a role that is adopted and fully discharged by the State. But so is tax collection. Citizens will be conscious of the risk of an overlap in operations between the two functions and the risk of information being used other than for the matter intended in its original provision.
- **The particular needs of the Customs workplace:** This reinforces the point made later in Chapter 13 that new hybrid types of technology expert will need to emerge. These hybrid experts will not only understand the application of technology but also the nuances of the particular sector that they are working in. Some might argue that all public sector industries are entitled to claim the same problem, that of relative uniqueness as a result of the spectrum of activities that the sector undertakes.

The challenge of using advanced technology in the Customs industry is such that South Korea already has in place a training school specifically for Customs officers who, working alongside academics, learn to understand the complexities of data, analytics, and their application to their particular line of work. There is already a wider trend for particular courses relative to the use of data, analytics, and the use of AI in administration, such as the UK Data Science Campus, which focuses on the use of data for public good.[28]

3.9   FIRE SAFETY AND AI

Another critically important element of public safety is that of the fire service. Fire safety principally falls into two categories:

1. Fire prevention
2. Effective extinguishment

3.9.1 Natural Fire Prevention

As data becomes more accessible, predicting the likelihood of both natural and urban fires becomes possible, even though prediction does not always lead to prevention, especially with the problem of climate change leading to volatility of the environment. Natural fires are often discovered when it is too late, as the fire has often already started and firefighters are immediately on the defensive. In the United States, where wildfires in California especially are a major problem, two 17-year-old California high school students were even able to build a system that would accurately predict the probability of a wildfire down to a 100-meter square by measuring moisture levels, available fuel, and other environmental factors. Called the Smart Wildfire Sensor, the project was entered in Google's AI for Social Good program.[29]

Overall, there are two main forms of detection:[30]

1. **Image detection:** This comprises a model that can identify the features or characteristics of fire, which can then be detected using a drone.
2. **Sensor-based approach:** Air sensors can be used to detect the amount of carbon dioxide, hydrogen sulfide, carbon monoxide, and oxygen in the atmosphere. When an anomaly is detected, forest officials are alerted and can initiate a course of action.

3.9.2 Prevention of Urban Fires

In Seoul, South Korea, Professor Jae Seung Lee of Hongik University also challenged his class to create solutions for real-world problems, leading to the creation of a model that predicted the probability of urban fires with 90% accuracy, based on the city's fire data. It showed which locations were most susceptible to fire risk, allowing the Seoul Metropolitan Fire and Disaster Management to patrol those areas at most risk.[31]

3.9.3 Smart Homes and Fire Detection

The increasing trend of the smart home is likely to accelerate as the advent of 5G triggers a proliferation of devices and greater connectivity. Already, smart smoke detectors can provide information not only to an owner's mobile device but also to a central agency or the local fire department. Additionally, the detector can be connected with a heating and ventilation system or air conditioning unit to restrict the spread of smoke.

It is also possible to link a smoke detector to a camera unit so that the source of a fire and hence the cause of the outbreak can be determined. With cooking fires being one of the most likely causes of domestic fire, smart stovetop devices can be used to detect motion in the kitchen and if there is no motion then they can switch off the fuel supply to the stove. (This may not be a solution that suits all cooks but is indicative of the possibilities available.)

While some of these devices might seem at first glance optional extras, domestic insurers are likely to play a significant part in encouraging their adoption by offering discounted premiums as an incentive to implement them.[32]

3.9.4 Commercial Fire Prevention

Commercial insurers are also especially keen to understand the impact of fire and increasingly more effort is being put into risk management. Effective risk management can also be rewarded by insurers through lower premiums but in some cases may also be a binding requirement or warranty of the insurance policy. The ability to detect fire at an early stage is critical not only to ensure the safety of occupants but also to put in place fire suppression techniques and technologies. These suppression systems, which initiate automatic extinguishment systems, can put out a fire without human intervention or can mitigate the problem until the fire department arrives.

Fire detection systems may comprise:

- Thermal imaging, which detects small changes in temperature
- Flame detection
- Spark detection, which is used in industries where dust and sparks are created that could lead to an explosion
- Ember detection, which is more sensitive than flame detection and is often used on production lines
- Rate of temperature change detection, which identifies sudden increases in heat

Fire suppression systems are usually specific to the type of industry involved and the particular working area but often encompass:

- **Mist systems.** These systems deluge the affected area with water mist, which cools the flames and surrounding areas, displacing oxygen and reducing radiant heat.
- **Water and foam systems.** These systems automatically start and are robotically controlled.[33]

3.9.5 Firefighting Using AI

Joint work being undertaken in the United States by NASA, the Jet Propulsion Laboratory, and the Department of Homeland Security has led to the development of a software program that creates detailed situational awareness for firefighters. The system is called AUDREY (Assistant for Understanding Data through Reasoning, Extraction and sYnthesis), which uses data analysis to better understand the behavior of fires, including how quickly one might develop, how what is burning affects the fire's heat, and how long firefighters have to do their job before the situation becomes untenable. AUDREY combines video and sensor data to predict what the fire is likely to do next. It potentially has the ability to see through poor visibility conditions such as smoke, fire, and heat to augment the natural senses of the firefighter.[34]

It is also possible to incorporate relatively simple visual recognition into the overall process by mounting a camera to the firefighter's helmet that enables edge and contour detection using filters like Sobel. Sobel is a process by which images are enhanced using an edge detection algorithm so that it creates an image emphasizing the edges of the object being viewed. In regard to the welfare of the firefighters themselves, personal devices can also measure oxygen levels to make sure that they are within the normal rate. ECG devices are additionally able to track the firefighters' physiological conditions, which may also impact their psychological decision making. Machine learning can pull all this information together and give a probabilistic output, or category of risk, so that the external support team can take appropriate action.

There are, however, some situations where it is simply too hazardous for humans to intervene, especially where fires occur in places of extreme heat or perhaps at height such as the case of a tower block. In these situations, the use of firefighting robots is becoming increasingly important. Examples to date include:[35]

- Thermite, which is a mini bulldozer capable of fitting through a normal door and of resisting extremely high temperatures.
- TAF-20, which can be operated at a distance of 500 meters and is used in Sydney, Australia, for extinguishing factory fires.
- Walk-Man, which is a humanoid robot created by the IIT – the Istituto Italiano di Tecnologia – in Italy to assess fire conditions and to activate extinguishment devices.

3.9.6   Fire Station Locations

The location of fire stations differs from that of police stations not only by virtue of their size and type but also the ability of the fire service to respond promptly and efficiently to emergencies. There are usually two criteria that need to be considered, which are:

1. Do current resources meet demand and also satisfy essential response key performance indicators? The answer may vary on a geographical basis, as the demands of the urban community differ from those of the rural community.
2. What are the future needs likely to be, taking into account issues such as urbanization, traffic accident levels, and industrialization?

Analysis can be complex and take into account issues such as new traffic systems, widths of roads, and perhaps even political and financial considerations. Experts normally need to collect both structured and unstructured data, bearing in mind potential limitations, and to use AI-based systems to predict demand and supply options.[36]

3.10   CONCLUSION

This chapter focuses on the three keys areas of policing, border control, and fire safety, which are linked by their joint need to provide public order and safety, albeit in quite different ways. All are affected by the use of data and analytics but to differing degrees, which are influenced by their required outcomes.

Fire safety is by far the least controversial in that it aims to use data and analytics not only to prevent fires but also to extinguish fires in an effective way that is less hazardous to the front-line firefighter. Early use of robotic devices is becoming more prevalent and it is likely that the firefighter of the future will become more technology-orientated than ever before.

The use of AI in the border control function seems to yield benefit, especially in the area of the automation of collection of import taxes and duty, but this is only one area of its broad remit. The other area is that of the management and control of the immigration or cross-border process in a way that is more efficient and less costly. However, this primarily requires the passive participation of the immigrant, whose personal biometric information needs to be supplied as part of the system. Facial recognition and the interpretation of nonverbal communication such as body movement are also key elements of a technologically orientated solution.

For many, the freedom to travel is considered an essential part of their liberty, although many would be prepared to tolerate some digital controls if they ensured their individual safety on a direct or indirect basis. And who would truly object to a system that speeds up the process after a long journey? There are, however, downsides that relate to the risk of how collected data will be retained and for what other purposes it might be used. The question of bias also arises in the case of algorithm-informed decisions as to whether to allow an individual to enter a country, even if one might argue that the problem of bias might be no more than a teething problem.

The issue of digitalization of the police force is a much more complex area but the nature of policing throughout its long history is that it has always had to move with the times. Civilization, which might be defined as a state of order and safety, inevitably depends on citizens complying with the rules, whether they agree with them or not. Issues such as bias and data management are key factors, but this is not really different from other parts of the public sector. Transparency, independent oversight, and a strong regulatory framework are essential elements that must be put in place and effectively maintained to help pacify any adverse public reaction. Data and AI-infused policing inevitably raise questions of civil liberties and the notion of the role of the state, which is an important enough topic to be considered in more detail in Chapter 11.

3.11 NOTES

1. Vizard, T. and Joloza, T. (2021). "Are We Facing a Mental Health Pandemic?" Office for National Statistics, May 5. blog.ons.gov.uk/2021/05/05/are-we-facing-a-mental-health-pandemic.
2. Salman, N. L. and Gill, P. (2020). "Terrorism During the COVID-19 Pandemic." UCL Jill Dando Institute of Security and Crime Science, May. https://www.ucl.ac.uk/jill-dando-institute/sites/jill-dando-institute/files/terrrosim_covid19_final_no_13.pdf.
3. UKEssays. (2018). "Stress in the Police Force: Causes and Effects," February 13. https://www .ukessays.com/essays/criminology/police-officer-stress.php?vref=1.
4. Gash, T. and Hobbs, R. (2018). "Policing 4.0: Deciding the Future of Policing in the UK." Deloitte. https://www2.deloitte.com/content/dam/Deloitte/uk/Documents/public-sector/deloitte-uk-future-of-policing.pdf.
5. Fritsvold, E. (2016). "12 Innovative Police Technologies." University of San Diego. https://onlinedegrees.sandiego.edu/10-innovative-police-technologies/ (accessed December 9, 2021).
6. Centre for Data Ethics and Innovation. (2020). "Review into Bias in Algorithmic Decision-Making." https://assets.publishing.service.gov.uk/government/uploads/system/uploads/attachment_data/file/957259/Review_into_bias_in_algorithmic_decision-making.pdf.
7. Fritsvold, "12 Innovative Police Technologies."

8. Shah, M. "The Many Different Ways AI Can Help to Detect Counterfeit Products." Good-Firms. https://www.goodfirms.co/blog/ways-ai-helps-detect-counterfeit-products (accessed December 9, 2021).

9. Hopkins, C. (2021). "Intelligent Automation: Have You Met Your New Colleagues?" Policing Insight, March 11. https://policinginsight.com/features/innovation/intelligent-automation-have-you-met-your-new-colleagues/.

10. You, T. (2019). "Robotic Traffic Policemen Equipped with Facial Recognition Cameras Start Patrolling the Streets of China." *Mail Online*, August 7. https://www.dailymail.co.uk/news/article-7332789/China-deploys-robotic-traffic-policemen-equipped-facial-recognition-cameras.html.

11. Reyes, G. (2021). "Report: China Using A.I. Emotion-Detection Software on Uyghurs." Breitbart, May 26. https://www.breitbart.com/asia/2021/05/26/report-china-police-using-a-i-emotion-detection-software/.

12. BBC. (2018). "Chinese Police Spot Suspects with Surveillance Sunglasses," February 7. https://www.bbc.com/news/world/asia-china-42973456.

13. Waters, D. (2008). "China's Battle to Police the Web." BBC News, March 25. news.bbc .co.uk/2/hi/technology/7312746.stm.

14. Yiwei, W. (2017). "Face Recognition Spots Wanted Suspects at Qingdao Beer Festival." Sixth Tone, August 31. www.sixthtone.com/news/1000773/face-recognition-spots-wanted-suspects-at-qingdao-beer-festival.

15. OSAC. (2020). "China 2020 Crime & Safety Report: Shanghai." U.S. Department of State, Bureau of Diplomatic Security, June 16. https://www.osac.gov/Country/China/Content/Detail/Report/f80b936a-f185-48d8-bbba-18f3cc377332.

16. Hopes, L. (2019). "Change Management Classics: Burning Platform." Resilience Alliance. https://resiliencealliance.com/change-management-classics-burning-platform/.

17. Knight, W. (2020). "If Done Right, AI Could Make Policing Fairer." *WIRED*, June 25. https://www.wired.com/story/done-right-ai-make-policing-fairer/.

18. CDS. "The Future of Policing." https://www.cds.co.uk/our-work/single-online-home.

19. National Police Chiefs' Council. (n.d.). "Digital Policing." www.npcc.police.uk/NPCCBusinessAreas/ReformandTransformation/Digitalpolicing.aspx.

20. ESRI. "Police." https://www.esriuk.com/en-gb/industries/police/overview (accessed December 9, 2021).

21. Pratt, A. (2019). "Police Stations: Are They a Thing of the Past?" UK Parliament, House of Commons Library, May 28. https://commonslibrary.parliament.uk/police-stations-are-they-a-thing-of-the-past/.

22. European Travel Information and Authorization System. (2021). "ETIAS & Artificial Intelligence: The Role of AI in Border Control." ETIAS, February 6. https://www.etiasvisa.com/etias-news/etias-artificial-intelligence-border-control.

23. Secunet. "Secure Borders with Secunet Border Gears." https://ees.secunet.com/en/complete-border-control-solutions/ (accessed December 9, 2021).

24. ETIAS, "ETIAS & Artificial Intelligence."

25. Gov.UK. (2021). "Ethics, Transparency and Accountability Framework for Automated Decision-Making." Cabinet Office, Central Digital & Data Office, and Office for Artificial Intelligence, May 13. www.gov.uk/government/publications//ethics-transparency-and-accountability-framework-for-automated-decision-making/ethics-transparency-and-accountability-framework-for-automated-decision-making.

26. Webb Fontaine. https://webbfontaine.com/solutions/customs-solutions/ (accessed December 9, 2021).

27. Mikuriya, K. and Cantens, T. (2020). "If Algorithms Dream of Customs, Do Customs Officials Dream of Algorithms? A Manifesto for Data Mobilisation in Customs." *World*

Customs Journal 14 (2). https://worldcustomsjournal.org/Archives/Volume%2014%2C%20Number%202%20(Oct%202020)/1902%2001%20WCJ%20v14n2%20Mikuriya%20%26%20Cantens.pdf?_t=1603239884.

28. Data Science Campus. https://datasciencecampus.ons.gov.uk/.
29. Bastone, N. (2018). "This Team of 17-Year-Old High-School Seniors in California Created a Device That Could Help Prevent Future Wildfires." *Business Insider*, November 19. https://www.businessinsider.com/california-high-school-students-create-device-to-prevent-wildfires-2018-11.
30. Kumar, V. (2020). "Applications of Artificial Intelligence in Fire & Safety." Towards Data Science, December 5. http://towardsdatascience.com/applications-of-artificial-intelligence-in-fire-safety-20f66f19bdf9.
31. Davis, J. (2019). "Could Artificial Intelligence Fight Fire Before It Starts?" Coopers Smoke and Fire Curtains, September 23. https://www.coopersfire.com/news/could-artificial-intelligence-fight-fire-before-it-starts/.
32. Travelers Risk Control. (n.d.). "The Use of Smart Home Technology in Fire Prevention and Detection [Video]." https://www.travelers.com/resources/home/smart-home/smart-home-technology-in-fire-prevention-and-detection.
33. "Fire Detection Systems." www.fireshieldsystemsltd.co.uk (accessed December 9, 2021).
34. McKinzie, K. (2018). "The Future of Artificial Intelligence in Firefighting." Fire Engineering, October 25. www.fireengineering.com/apparatus-equipment/artificial-intelligence-firefighting/#gref.
35. WiredBugs. "Firefighting Robots: Meet 7 Robot Firefighters That Can Save The Day." https://wiredbugs.com/firefighting-robots/ (accessed December 9, 2021).
36. Center for Public Safety Management, LLC. "Fire Station Location Analysis." www.cpsm.us/services/fire-station-location-analysis (accessed December 9, 2021).

Personal Social Services

4.1 INTRODUCTION

The concept of personal social services relates to the provision of care for those in the community who can't look after themselves. The delivery of these services doesn't fall into clear demarcations as there are often overlaps in terms of the type of service provided. How this support is provided falls to either voluntary or statutory agencies and, as a result, there are often considerable differences in the type of training needed. Additionally, there are also differences in the way these services are offered on a country-by-country basis and, even within countries, there are variations on a regional basis as well. Most voluntary and private companies are registered charities and they are obliged by statute to meet strict criteria. The main personal social services are government funded, although the management of these funds is usually devolved to the local level.

Personal social services generally comprise four key categories (adult care, children's social care, healthcare, and social housing) and, although not exclusively, cover the following categories:

- Mental illness
- Elderly and those with infirmity
- Physical sickness
- Those with disability
- Criminal offenders
- Abused and at-risk children

Services may be provided in different ways, typically through:

- Day care
- Residential care
- Hospitals
- Services provided at home
- Children's courts

Social work tends to be defined by the particular type of work that is undertaken, be it case work (or individual care), field work, or broader community services. Community services comprises either care "in" the community or care "by" the community.[1]

The inclusion of criminal justice in this category might seem at first glance to sit rather uncomfortably with other social services, which are more focused on well-being. In reality, issues such as probation and rehabilitation are often associated with broader welfare issues, and in many cases, the idea of punishment coexists with the desire to improve the personal welfare of offenders.

Some of the broader issues related to social protection are also considered, these being the services that are provided in a proactive way to prevent, manage, and overcome situations that adversely affect people's well-being at a more macro level. Finally, the chapter considers the use of technology not only in the recruitment process, but also in the management and payment of unemployment and other benefits.

4.2   CARE HOMES

To understand the likely impact of technology in the care home system, a good place to start is by understanding the background of that sector. As the aging population grows, so does the need to provide nursing home care for those whose needs cannot be met by home-based care or by the community. Modern care homes not only care for the elderly but also look after those with particular needs, such as those rehabilitating between hospitalization and going home, or those with more specific needs such as suffering from dementia or Alzheimer's disease. Overall they provide skilled nursing facilities that not only offer care but also aim to keep residents occupied and interested.

It's a concept that is far removed from its origin, which rests in the establishment of almshouses for the poor and needy. In their day, almshouses provided shelter and food for the impoverished old, those who were disabled, and those who were orphaned. Toward the end of the nineteenth century, almshouses also provided accommodation for those with addictions such as alcoholism and those with mental health issues. There were, however, other, better places for the "worthy poor," such as widows with no work skills, and as a result a new care model arose called "old age homes," which were usually operated by religious or ethnic groups.

In the United States, the Great Depression led to a need for more housing while at the same time the conditions within traditional almshouses deteriorated. There was a demand for something better, leading to the Social Security Act of 1935, which included the Old Age Assistance (OAA) program. This comprised the government giving money to the needy but with the caveat that those staying in almshouses did not receive anything by way of funding. In effect this was the death knell for almshouses, and the idea of spending OAA money on privately run old age homes came into existence. This was the first step in the idea of governmental intervention and the setting of standards.

The passing of the Medicare and Medicaid Act, also known as the Social Security Amendments of 1965, effectively paid for residential care for those with low incomes. This meant that the elderly could go into nursing care at the expense of the government. Following the establishment of the law, there was a huge increase in the number of care homes. For those who could afford better, the quality of these nursing homes was, however, insufficient and, as a result, the concept of "assisted living" was introduced in the mid-1970s for those who needed support without medical care. This change of ethos led increasingly to the model of a nursing home as a business, albeit a regulated one, and is now one that in the United States alone is a $100 billion industry paid mainly by Medicare and personal financing.[2]

4.2.1 The UK Model

Mirroring the commercialization approach of US care homes, the UK introduced the concept of the "social care market" under Margaret Thatcher's government. This involved (under the National Health Service Community Care Act 1990) the idea that these services could be tendered out to both the public and private sector or, in other words, undertaken by either of them.[3] As a result, the role of local authorities shifted from being one of providers of social care to one of acting as an agency. Local authorities therefore became a combination of a broker of services, a purchaser of those services, a regulator of the same, and ultimately also of being care manager. By 2019 private for-profit firms owned and managed 84% of adult social care beds in the UK,[4] compared to the 1980s when over 60% of beds were run on a not-for-profit basis by the local authority or by the National Health Service.[5]

There were two other important considerations affecting the UK model:

1. The Care Act 2014 left the ultimate responsibility for care in the hands of the local authority if the care home could not carry out its duties.
2. The use of holding companies and the way they were structured financially protected any investors from financial or legal risk if a subsidiary failed or caused harm. This meant that cleverly structured companies could mainly avoid all but a small proportion of losses and damages that might be associated with poor care and home closures, with the overall impact of making the social care system vulnerable to what some describe as predatory practices, including financial engineering.

One of the main issues in the UK is that although there are many care homes, they are, on balance, not keeping up with the aging population. Overall, the picture is one of care homes generally increasing in physical size and capacity but with fewer of them, leading to less choice and consolidation in the market. This is only one of the problems. Overall, review of the UK sector (as a case study[6]) starts from a low place:

- Between 2010 and 2016, adult social care expenditure in the UK fell in real terms by 37% nationally.
- 16% of care homes in England were rated inadequate or requiring improvement.
- At least 1.5 million people aged 65+ in the UK (8% of all over 65 years) are reported to have some level of unmet care needs.
- Data from Public Health England shows that the total number of residential and nursing home beds, per 100 people aged 75+, declined between 2012 and 2020 by 15% and 10%, respectively.

- On the staffing side, according to Skills for Care, in 2019 there were more than 120,000 vacancies across the sector and a staff turnover rate of more than 30%.
- Care work is identified as one of the lowest-paid sectors in the economy, with almost a quarter of the workforce on zero-hours contracts.
- The problem of poor pay is made worse by restrictions on leave, increasing staff-to-resident ratios, loss of sick pay, and other losses of employee benefits.

There is an immediate tendency to suggest that the private care home system is, by definition, a private and not a public service, and therefore should be considered to be out of the scope of this book. The reality is, however, that there is a public/private interlock in this sector that justifies its inclusion. In the UK, the social care sector receives almost half its income from local authority-funded residents, and as a result it is highly vulnerable to government spending cuts. Of approximately 439,000 care home beds in the UK, 37% are fully funded by local authorities, and a further 12% are partially funded.

In their March 2021 paper "Careless Finance," the Centre for the Understanding of Sustainable Prosperity (CUSP)[7] considered the challenge of the provision of adult social care in the OECD (Organisation for Economic Co-operation and Development, an intergovernmental economic organization with 38 member countries), especially against a backdrop of COVID-19, which placed significant stresses on the care home system. CUSP's particular focus, which was the subject of the paper, was to highlight the unsuitable nature of the private adult care system, principally private care homes, and to point an accusatory finger at what it described as the marketization and financialization of the social care sector. Its particular argument was that the UK private sector care system was unsuitable to be operated as a market because:

- There was no scope to improve labor productivity, as the main input of the care service is time spent with the care worker with little or no scope for productivity increase. Staffing costs make up the largest line item in care homes, representing 60% of operating costs and, as a result, there is little room for increases. In effect, this opens the door for some sort of automation although, as considered later, there are important ethical issues to reflect on.
- Local authorities are able to set prices at unsustainably low levels, which creates financial pressure and, consequently, there is a desire by care homes to reduce costs. The buying power of local authorities who represent many different service users also means that the authorities can hold the price down. As a result, care provision within single establishments has to be subsidized by private patients, with an absence of transparency into cost allocation. Increased pressures on local authority budgets will only place more pressure on the care home sector, which, some argue, is already at an unsustainable level.
- There is a lack of consumer access to information, especially about price, and availability of detailed care home price information is relatively scarce. This results in a limited ability for customers to exercise a more informed choice. It should be noted that there are some websites that exist, such as Caredata, Which?, and TrustedCare, that provide detail on some individual care home fees and list average fees for residential, nursing, or self-funding in local authorities.

The response of private care to consistently inadequate funding and the impact of operational stress because of the pandemic has exposed care homes' vulnerability and fragility, especially as they have had to cope with rising costs as a result of the Covid pandemic. This problem was made even worse by high levels of staff absenteeism through the need to quarantine. CUSP reminds us, however, that inadequate funding is only part of the problem, pointing out that "10% of the sector's £15bn annual income (in the UK alone) leaks out in the form of rent, dividend payment, net interest payments out, directors fees and profits before tax." The apparent lack of transparency adds to the problem. CUSP says that not only is the time right, but that it is essential that the care home model is reviewed going forward.

In their 2020 report "Care Home Markets in England: Changes over Time and Impact of Local Authority Expenditure on Supply," the Personal Social Services Research Unit of the University of Kent more specifically considered the impact of local authority cuts on care homes in England, and how price and quality are affected by competition. Although one might imagine that greater competition would lead to improvements in quality, the findings indicated the opposite, in that more competition led to a 4% drop in quality of service (of those described as excellent). Beyond this, the Unit discovered that a reduction in quality coupled with more competition was more likely to lead to closure of individual care homes, placing even more pressure on the supply side.

It is against this challenging and problematic background that the issue of automation and the use of robots needs to be considered.

4.2.2 Care Homes in Japan

Japan has been a leading proponent of robots in care homes for many years. In response to their own problem of an increasingly aging population and a reduced number of helpers (a predicted shortfall of 370,000 caregivers by 2025), the Japanese government has adopted a robotic approach that has been in operation since 2015 and is currently used by about 15% of nursing homes.

Different types of robots are used for different needs:[8]

- Pepper, the world's first humanoid robot, from manufacturer Softbank, is being used in 500 care homes for games, exercises, and routines.
- PARO is a therapeutic robot resembling a seal and is used to relax people. It responds to sound and touch and is especially calming to patients with dementia and Alzheimer's disease.
- Robear is a bear-like nursing robot that is able to lift patients and helps them sit and stand.
- Telenoid is a lap-based robot that focuses on communication and is helpful for people with advanced dementia.

The Japanese government has also created a list of priorities for robotic use in care homes, including predicting when a patient might want to go to the toilet. This rather basic but critical capability assumes a disproportionate importance in terms of practicality and human dignity. Ongoing research seeks to gain better understanding of issues of productivity and outcomes,[9] considering issues such as:

- Types of robot adoption, in terms of type, cost, and how they are used.
- Staffing, in terms of number and type of nurse, hours worked, and other operational factors.
- Quality of care, in terms of patient pain rate and specific medical conditions.

There are some skeptics. Judy Downey from the London-based Relatives and Residents Association says that the key to looking after someone "is having a relationship" with them, adding that what matters "is the smile, the human touch."[10] Elsewhere, the toymaker Hasbro discovered that many elderly people were using pet toys and they have created a robotic pet companion.

4.2.3 The Canadian Picture

The population of Canada is about the same as that of California, numbering about 38 million, and it has a similar number of older adults at about 6 million. Older adults represent 17% of Canada's population but 47% of healthcare costs. By 2030 that figure is expected to increase to 23% and the cost of long-term care is expected to double. The scale of Canada's older population is placing major pressure on the system; in 2019 there were nearly 80,000 older people looking for long-term support.[11]

As a result, Canada has adopted the Aging in Place program, which aims to reduce the number of people in nursing homes by 20% by 2031. Aging in Place aims to create a sustainable model for long-term care by moving the emphasis to home and community care, with the key objective being to utilize nursing homes for those with the greatest need while at the same time reducing care home costs.[12]

4.2.4 The Emergence of AgeTech

Overall, as evidenced by the Canadian model, there is an increasing move toward a three-tier approach comprising:

- Prevention
- Care at home
- Care in the community

Part of the Canadian solution rests with AgeTech companies that focus on Canada's aging problem and are part of an emerging technology community. Home Care Pulse is a company that examines trends in the Canadian healthcare systems and that has identified a series of key Canadian companies working in this space, which provide a good illustration of typical capabilities emerging in this sector:[13]

- Alayacare provides workload scheduling specifically for nursing homes.[14]
- Steadiwear provides a smart glove for people with tremors that contains a fluid that moves in the opposite direction to the tremor, providing stabilization.[15]

- Tochtech provides devices that detect movement around the home, identifying normal patterns and signaling abnormalities, therefore promoting independence.[16]
- AceAge has developed tools that dispense medication, including integrating a facial recognition capability to ensure that the right dosage is given to the right person.[17]
- uCarenet provides a solution that helps older people with scheduling appointments, including managing visits from paid care workers. It includes a voice translation capability to facilitate the use of care workers from other countries, as the sector increasingly recognizes the need for international staff resourcing. (This capability was developed in response to the founder's own mother, who normally had spoken French and English but reverted back to her childhood language of Greek as a result of Alzheimer's disease.)[18]
- In Canada, there are two also specific AgeTech hubs, the Centre for Aging + Brain Health Innovation' (CABHI)[19] and AGE-WELL.[20]

4.2.5 Going Forward

How can technology and AI help provide better care for the elderly but at lower cost? The risk is that automating some of the interactive tasks might lead to a reduction in quality time spent with the resident rather than improving it. Perhaps matters aren't so clear. Research by Dr. Chris Papadopoulos at the University of Bedfordshire in the UK and Japan revealed in a 2020 report that older adults who interacted with robots for 18 hours over two weeks had a significant improvement in their mental health.[21] Researchers affirmed that the intention was not to replace human workers with robots but rather to supplement the human intervention when there were pressures on staff time. The robots that were used, such as Pepper, were conversational in nature, although users said that the conversations were superficial and that they lacked richness, personalization, and cultural awareness.

The impact of all these issues should force care homes to innovate, rather than be squeezed by lack of funding and their need to provide service to a vulnerable part of society. In reality, much of the innovation in this sector to date has happened not in service provision but in financial engineering; this is one of the main conclusions of the CUSP report, which says that the UK Government needs to "get a better grip on the scale of these accountability issues, and to take action where necessary." This means the creation of "a system which is economically resilient, socially just, and which meets the needs of all within the means of the planet."

4.2.6 Conclusion

Against enormous pressures in the care home system, exacerbated by demographic changes, there is an increasing need not only to improve capacity but also to reinvent the business model. This may happen both through the improved use of technology to support care homes and through the provision of better care for the elderly at home. AI and robots appear to be one of the few ways that a care system that is heavily dependent on labor can genuinely obtain productivity benefits within the sector.

There are, however, major cultural issues to address as well, especially that of accepting that there is a place for AI and robots in the solution of this problem. According to Dr. Hirohisa Hirukawa, director of robot innovation research at Japan's National Institute of Advanced Industrial Science and Technology, "the mindset by the people on the frontline of caregiving [is] that after all it must be human beings who provide this kind of care."[22] Can we be so sure?

One problem is that we usually consider robots to be "robotic" in their mannerisms, speech patterns, and conversational ability. We are stuck in the mindset of today rather than in the mindset of tomorrow, especially as the development of more humanoid robots is inevitable. An expectation of humanoid robots is founded in the science fiction of *Westworld* and *Blade Runner* rather than rooted in reality, but we cannot overlook the potential of more humanoid, AI-infused robotic helpers as part of the care home and of homecare solutions.

It seems the issue is not one of functionality or the capability of technology but rather uncertainty that a robot might truly be able to give the care and empathy our elders deserve. There is no doubt that future systems can be programmed to be empathetic, and perhaps even to be programmed to be interesting and have a personality. Perhaps the hardest question to address is how, with whom, or with what, we should expect to live out our final days.

4.3 IMPACT ON CHILDREN

Another of the more sensitive areas of social services is the protection and support of at-risk children. Key issues include:

- The likelihood that post-pandemic, where there might be work shortages following job cuts, children will increasingly be the victims of violence and sexual exploitation.
- That there will be fewer human case workers on the job as a result of budgetary cuts despite the growth in child care issues.
- That the administrative demands on human case workers will increase, taking them away from front-line duties.

The aim of the use of analytics in this area is to use data to help identify and profile those at the most risk, including children, and to support professionals in the next steps. There is more to the challenge than just the matter of data quality and its interpretation. Beyond coming to terms with the technology, including understanding issues of terminology (e.g., distinguishing between predictive analytics, machine learning, and AI), social workers need to consider:

- Ethical aspects of the application of such technologies
- Challenges in obtaining consent from families
- How to secure cooperation and coproduction within participating families

The issue of ethics is particularly challenging. Some suggest that local authorities have given no more than lip service to ethics, especially in terms of consent and how data is used. Around the UK, local authorities have since 2012 explored the use of algorithms that focus on their use relative to individual children and specific families.[23] This is an extension of their risk-focused work such as the Troubled Families program. The concept was that by identifying troubled families it might be possible to turn them around, thereby avoiding more costly interventions at a later stage.

Lisa Holmes of the University of Oxford Rees Centre, which focuses on children's social care research, suggests that the program has tended to suffer from adopting an individualistic risk management approach using predictive analytics rather than taking a step back and understanding some of the more strategic issues involved. She makes the point that any solution needs to be multifaceted, as families operate normally within a range of risk and protective factors'. This suggests that to create a meaningful picture requires huge, complex datasets. On the one hand it might be possible to use large datasets such as census information or other linked data, but on the other hand, individual data may be used. It is a question of how that mixed data can be mashed together in some way to provide meaningful insight, especially taking into account variations in data quality and completeness.

Typical analysis of data might include the examination of case workers' case notes through the use of text analytics, and which particular text or combination of words might give an indication of whether a case should remain open or be closed. While it is recognized that algorithms can remove some of the biases, nevertheless there are still subjective elements from those who have completed the forms. "The risk," says Cathy Ashley, group chief executive of the Family Rights Group, is that "case files reflect the inherent subjectivity of those filling them. You are in danger of reinforcing, of the machine picking up on those." Beyond this is the issue of risk aversion through using an intelligent alert system. If predictive analytics indicates an amber warning, authorities are more likely to act "because you'll be worried that, if something goes wrong, then it will be on you." She describes it as the system having "institutionalized risk aversion." In other words, where there are alternatives that might have different levels of potential risk, social services as an institution is most likely to adopt the option that carries the lowest probability of failure.

The focus must inevitably be on the benefits that accrue. One argument submitted by technology companies is that they are able to predict an outcome better than the social workers themselves. The challenge in this particular sector is that of how much better? In 2018, the London borough of Hackney worked with a private provider to create a system known as the Early Help Profiling System (or EHPS). Its simple aim was to identify those children who were most at risk of harm; however, it was dropped in 2019 as it did not realize the expected benefits.

With most models being built by the authorities themselves, there are often problems in benchmarking due to the enormous variance between case studies: inner city versus rural; predominantly white versus predominantly black, for example.

One particular issue of implementation is stakeholder management, especially in the form of user acceptance. UK councils such as Bristol have sought to bring these techniques more to the attention of the media, suggesting that the more that people are aware of them the more comfortable they will be with their usage. Bristol created an analytics hub that builds lists from a profile of individuals, using data points such as the extent of absenteeism from school, going missing, or being a victim of crime. These characteristics are then used to highlight the risk of an individual being sexually or criminally exploited. The methodology is that if a young person reaches the top of that list, then the local social worker receives an email that suggests that their support plan be reviewed, including whether a multiagency approach is appropriate.

Gary Davies, the head of Early Intervention and Targeted Services for families, suggests that the system is not intended to make decisions but rather to "refresh corporate memory." The approach also supports strategic intervention, for example in a particular school or neighborhood. Bristol's experience was that they discovered that the demand for their services had increased and as a result they needed to commit more money to support it, which, Davies says, "means more social workers and family support workers."

The reality is that, despite its current perceived shortcomings, there is likely to be a growing move toward the use of predictive analytics in child care, although there are major hurdles of consent and ethics to overcome. Additionally, at a time when case volumes are rising and the nature of child protection is more complicated, the early use of these systems seems to increase the administrative burden on case workers rather than making the process simpler. The paradox also is that greater and better use of analytics appears to have resulted in the discovery of more vulnerable children and therefore more cases, rather than fewer. This has placed even greater demands on the service at a time when budgetary cuts are pushing headcounts down.

4.4 MENTAL HEALTH

The challenge of mental health in the community has never been more real. Mental illness is characterized in many different ways, from having abnormal thoughts and emotions to the way that we deal with other people. It also comes in many different forms, such as depression, bipolar disorder, and dementia. According to the World Health Organization, 264 million people are affected by depression, with more women affected than men.[24] Strategies already exist for preventing depression and treating mental problems, although each different form of mental illness gives rise to different forms of treatment, ranging from medication and psychological support to talking therapies such as cognitive behavior therapy. There is not one single answer to a complex problem.

Social attitudes stigmatize mental illness. According to a 2018 survey, nearly 1 in 3 Americans worry about what people would think, and 21% have concealed the fact that they are taking treatment from friends and family.[25] The Covid pandemic has also heavily affected the problem of mental health, leading to problems such as anxiety, stress, fear, denial, and anger. Mental illness is described by some as being the hidden pandemic. Despite the scale of this problem, many do not receive the treatment they need and this can be due to many factors, typically that there are:

- Demands for help that far exceed the available supply of professionals
- Gaps in insurance coverage for private treatment
- Disconnects between primary care systems and behavioral care systems
- Inadequacies in self-help solutions

In many cases, delays are a contributing factor. These particular problems (and others) oblige us to consider what solutions might be available through technology. At the heart of diagnosis rests the clinical interview, and scientists are already exploring whether this can be automated, and, if so, to what degree. The use of VH (virtual human) support as a conversational agent, infused by AI, could be a factor in improving clinical productivity and ensuring more accurate and appropriate diagnoses. Techniques such as SimSensei comprises "a new generation of clinical decision support tools and interactive virtual agent-based healthcare dissemination/delivery systems that are able to recognize and identify psychological distress from multimodal signals."[26] In other words, the system analyzes human behaviors (such as facial expressions, body posture, attention, and fidgeting) in order to identify possible psychological issues. The originators recognize that this technology does not provide an exact diagnosis but provides a number of indicators that might stimulate further action being taken.

In effect, these are systems that go beyond detecting the obvious symptoms such as blood pressure or heartbeat and investigate what previously had been undetectable, such as a patient's mental state. Some might suggest that there are considerable and significant ethical issues in such a process. As work increasingly takes place in an online environment either at home or in the workplace, the idea that employers might use technology to evaluate our mental condition and perhaps our ability to make correct decisions might seem especially worrying. We should not be entirely surprised by this degree of invasion of privacy. Already companies are able to use AI-infused software to flag anomalies in employee behaviors (e.g., if they are copying large numbers of files that they do not usually access). The "burning platform" is one of security, but the reality is that to be able to detect one wrongdoer, everyone has to be monitored. In effect, AI creates a digital fingerprint of an employee and if behavior doesn't match a typical safe fingerprint, then an alarm is raised.[27]

The use of robotics to help those with mental disorders such as dementia was mentioned earlier in this chapter. Not only might robotics help with issues such as companionship but appropriate data collection and analytics could also help with clinical diagnosis and treatment. One issue to address is how individuals suffering from mental illness might feel if they are knowingly interacting with a machine or system rather than a human being. Although it is unlikely that robotic systems would cause actual harm, it remains critical that appropriate clinical trials are carried out to measure their effectiveness.

Beyond all this, in a world of increased gaming, especially among younger people, there is no shortage of therapeutic and mental health games that aim to improve resilience. Intelligent systems could also be used to align the need of users with what beneficial gaming solutions might be available.[28]

In the case of mental health, the relationship between contributing factors and eventual symptoms are especially complex. For example, according to UK Government information, there are associations between depression, income, and unemployment, and they report that "any connection to a job or income is better than none for good mental health and well-being. . . ."[29] In this most emotional of subjects, at a time when the numbers of those affected by both mental health issue and potential unemployment are increasing, the threat of financial cuts can only lead to fewer professionals who are able to help. It is unlikely that humans can be entirely replaced in this most sensitive of areas but there is a probability that what humans do can be supplemented in some way by intelligent systems.

In addition, much can also be done to anticipate mental problems. AI systems can be used not only to monitor working hours but perhaps even the words used in individual emails. Many, on ethical grounds, may draw the line at work systems looking at behavioral traits to predict the mental wellness of an employee; nevertheless, prevention is usually recognized as being better than cure. Despite ethical and privacy issues, many might consider this level of intrusion to be a price worth paying.

4.5   SOCIAL PROTECTION

The broader concept of social protection is as a function aimed at preventing, managing, and overcoming situations that adversely affect people's well-being. The aim of social protection is to avoid poverty and vulnerability at an individual level by having a stable and secure labor market; reducing people's exposure to risks such as illness, unemployment, disability, and susceptibility to disadvantage in old age; and ultimately to provide greater equality. In addition, social protection systems provide financial support to those in need, such as single mothers and others with low income, as well as the physically and mentally challenged.

More projects that are infused with advanced analytics and AI are emerging. Social protection strategies generally fall into the categories described in Table 4.1.[30]

TABLE 4.1   Social Protection Strategies

Social Protection Strategies	Intervention Type	Description
Labor intervention	Employment services	Improvement of the functioning of the labor market through a combination of counseling, placement assistance, job matching, and other related services.
Labor intervention	Job training	Increases the quantity and quality of those people available for work by training/retraining those who are unemployed, those involved in layoffs and who have been made redundant, as well as youth.
Labor intervention	Direct employment generation	Comprises the support of small and medium enterprises through subsidies and public work projects to increase the demand for more labor.

Social Protection Strategies	Intervention Type	Description
Social insurances	Provision of affordable compensation schemes	For many with low income, these schemes still remain unaffordable. One possible option is the use of micro-insurance schemes, where some limited benefit is provided in return for a very low premium payment.
Social assistance	Universal or targeted	Universal payment avoids the challenge of means testing and provides a level benchmark for the population to benefit. In a targeted approach, the main issue is who is entitled to benefits.
Social assistance	Capability versus income	In this context, "capability" refers to improving the ability of the individual to find employment through providing a minimum level of support through education and health, as opposed to a financial payout. One particular challenge is how quickly this approach can make a difference, given the time between training and entry into the workplace.
Social assistance	Distribution of social provision	The way in which social care is distributed and allocated is critical, and can be linked not only to the nature of individual circumstances but can also relate to the culture of particular countries and the "informal economy." In many cases there are concerns as to how well the state can act effectively, placing greater dependence on NGOs and other philanthropic groups.

4.5.1 Social Risk Framework

The social risk framework, or SRM, is a conceptual framework tool used by the World Bank to support developing countries. In comparison to the earlier approaches, which are relatively micro in nature, the social risk framework takes a much more expansive and "macro" viewpoint. The SRM focuses on the management of risks before they occur and has two basic principles, which are:

1. That the poor are most likely to be affected by risks.
2. The poor are most likely not to have tools to cope.

TABLE 4.2   Social Risk Framework Tool

Social Risk Framework Element	Description	Explanation
Prevention strategies	Strategies that reduce the risk of an event occurring which might affect income.	These comprise skill training, building of care homes, and implementation of educational health programs.
Mitigation strategies	Similar to prevention strategies but are put into operation so that when an event happens the impact is reduced.	Typically these comprise mandatory insurance for unemployment, better financial education, and micro-insurance that formalizes existing informal insurance arrangements
Coping strategies	These are aimed at lessening the impact once an event has occurred.	These include, for example, disaster relief or social assistance in the form of cash or noncash transfers, or subsidies.

The main elements of the tool, according to the World Bank,[31] are shown in Table 4.2.

The World Bank has also tabulated what it considers to be the main sources of social risk (Table 4.3).

One particular problem the World Bank is struggling with is how to make the framework apply in operational terms. Its Social Protection and Labor Strategy 2012–2022 is intended to respond to operational issues by placing greater focus on the following four key strategic directions:

1. Focus on systems rather than individual programs
2. Focus on low-income states
3. Place greater emphasis on opportunities and livelihoods
4. Build on its core strengths of knowledge, innovation, and results

It is probably in the "social protection delivery chain" that advanced analytics and AI could have the greatest part to play (although there are potential applications in multiple areas). This delivery chain is the mechanism or bridge that links the citizen with the institution through the use of effective information systems, typically:

- **Citizen:** Communication in person through social workers, teams and service providers, or digitally through online systems, mobile devices, chatbots, and ATMs.
- **Information systems:** Systems that determine eligibility through access to social records, ID systems, case management, and payment systems.
- **Institutions:** Interactions with local and national institutions, access to appropriate financing, and provision overall of an effective governance framework.

TABLE 4.3 Main Sources of Risk

Nature of Risk	Micro Risk	Intermediate Risk	Macro Risk
Natural		Rainfall, landslide, volcanic eruption	Earthquake, flood, drought, tornado, asteroid impact
Health	Illness, injury, disability, food poisoning	Pandemic, food poisoning (dependent on scale and extent)	Pandemic (dependent on scale and extent)
Lifecycle issues	Changes in birth rate, old age, death		
Social	Crimes, domestic violence, drug trafficking	Terrorism, gangs	Civil strife, war, social upheaval, drug addiction, child abuse
Economic	Unemployment, harvest failure	Unemployment, harvest failure, resettlement	Financial crisis, collapse of blue chip companies, massive shock to trading market
Administration and political	Ethnic discrimination	Ethnic conflict, rioting, chemical and biological mass destruction, administration-induced disasters and collapses	Politically induced malfunction of social programs, military coup
Environment		Pollution, deforestation, nuclear disaster, soil salinities, acid rains	Global warming

Effective use of technology in this area can more accurately manage the criteria for inclusion in such a program, as well as coordinate a more effective response. The challenges of inclusion are that the system needs to be:

- Dynamic and be able to rapidly reflect sociological changes over time
- Scalable
- Able to reach hard-to-serve populations, overcoming barriers of geography, language, and ethnicity, and those with very limited (or no) access to technology
- Adaptive and able to respond to shocks
- Able to promote higher take-up rates, especially by avoiding bureaucratic barriers

The challenges of coordination in such a broad-based model are such that a fragmented approach is likely to be ineffective and costly, and will ultimately fail to provide help to those most in need. Key issues that arise through a lack of coordination include:

- For citizens: Bureaucracy, duplication, long queues and delays, lost access to benefits
- For administrators: Multiple processes and rules, excessive and costly administration and paperwork, lack of information, inability to prioritize
- For agencies: Lack of visibility of the benefits of and gaps in programs, duplication, lack of transparency, inability to manage synergies

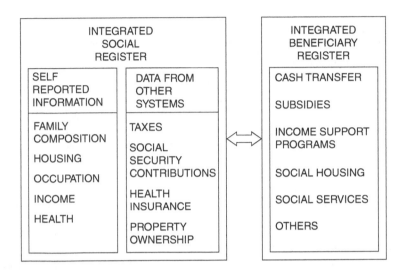

FIGURE 4.1   Chilean Social Register
Source: World Bank Group, https://thedocs.worldbank.org/en/doc/575621575490523237-01600
22019/original/SPJCC19SSND4S1GeorgeLeiteSocialRegistriesandIntInformationSystems.pdf.

Considering technology specifically, many countries already use a social registry as a platform for both registration and eligibility for benefits. Some countries also use an integrated beneficiary registry to coordinate who gets what across multiple programs, typically from cash transfers, pensions, and other social support. Optimum benefit management is obtained when countries are able to align their social registry with their beneficiary registry in a form of converged technological platform, such as in Chile, for example (Figure 4.1).

Despite the use of increasing technology, not all benefits are digital. Some countries, such as Nepal and Jamaica, still make payments in cash. This is an operational payments issue known as G2P (government to person), which is capable of transformation but is deeply rooted in local attitudes. In what is already the third phase of progress (G2P 3.0), effective implementation of G2P is expected to eventually "expand financial inclusion, increase economic development, empower women, and reduce inequality."[32]

Table 4.4 sets out a series of case studies that illustrate some of the uses of technology in social care programs.

4.6   EMPLOYMENT AND BENEFIT MANAGEMENT

This final section considers the matter of recruitment for the labor market and then the management of the benefit system for those who are unable to find suitable work. Although often the recruitment process typically takes the form of self-help, the public sector also has a role to play in trying to place unemployed people in the workplace.

TABLE 4.4 Use of Technology in Social Care Programs[33]

Case Study	Technique	Benefit
Harambee Youth Employment Accelerators, South Africa	Aims to solve youth unemployment through effective partnerships. Uses machine learning to improve conversion rates and matching of candidates to opportunities.	Not specified/quantified
"Give Directly." Provides unconditional cash transfers to those in poverty in Uganda, Kenya.	Uses satellite imagery to identify which homes have roofs, as a measure of poverty. Uses remote sensing.	Not specified/quantified
Pula Advisors, who provide agricultural insurance and bundle their insurance products with other sales, such as seed and fertilizer.	AI is used to identify yield patterns of crops, which trigger payments to those farmers suffering from drought conditions.	Prediction can only identify 60–80% yield outcomes but can identify which areas should be given more attention.
Red Cross Togo uses a FUNES prediction system to identify possible flooding.	The FUNES method predicts flooding for the current and next two days.	Allows relief to be planned and coordinated in advance using a data-driven, algorithmic approach.

The willingness of individuals to participate is often a prerequisite of being eligible for unemployment benefits.

The use of technology in the recruitment process is already a well-refined approach by both recruiters and those looking for the right position. Already, online tools help prospective candidates improve their résumés and target suitable jobs. Platforms such as LinkedIn Recruiter help employers find suitable people based on their work experience, skills, location, and other key characteristics. This automated approach has become so important and so commonplace that there are specialist consultants who are able to help an individual craft a compelling résumé.[34]

Recruitment bias can also be an issue. To avoid accusations of bias, employers are increasingly considering the use of employment robots, such as Tengai in Sweden, which has been programmed to ask the candidate, among other questions, "Have you ever been interviewed by a robot before?"[35] Other companies collect behavioral data that is obtained from game-based challenges to evaluate candidates as part of their wider assessment.

There are some for whom suitable positions cannot be found, for one reason or another, and as a result they need the protection of the Benefits System. Even in this scenario, they are unlikely to be able to hide from technology as they encounter benefits robots,[36] systems that are used to gain straightforward but key information on incomes, housing, and dependents, which help the case officer make an informed human decision. The probability is that this is only an interim measure. By 2018, UK systems were already automatically processing 42% of all benefit claimants' documentation and this figure is set to increase.[37]

Elsewhere, the UK Government is also using AI-based systems to investigate benefit fraud and overpayment by using algorithms to check on applications made using the same style or where patterns emerge of the use of the same phone number for different applications. In its 2020 report, the Government estimated the monetary effect of overpayments to be £4.6 billion 2019/2020 (based on a total benefit bill of £191.7 billion).[38] Algorithms also check on a claimant's social media site in search of inconsistencies, such as an applicant declaring an inability to work yet posting photographs of skiing holidays.[39]

As with policing and immigrations services, the challenge is not only to effectively automate repetitive tasks but also to be able to make informed recommendations on individual cases. The opportunity exists for improved and more consistent productivity at reduced cost, but the risk is that some of the most vulnerable might be adversely affected if there is unconscious bias within the system. On the other hand, the ability of intelligent systems to track and prevent benefit fraud and overpayment can only be seen as a good thing that is ultimately to the advantage of the taxpayer.

4.7 CONCLUSION

The grouping of the individual parts of this chapter might seem at face value to be strange bedfellows but they have a common theme, which is the care and protection of the individual within the wider context of service to the public. Each individual area already seems to have its fair share of problems and challenges as a combination of societal and demographic factors, and there is every probability that in some cases these problems and challenges could get worse. One temptation is to believe that the solution can only be one of spending even more money, but this cannot prove a sustainable answer, as the problem is partly that of dealing with some underlying structural matters. The use of data and AI are not the panacea to solving these major social issues, but might prove to be important contributors to the solution.

As with other sectors, there are key matters of bias, ethics, and safety to be considered. It is a repeating theme that is seen across all areas of public sector transformation. Certain elements of the service naturally lend themselves to self-service, but it's not a solution that is appropriate everywhere and for everyone. Should those suffering from mental illness really be expected to self-diagnose and obtain self-service therapy from anonymous systems?

The sectors dealt with in this chapter are, on the whole, those in which soft skills are especially important. These personal skills are in short supply and the pressure on individuals with those competences is likely to increase. Automation offers the chance for some of the routine tasks to be automated and, in doing so, relieve some of the burden on humans. However, it only starts to become feasible, at least in the short term, when robotically-made final decisions are subject to appropriate human oversight.

The challenge of looking after the elderly is a different sort of issue. Technology potentially opens the door to a different type of care, either at home or in a more structured community, especially in a 5G and even quantum computing world, but is this sufficient to replace human contact? The need for a different, more technological, type of care has arisen not as a result of some attitudinal shift toward respect for the old, but rather predominantly because of structural inadequacies within the system that include financial pressures on the care system itself.

The answer is not one of digitalizing existing processes, using technology where we can, and replacing the human component with robots; rather, there is a need to consider what we as a society really want, and how to sensitively deal with the most vulnerable in society. This may require not only changing some of the operational models but perhaps, in the case of care homes, revisiting the financial model as well. It's a topic that is considered later when we deal with social housing.

4.8 NOTES

1. Spicker, P. (2021). "The Personal Social Services: Social Work and Social Care." In *An Introduction to Social Policy*, http://spicker.uk/social-policy/pss.htm (accessed December 8, 2021).
2. Birnstengel, G. (2021). "How'd We Get Here? The History of Nursing Homes." Next Avenue, March 5. www.nextavenue.org/history-of-nursing-homes.
3. Walker, C. C., Druckman, A., and Jackson, T. (2021). "Careless Finance—Operational and Economic Fragility in Adult Social Care." CUSP Working Paper No 26. Guildford: Centre for the Understanding of Sustainable Prosperity. Available at https://www.cusp.ac.uk/wp-content/uploads/Careless-finance-final.pdf.
4. Blakeley, G. and Quilter-Pinner, H. (2019). "Who Cares? The Financialisation of Adult Social Care." London, UK: Institute for Public Policy Research, pp. 1–12. Available at: www.ippr.org/research/publications/financialisation-in-social-care.
5. Bayliss, K. and Gideon, J. (2020). "The Privatisation and Financialisation of Social Care in the UK." Working Paper 238, pp. 1–47. Available at: https://ideas.repec.org/p/soa/wpaper/238.html.
6. Allan, S. and Nizalova, O. (2020). "Care Home Markets in England: Changes over Time and Impact of Local Authority Expenditure on Supply." Personal Social Services Research Unit University of Kent, PSSRU Discussion Paper 2020-04.
7. Walker, Druckman, and Jackson, "Careless Finance—Operational and Economic Fragility in Adult Social Care."
8. "Robots Take Care of the Elderly in Japan." Aerobotics Global. https://www.aeroboticsglobal.com/robots-for-elderly-care (accessed December 1, 2021).
9. "The Impact of Robots on Nursing Home Care in Japan." Walter H. Shorenstein Asia-Pacific Research Center. https://aparc.fsi.stanford.edu/research/impact-robots-nursing-home-care-japan (accessed December 1, 2021).
10. Learner, S. (2019). "Fear Is Stifling Potential Use of Robots in UK Care Homes, Says AI Researcher." www.homecare.co.uk, April 25. https://www.homecare.co.uk/news/article.cfm/id/1609000/fear-stifling-potential-robots-uk-care-homes-AI.
11. Etkin, K. (n.d.). "Can Canada's Age Tech Startups Seize the Opportunity Posed by the Country's Growing Care Gap?" The Gerontechnologist. https://www.thegerontechnologist.com/can-canadas-age-tech-startups-seize-the-opportunity-posed-by-the-countrys-growing-care-gap/ (accessed December 1, 2021).
12. National Research Council Canada. (2021). "Aging in Place Challenge program." Government of Canada. https://nrc.canada.ca/en/research-development/research-collaboration/programs/aging-place-challenge-program (accessed December 1, 2021).

13. Home Care Pulse. (2020). "The Annual Home Care Industry Report." https://www.homecarepulse.com/benchmarking/2020-study/.
14. AlayaCare. www.alayacare.com.
15. Steadiwear. https://steadiwear.com.
16. Tochtech Technologies. www.tochtech.com.
17. AceAge. aceage.com.
18. uCarenet. https://ucarenet-technologies.com.
19. Centre for Aging + Brain Health Innovation (CABHI). https://www.cabhi.com.
20. AGE-WELL: Canada's technology and aging network. https://agewell-nce.ca.
21. "Culturally Competent Robots Could Improve Mental Health and Loneliness in Older People." University of Bedfordshire, September 7. www.beds.ac.uk/news/2020/september/culturally-competent-robots-could-improve-mental-health-and-loneliness-in-older-people/.
22. Hurst, D. (2018). "Japan Lays Groundwork for Boom in Robot Carers." *The Guardian*, February 6. https://www.theguardian.com/world/2018/feb/06/japan-robots-will-care-for-80-of-elderly-by-2020.
23. Turner, A. (2019). "Using Algorithms in Children's Social Care: Experts Call for Better Understanding of Risks and Benefits." Community Care, November 15. https://www.communitycare.co.uk/2019/11/15/using-algorithms-childrens-social-care-experts-call-better-understanding-risks-benefits/.
24. "Mental Disorders." (2019). World Health Organization, November 27. www.who.int/news-room/fact-sheets/detail/mental-disorders.
25. National Council for Mental Wellbeing. (2018). "New Study Reveals Lack of Access as Root Cause for Mental Health Crisis in America." Press Release, October 10. https://www.thenationalcouncil.org/press-releases/new-study-reveals-lack-of-access-as-root-cause-for-mental-health-crisis-in-america/.
26. University of Southern California Institute for Creative Technologies (ICT). (2015). "NPR Covers SimSensei: Using Virtual Humans to Help Detect Depression and PTSD." May 20. https://ict.usc.edu/news/npr-covers-simsensei-using-virtual-humans-to-help-detect-depression-and-ptsd/.
27. Revell, T. (2017). "AI Tracks Your Every Move and Tells Your Boss If You're Slacking." New Scientist, January 30. https://www.newscientist.com/article/2119734-ai-tracks-your-every-move-and-tells-your-boss-if-youre-slacking/.
28. Luxton, D.D. (2016). *Artificial Intelligence in Behavioral and Mental Health Care*. Academic Press/Elsevier.
29. "Employment and Income Spotlight." (2021). gov.uk, updated November 18. https://www.gov.uk/government/publications/covid-19-mental-health-and-wellbeing-surveillance-spotlights/employment-and-income-spotlight.
30. Lunau, T., Siegrist, J., Dragano, N., and Wahrendorf, M. (2015). "The Association between Education and Work Stress: Does the Policy Context Matter?" *PLoS One* 10, no. 3: e0121573.
31. The World Bank Group. (2018). "Social Protection Delivery Systems & the Dual Challenges of Inclusion & Coordination." Presentation. https://thedocs.worldbank.org/en/doc/201161528813030225-0160022018/original/SSNDay49amDeliverySystemsFramework.pdf (accessed December 1, 2021).
32. "Amplifying Beneficiary Impact and Experience in the G2P Digital Transformation" (Event Summary). a2i. https://a2i.gov.bd/wp-content/uploads/2019/09/Amplifying-Beneficiary-Impact-and-Experience-in-G2P-digital-Transformation.pdf (accessed December 1, 2021).
33. Ohlenburg, T. (2020). "AI in Social Protection – Exploring Opportunities snd Mitigating Risks." Bonn: Deutsche Gesellschaft für Internationale Zusammenarbeit (GIZ) GmbH, April 20. https://socialprotection.org/sites/default/files/publications_files/GIZ_ADB_AI%20in%20social%20protection.pdf.

34. Vari, G. (2020). "Can AI Improve Your Job Search? It Already Has." *Forbes*, July 10. https://www.forbes.com/sites/forbestechcouncil/2020/07/10/can-ai-improve-your-job-search-it-already-has/.

35. Savage, M. (2019). "Meet Tengai, the Job Interview Robot Who Won't Judge You." BBC News, March 12. https://www.bbc.com/news/business-47442953.

36. "Benefits of 'Welfare Robots' and the Need for Human Oversight" (2019). *The Guardian*, October 17. https://www.theguardian.com/society/2019/oct/17/benefits-of-welfare-robots-and-the-need-for-human-oversight.

37. Booth, R. (2019). "Benefits System Automation Could Plunge Claimants Deeper into Poverty." *The Guardian*, October 14. https://www.theguardian.com/technology/2019/oct/14/fears-rise-in-benefits-system-automation-could-plunge-claimants-deeper-into-poverty.

38. Department for Work and Pensions. UK Government (2020). "Fraud and Error in the Benefit System 2019 to 2020." May 13. https://www.gov.uk/government/statistics/fraud-and-error-in-the-benefit-system-financial-year-2020-to-2021-estimates.

39. Marr, B. (2019). "How the UK Government Uses Artificial Intelligence to Identify Welfare and State Benefits Fraud." *Forbes*, October 19. https://www.forbes.com/sites/bernardmarr/2018/10/29/how-the-uk-government-uses-artificial-intelligence-to-identify-welfare-and-state-benefits-fraud/.

5

Health

5.1 INTRODUCTION

The mantra of healthcare over the COVID-19 pandemic was "data-driven decision-ing," on which basis doctors, experts, and politicians were prepared to shut down large parts of the economy to ensure that the spread of the virus was contained. While it is relatively easy to look back and consider whether the right decisions were made at the time, what is more critical perhaps is the general acceptance by both the medical profession and, more importantly, the general public, about the acceptance of the use of data to inform decision making. In many ways this may prove to be a watershed moment in healthcare.

The mood also is one of digitalization of health, especially at a personal level, as evidenced by the movement of health and life insurance companies toward the capture of personal data. The idea has been around for a while, but recent events are also likely to add greater impetus to this approach. This chapter therefore considers the uses and subsequent impact of data in the management of health at the present and going forward.

5.2 DIGITALIZATION AND ITS IMPORTANCE IN HEALTHCARE

The cost of healthcare was already extremely high even before the pandemic. Health-care spending in the western world is already estimated at between 10% and 15% of GDP, and as high as 17% of GDP in the United States.[1] In almost all countries world-wide, the cost of healthcare is increasing, and it is expected to double in 20–30 years due to aging populations.[2]

These levels of expenditure are unsustainable, especially in a post-pandemic era in which many countries will face a massive debt burden. As a result, there is likely to be a transformation in healthcare, with a massive shift away from responding to illness by providing treatment to a new proactive point of view, where patients are encouraged to actively monitor and maintain their well-being. In addition, there will be an increasing trend of the use of advanced analytics and AI to drive greater efficiency through prediction of illness and adoption of early diagnosis and intervention.

	STRUCTURED DATA	UNSTRUCTURED DATA
EXTERNAL DATA CREATED BY PATIENTS, INFORMATION THAT CAN AFFECT PEOPLE'S HEALTH	GEOLOCATION GOVERNMENT STATISTICS MEDICAL TRENDS PRIVATE HEALTHCARE DATA CLIMATE AND POLLUTION DATA	SOCIAL MEDIA DATA LIFESTYLE & HEALTHCARE TELEMATICS CATASTROPHE / EPIDEMIC DATA AGING AND MULTI-MORBIDITY PHARMA RESEARCH
INTERNAL DATA CREATED BY HEALTHCARE PROVIDERS AND HEALTHCARE PROGRAMS	PATIENT DATA WORKFLOW DATA HOSPITAL PERFORMANCE PRESCRIPTION HISTORY	CALL RECORDING COMPLAINTS IMAGERY I.E. MRI WEB ACTIVITY
	STRUCTURED DATA (HELD IN PRE-DEFINED DATA MODELS)	UNSTRUCTURED DATA (NOT ORGANIZED IN PRE-DEFINED MANNER)

FIGURE 5.1   Examples of Healthcare Data

The key drivers of efficient healthcare are:

- Cost constraints
- Pressure on staff, principally doctors but also nursing and support staff
- Speed of delivery, especially as the services provided do not have the luxury of elasticity because treatment of illness is time-critical
- Political pressures, especially where regulators are involved.
- Customer expectations, as health services are increasingly benchmarked against other services (e.g., retail)

There is also a need to take into account what are described as "megatrends." The most relevant megatrend is urbanization, which is the increasing rate of movement of people from rural locations into the city, and consequently the pressure on urban medical services.[3]

5.2.1   Different Categories of Data Sources in Healthcare

There are already multiple sources of both structured and unstructured data in the healthcare system (Figure 5.1).[4] These include, but are not limited to:

- Healthcare encounter data, which is information submitted by healthcare providers that records clinical diagnoses and treatments.
- Claims data, where treatment is the subject of a healthcare insurance claim.

- 24/7 biometric data, which comprises digitized information linked to a person's physical characteristics and physiological traits.
- Patient-reported outcomes data, which is information based on outcomes as reported by a patient, as opposed to that reported by a medical professional.
- Consumer data, which includes personal, behavioral, and attitudinal data.
- Socioeconomic data, which is about humans, their activities, and where these activities are undergone.
- Genome data, which provides insight into DNA-type tracking of genetic structures.
- Epigenetic data, which studies how genetics and environment affect genes.
- Microbiome data, which is used for understanding microbial communities and their impacts in health and disease.

Digitalization in healthcare is not a new concept. In his book *Reimagine*, Tom Peters quotes David Veilette, CEO of the Indiana Heart Hospital:

> *Our entire facility is digital. No paper, no film, no medical records. And it's all integrated – from the lab to X-ray to records, to physician order entry. . . . Patients don't have to wait for anything. . . . Physicians can walk around with a notebook that's pre-programmed . . . they can review a chart from 100 miles away.*[5]

From this vast amount of data and information there are a series of challenges that emerge, including:

- Making sense of all the information, and needing to use expert systems to obtain insights.
- The continuing challenge of data and security in this most private of subject matter areas.
- The temptation to monetize this data, recognizing that almost all data has financial value, and to avoid the risk of it being sold to third parties to offset other expenses.
- The relevance of individual datasets in respect of particular problems – for example, that of the cause of cancer and the uncertainty as to whether it is genetic or due to external issues such as stress (or perhaps a combination of both, or neither).

5.3 MEDICAL MONITORING AND BIOSENSORS

The essence of biosensors is that they are bidirectional. That is, the benefit of any generated data flows two ways, both in the direction of the medical authority and in the direction of the patient.

1. Data provides the hosting organization, for example a healthcare service, with information about its patient or customer. In a public service, this provides healthcare organizations with an early warning both about trends and about the condition of the individual patient. In a more commercial context, the health insurance

sector, for example, this could contribute to more accurate underwriting decisions, pricing, risk management, and, ultimately, greater profitability.

2. It engages the patient more directly in the health process. Through this monitoring they can recognize whether they are getting enough exercise or sleeping well. Self-monitoring effectively leads to greater self-awareness, and to some degree to limited self-medication.

In many cases the devices are unattractive and are usually wristband-type devices, although there is increasingly a move to incorporate these into standard-looking wristwatches or even higher-end jewelry. This approach on balance might seem relatively crude. By comparison, John Rogers of the Center for Bio-Integrated Electronics at Northwestern University is currently working on creating microns-thin, one-inch-square, skin-pliable sensors, in an approach known as bio-integration.

Bio-integration is where "a suitable implant biomaterial integrates into the body to perform a key function, while minimizing negative immune response."[6] It's a technique with origins in dentistry. The well-established use of dental implants for tooth replacement already requires a balance between bodily response, mechanical structure and performance, and aesthetics. These new tiny biosensor wafers have a Bluetooth antenna, a central processing unit (CPU), physiologic monitors, and a wireless power system. Some professional sports teams are already starting to wear these during competition to measure individual performance. The aim is for these sensors to ultimately even be printed onto the skin as a dissolvable tattoo.

Biosensors are already being investigated for many rapid, sensitive, specific, stable, cost-effective, and noninvasive detections, such as the detection and management of breast cancer, which is the leading common cancer among women worldwide.

As with most types of monitoring, effective patient engagement depends on the degree of trust between the provider of the data and the user (or consumer) of the data. There are not just ethical considerations but also matters of patient management. At a time both when medical services are under financial pressure and data has become a valuable commodity, patients will be anxious to ensure that data they provide either on a direct or indirect basis will be used for the right purpose and not be unreasonably shared with a third party.

The impact of the data-driven response to the recent pandemic is that a large part of the population (on the whole) was prepared to comply with directions given by the Government regarding meetings and traveling. Even before these instructions were mandated rather than provided by way of general guidance, there was already a high degree of compliance (even if the overall response was not unanimous). It's a topic that will be the subject of discussion going forward and has particular relevance in the willingness of the public to use devices that collect data in this way for medical reasons. According to one report, there were two main indicators of who were *most likely* to comply:

1. Those with a perceived duty to obey the government.
2. Those who felt a moral responsibility, thinking there was a moral obligation to not flout the rules in order to protect both themselves and others.

For these reasons, transparency of government decisioning is an important factor even on a limited basis, as is a sense of responsibility to fellow citizens. While these issues might seem to be more specific to the pandemic, they have wider implications in the public's willingness to adopt a more data-driven health service, including the increased use of devices.[7]

5.3.1 Use of Biosensors in Mental Health

The major healthcare concern of mental health (dealt with in part in Chapter 4) reinforces the idea that there are overlaps in providing healthcare to different parts of the public sector. Stress and anxiety, which are major contributors to mental health problems, occur at many levels. Their causes are unclear but may be due to factors such as a major change in lifestyle (job, house, or partner) or perhaps as a side effect of stimulants such as caffeine and alcohol. Increasing use of digitalization may help assist in understanding the external characteristics that might be key triggers of mental illness.

Specifically in the workplace, stress and anxiety may be evidenced (and measured) by signs of:

- Excessive and/or abnormal working hours
- Use of particular language in email and other digital responses
- Changes in productivity and decline in work quality

Employers, who have a legal duty of care to their employees, may be able in some circumstances to detect when there are possible mental health issues and be proactive in their support. The use of employee monitoring (or employee surveillance) is not new and has been used to date principally to manage nonproductivity.[8] There are issues of ethics and consent to consider in this type of managerial oversight, as well as compliance with legal requirements. With one fifth of the workforce working in the public sector, one might usefully debate the feasibility and ethical aspect of some sort of shared approach between the surveillance of public sector employees and the management of their mental health, which is usually treated by a different part of the same sector. In other words, these employees are all part of the same organization albeit in different departmental silos.

Mental health issues and stress do not occur solely in the workplace, and in any event there are many public sector jobs that are not computer-oriented, such as trash collection, for example. Outside the workplace, it may also be difficult to capture data in a home situation that might give clues about mental health conditions.

Already, attention is being given to the monitoring of brain waves, such as with Elon Musk's Neuralink process, which has been described as a Fitbit in the skull.[9] This physical approach involves drilling a hole in the skull and inserting a device that then relays information to a computer. The idea seems not only dystopian but perhaps also mildly terrifying. It also seems unnecessarily intrusive. On the other hand, patients with heart conditions are already readily prepared to accept the invasive use of a pacemaker or stent to ensure the continued circulation of their blood, so ethically it seems that a precedent for physical intrusion may have already been set to some degree.

Perhaps more realistic is brain electroencephalography or EEG, most often seen in the form of headgear or cap with wires attached, which monitors brain signals. It's an approach that has some advantages in that it is noninvasive, portable, and less subject to regulatory oversight. One particular downside is that the patient usually needs to have some of their hair shaved off in order to provide a good electrode contact. In medicine, EEG is mostly used for the management of epilepsy and the management of neural networks due to compulsive disorders, but the number of types of use is expected to grow in the future.[10]

5.4 INNOVATING TO ZERO IN HEALTHCARE

Another megatrend is the use of data and analytics to "innovate to zero." The expression relates to a mindset of zero waste, zero environmental impact, zero defects, zero crime, zero accidents, zero friction in processes, and zero carbon emissions, and many others. In the context of healthcare, the idea of net zero hospitals are those that have been built to be efficient in their construction through effective use of natural lighting, solar control, smart heating, and smart ventilation systems.

Beyond the physical structure and performance of the building, innovating to zero is an expression that also relates to the medical functioning of the hospital, perhaps embracing ideas such as:

- Zero invasive surgery
- Zero medical waste
- Zero surgical errors

These are not impossible targets. For example, on a preventive basis, the World Health Organization (WHO) set and achieved a target of zero deaths from malaria by 2015, and also have aimed for a polio-free world. It might even be possible to aim for zero obesity, suggests Sarwant Singh, author of *Innovating to Zero*, by increasing taxes on fatty foods and offering incentives for gym membership or lower insurance premiums for those who are healthy. The solutions to these zero states are not always obvious.

What then are the practicalities of these "zero" ambitions for healthcare that might be achieved in an AI-infused world?

5.4.1 Zero Invasive Surgery

It is estimated that 10 million different types of operations take place every year and that this figure could go up to 300 million. Robots are already used in invasive surgery and it is estimated that as many as 1 million operations using some form of robotic systems are already undertaken annually. Collaborative robots (cobots) assist experienced surgeons; although expensive, they bring greater accuracy and standardization to invasive processes. The use of AI systems would allow robots to respond differently in some way to the physical conditions around them during the course of invasive surgery.

There are five levels of medical robot:

- Level 1. Telemanipulation with local support. Some elements of invasive surgery also include an element of automation.
- Level 2. Part automated system, for example, the orientation of a camera to a particular tool.
- Level 3. Highly automated, working independently but only to agreed limits, and then handing over to operator intervention once it is working outside its defined area.
- Level 4. Fully automated, but under the supervision of an operator. These machines, such as radio-surgical knives, operate in accordance with trajectories that have been agreed before the operation starts.
- Level 5. Fully autonomous, making independent decisions and undertaking tasks relative to its specialization. Currently there are no such robots.

There are major ethical and practical considerations that need to be considered, but there seems to be an inevitable convergence between effective healthcare and advanced AI-infused engineering. Advanced intelligent systems will also force a rethinking of both the function and the location of hospitals. In matters of morality and legality, important questions such as where the blame might lie should there be failure or a mistake somewhere between man and machine, have yet to be fully tested and debated, as they will also need to be in the case of accidents involving autonomous vehicles.[11]

5.4.2 Zero Waste Management

Waste is one of the major problems in healthcare and can often be used as a key indicator of efficiency. Prevention and management of medical waste is not only environmentally desirable, but can also be a key cost saver. According to a 2015 report, 5,000 US hospitals individually each generate 7,000 tons of waste every day, and disposal costs total US$10 billion annually.[12] Waste disposal can be both regulated and streamed, as different types of hospital waste need to be disposed of in different ways. Much depends on:

- The size and nature of hospital
- Local disposal facilities
- Management techniques

The recent pandemic caused major issues not only of sourcing personal protective equipment (PPE) but also of disposing of it. With such an interest in this area, hospitals are increasingly focusing on programs of waste management, typically:

- Better collaboration between hospitals that focuses, for example, on waste management cultures and improved knowledge transfer
- Improved management within the supply chain, one example being sourcing goods with less nonrecyclable packaging

- Improved hospital/supplier engagement, from creating less wasteful goods to improving tracking of waste
- Use of dashboard tracking tools that analyze and manage disposal rates

There is already evidence of the limited use of AI in some areas of waste management, including intelligent bins and smart sorting, although these systems are more focused at general than medical waste. Going forward, AI, machine learning, and robotics are likely to form part of a solution that, while not eliminating waste entirely, will significantly reduce operational costs and improve efficiencies.

5.4.3 Zero Surgical Errors

Preventable surgical errors are said to cost the US healthcare system $36 billion per year and cause over 400,000 avoidable deaths annually, according to one report.[13] The overriding goal is to integrate AI in the form of real-time intelligence to support human diagnosis of illness and treatment. In effect, the target is one of improving clinical effectiveness to 100%. Doctors and technicians increasingly see the use of AI in clinical diagnosis as comprising machine learning, natural language processing, neural networks, and advanced visualization tools. As with the issue of surgery, there is an inevitable nervousness as to where responsibility rests, especially in the matter of misdiagnosis.

Notwithstanding, the use of AI-infused surgical systems might still give valuable insight into patient-specific solutions for types of treatment, including surgery and postoperative care. These systems also make it possible to integrate hospital systems with personal mobile devices in order to track welfare and other postoperative care such as weight management.[14]

In effect, an integrated system has the potential to provide a more customer-centric, personalized form of sustainable care. There are, however, questions about the reliance by doctors on "black box" techniques, especially where the workings of an algorithm that converges multiple and varied data sets is both unseen and not understood by clinicians. Even so, financial efficiency will remain a key driver for change. According to a 2016 survey, the effective use of data and analytics could provide the US healthcare system alone with savings of US$300 billion–$400 billion per year.[15] The disappointing reality is that many of the early promises made in this area, especially in the emotional area of cancer treatment, have failed to come to fruition – but this should not be a reason for not trying.[16] In this most personal and emotional area of the public sector, where enormous financial pressures exist that are unlikely to ease, it is especially important to consider the technology cup half full rather than half empty.

5.5 TISSUE ENGINEERING

Tissue engineering is a process that combines cells, bioengineering, and other materials built on a biological scaffold to restore, maintain, or replace biological (i.e., natural) tissue. The challenge for tissue engineers is creating an efficient, economic, and secure scheme for tissue creation. The ultimate goal is creating replacement organs in order to reduce the problem of donor shortages. In some way, newly grown tissues could also be customized by being linked to an individual's DNA to reduce rejection rates.

Instead of using human intelligence, scientists are experimenting with using AI in the form of standardized and centralized databases, coupled with machine learning and neural networks.[17] Scientists overall recognize that the traditional approach to tissue engineering has certain drawbacks that AI can improve on, in terms of high accuracy, speedy results, and at lower cost.[18]

In this highly specialized area, scientists are already using AI for:

- Improved prediction of the likelihood of matched tissue, currently with 94% accuracy.
- Automatic robots that process new replacement cells for new tissue by using image processing.
- Creation of higher-quality tissue cell types.
- More efficient and speedy development of suitable tissue.
- Improved cell culturing for regenerative treatments.
- Assistance in creating 3D scaffolds for cell regeneration.

5.6 CYBERNETICS

The concept of cybernetics has been around since AI was first introduced back in the 1940s. Purists consider cybernetics to be a form of bidirectional science that integrates mankind and computer. This refers not only to humans having technical or robotic implants to help personal performance but equally robots having human-based neurons as part of their processing units. The idea that robots of some kind might ultimately have human elements somehow integrated into their systems seems straight out of the realms of science fiction, and opens the door to significant and substantial ethical questions.

Scientists are also considering the potential for humans to have some sort of implanted chip that has the ability not only to control muscles but also to enhance our senses. Kevin Warwick, professor of cybernetics at the University of Reading, has already taken the step of becoming a human guinea pig by having several implanted chips. He is, by his own definition, half-man and half-machine; in other words, he is a cybernetic organization, or cyborg.[19]

From a public health viewpoint, cybernetics comprise the integration of the inanimate with living organisms. Although it has been a problematic science, the technology's recent developments in areas such as strength, flexibility, temperature resistance, and their ability to match the human body make this a promising area of innovation. Many might view this as being mainly a way of making high-quality prosthetics. However, these are sophisticated mechanical devices infused with AI that replace upper and lower extremities; there are other uses as well, such as retina replacement. As this technology develops, it creates a real opportunity to transform the lives of disabled people.[20]

It is worth reflecting a little on the training of these future cybernetic specialists. One university already offers a six-year master's degree in cybernetics, describing it as the "the science of control in complex dynamic medical systems." The course directors there admit that this may be a problematic topic for those whose interest is "exclusively on medicine with a natural and humanitarian focus," due to the high degree of mathematics and other specializations needed. This is just one example of the changing nature of medicine, the blurring of healthcare and technology, and the changing competences of the medical profession.[21]

5.7   ADVANCEMENTS IN DRUG CREATION AND TREATMENT

In 2020, a drug was used for the first time in Japan that was created by AI for patients with obsessive compulsive disorder (OCD) with a development time of only 12 months compared to the usual much longer cycle. An algorithm was used to sift through potential compounds and then to match them against a list of desirable parameters, and from this to create a new medication for that particular illness.[22]

The traditional method of developing drugs is long and expensive, and can sometimes take up to 15 years. Before coming to market, new drugs have to undergo clinical trials in respect of efficacy, dosage, and potential side effects, so it's not surprising that perhaps only 10% of new drugs ever make it to the marketplace. According to McKinsey, the use of AI and machine learning could create savings of up to US$100 billion per year.

Not only does AI provide the ability to create and test new drugs, it is also possible to "sunset" them more quickly if there are side effects. There are important ethical issues to consider, not least those of which might be tolerable side effects, in this fast-tracked approach to the advancement of medicine. The fast-tracking of drugs to cope with the pandemic met with considerable resistance, less so due to the view of some that there were sinister motives at work but more so because of the uncertainty of side effects. The sad echoes of the thalidomide disaster leading to birth defects haven't yet been erased from public memory.

Even if there are concerns from the public about rapid drug development in a machine learning environment, there is active support for the approach among academics and manufacturers. In 2018 the Machine Learning for Pharmaceutical Discovery and Synthetic Consortium was founded by eight pharma companies plus MIT. "The main goal of the PharmaAI consortium at MIT is to bring the latest machine learning tools to drug discovery," says Regina Barzailay, Delta Electronics Professor, EEC, at MIT. "These tools range from deep learning models for property prediction to retrosynthesis algorithms that propose optimal recipes for generating target molecules."

According to Dr. Jake Wilson, consulting director at Elsevier, one of the key issues to address is bias in either the model data set or the real one used for development. "This can lead to the development of drugs that work for one set of patients with a similar genetic background, but not another."

Xinqiang Ding, a postdoc in MIT's department of chemistry, adds, "This research is an example of combining traditional computational chemistry methods, developed over decades, with the latest developments in machine learning so we achieved something that would have been impossible before now."[23]

AI also has applications in stem cell treatment. Stem cell treatment activates dormant cells that can then be used to replace damaged cells and can be used to treat ailments with pain and inflammation, such as arthritis and burns. It is part of a wider regenerative medicine approach. In 2021, Japanese scientists used AI to create a capability called DeepACT, which identifies healthy stem cells for reuse. These cells are usually detected by the human eye under a microscope, but DeepACT uses a system that does this more quickly and efficiently. The approach is considered to be a major step on the road to industrial stem cell manufacture, at higher standards and lower cost.[24]

5.8   CASE STUDIES IN HEALTHCARE

5.8.1   Ping An Good Doctor

There are multiple case studies that are of interest in this area. One of particular interest is that of the Ping An "Good Doctor" technology solution, which was created in China in 2014 to provide an integrated online solution to medical care (Figure 5.2). It was a response not only to the challenge of urbanization but also as a way of relieving pressure on overextended doctors and the public healthcare system.

In 2020 Ping An released their Global Medical Consultation Platform, which gives access to doctors and experts across the world through either a browser interface or through their mobile device, allowing consultations to take place using a sophisticated tiered system in terms of access to specialists. Currently the system has 400+ million registered users and by 2025 is estimated to have 1.8 billion e-visits annually. Ping An refers to its customer base as Netizens, and the system is networked to 3,000+ hospitals and 163,000 pharmacies, with superfast two-hour drug delivery. Beyond being a platform to respond to illnesses, Ping An also describes itself as a health maintenance organization that provides services for both corporations and individuals, including dental, health checkups, and even beauty care services.

5.8.2   Cancer Screening Case Study

In a more limited but equally important approach, AI can be used in mammogram screening. According to the WHO, breast cancer is the world's most common cancer, with 2.3 million women diagnosed and 685,000 deaths in 2020. Over the past five years, 7.8 million women have been diagnosed with the disease. Currently, the diagnostic process is that two radiologists are required to examine an X-ray image, known as a mammogram, with a third radiologist sometimes required to provide unanimity. This is a major constraint on resources, and AI systems are capable of performing the second mammogram reading, which can establish whether a radiologist assessment is needed. Not only does this reduce radiologists' workload, but automated decisioning permits earlier treatment and intervention, with potentially life-changing implications.[25]

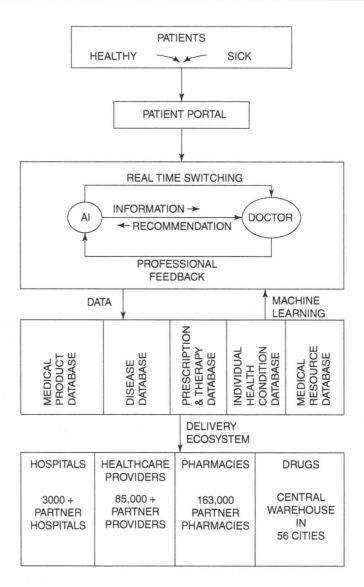

FIGURE 5.2   Ping An Good Doctor
Source: Ping An Good Doctor investor reports. Adapted from http://www.pagd.net/media/pdf/
us/presentation/pagd-presentation_-en-website-version-final.pdf.

5.9 PARAMEDICS AND AI

A great deal of medical knowledge about the treatment of traumatic injuries comes
from battlefield experiences. During the Vietnam War (1959–1975), surgeons in small
units located close to the battlefield were able to quickly provide special care and were
able to improve the chances of the victim's survival. The aim was to provide treatment

within one to two hours, although five to six hours was more common.[26] In many ways, this was the forerunner of the paramedic service as we currently know it, which itself is transforming through the use of AI.

In a cross-border collaboration between the United States and Canada, paramedics have tested a system for the emergency treatment of patients called AUDREY (Assistant for Understanding Data through Reasoning, Extraction and Synthesis), an approach that has also been used in firefighting. Not only does it provide assistance to those in the field, but the system also has learning capabilities and can make predictions about what resources might be needed next. It is being used in an area that is a mixture of urban and rural communities, and one of the key issues of this test was the availability of connectivity for the cloud-based system. Urban areas usually have strong connectivity but rural locations are usually less fortunate. The case studies model a patient complaining of chest pains where the system was linked to the cardiac center, a disaster situation, and video to a search-and-rescue process. Also, the system replaced the use of cell phone communication between the paramedic and the doctor in the hospital emergency room. Arguably, this is not AI but rather the use of advanced technology and communications in a paramedic environment. It is likely that, in time, AI will be able to advise front-line responders even before initial engagement with the doctors.[27]

5.10 CYBERSECURITY IN HEALTHCARE

The topic of cybersecurity has been covered to some degree elsewhere in this book but it is important to reaffirm its importance in the area of healthcare, where there is data relative to our most personal and intimate of circumstances. Breaches of cybersecurity not only affect the effective operation of the system but also attack the most vulnerable in society. In 2021, the Irish Health Service was attacked by ransomware, leading to what was described as a catastrophic impact, especially on healthcare workers who had been working so diligently during the pandemic. The attack affected 2,000 systems used by the Irish Health Service, and more than 4,500 servers.[28]

The challenge of cybersecurity in the healthcare sector is unlikely to go away in a hurry. Virtual healthcare is increasingly becoming normal, with many of the new processes introduced during the pandemic, such as remote triage, unlikely to disappear in their entirety going forward. At the beginning of 2020 there was a 600% increase in the use of virtual healthcare and UK patients, for example, are three times more likely to use it now than before. 91% of patients are now prepared to use their mobile devices to interact with their healthcare provider. Nevertheless, healthcare in all its many forms is complicated, and with complexity comes vulnerability. According to one report, 41 million patient records were breached in 2019, three times the amount than in 2018.[29]

As advanced analytics and AI are increasingly used going forward, new opportunities are inevitably created for those who wish to take advantage not only of the most vulnerable in society but also to seriously disrupt those healthcare workers to whom the general public owe a considerable debt and gratitude.

5.11   CONCLUSION

The issues discussed in this chapter, including cyber risk, serve to remind us that a technologically advanced and AI-infused health service will become more commonplace, partly through choice and partly through financial necessity. At the same time, this new approach to healthcare has important technical, ethical, and operational issues to contend with.

These issues include, but are not restricted to, aspects such as:

- **Affordability:** Better and more advanced systems will be more likely to be available to those healthcare providers who are best placed to afford them, such as in the private sector rather than in the public sector. If an AI future is to provide a better future for all, the benefits of technology need to be spread evenly or a two-tier or even a three-tier system will increasingly become normal.
- **Data Privacy:** AI and analytically infused healthcare systems are intrinsically data driven. However, data has value and those who own the data will use it to their own advantage. This may happen in one of two ways: either to improve operational and clinical efficiency for their own patient base, or to monetize it in some way. Systems that require the patient to opt out of sharing data to third parties rather than opt in (especially if the options are buried in small print) are probably on firm ground legally, but some might say that such an approach is open to question.
- **Speed of Change:** The apparently obvious attractions of bringing new drugs and remedies to market need to be considered against the risks involved. Pharmaceutical companies have often justified their high prices as being as a result of their high R&D cost base, but to what degree might an AI-infused drug development program undermine their traditional business model, and what might the future of the pharma industry look like?
- **Clinical Diagnosis:** To what degree should we be prepared to let a machine make a decision about our personal wellness and welfare? Many people already use internet search engines as their first port of call before consulting their local physician. The reality is that in many situations, we already allow machines to offer advice and make recommendations (if not actual decisions) about our journey home, our preferred viewing, what we might buy for our partners at Christmas, and our finances. Perhaps it is only a short journey before robotic medical advice is readily accepted as being normal.
- **Surveillance:** With illness being such a prevalent issue, how happy might workers be that allow their employer to look at the way they behave before a screen and from this decide not only on their mental state, but also on their fitness to make decisions? For those working in the public sector, their employer is in many cases also their healthcare provider, albeit operating in a different silo. What is the wider implication of this in terms of employee contracts and ethical concerns?

Overall, the healthcare sector is in the same position as almost everyone else who works in the public sector. They provide the service, yet in many cases are also beneficiaries of the same benefit. The public healthcare system sits in alliance with the private sector and both have an important role in providing a service, although inevitably a tiered arrangement is in place. Even so, it is likely that a cascade of technology will occur, with the private sector as front runners but with new advanced systems trickling down in time to the public sector and the population as a whole.

Finally, it needs be recognized that the healthcare system does not exist in isolation but is part of a complex and interconnected ecosystem that forms the totality of the public sector. As in other areas, the impact of technology will not only affect the treatment that the citizen receives but also inevitably affects the training that future medical professionals at almost all levels will need to receive. It is natural therefore that the next chapter considers the matter of education.

5.12 NOTES

1. The World Bank. "Current Health Expenditure (% of GDP) Data." https://data.worldbank .org/indicator/SH.XPD.CHEX.GD.ZS (accessed December 8, 2021).
2. Appleby, J. (2013). "Spending on Health and Social Care over the Next 50 Years: Why Think Long Term?" The King's Fund. https://www.kingsfund.org.uk/sites/default/files/field/field _publication_file/Spending%20on%20health%20 . . . %2050%20years%20low%20res%20for% 20web.pdf.
3. Singh, S. (2012). *New Mega Trends: Implications for Our Future Lives*. London: Palgrave Macmillan.
4. Health Catalyst Editors. (2018). "The Digitization of Healthcare: Why the Right Approach Matters and Five Steps to Get There." Health Catalyst, December 27. https://www .healthcatalyst.com/insights/digitization-healthcare-5-keys-progress/.
5. Peters, T. (2003). *Re-Imagine! Business Excellence in a Disruptive Age*. London: Dorling Kindersley Publishing.
6. Semisch-Dieter, O., Choi, A.H., Ben-Nissan, B., and Stewart, M. (2021). "Modifying an Implant: A Mini-review of Dental Implant Biomaterials." *BIO Integration* 2, no. (1): 12–21.
7. Barbour, S. (2020). "Coronavirus Spike: Why Getting People to Follow Restrictions Is Harder the Second Time Around." The Conversation, updated June 30. https://theconversation .com/coronavirus-spike-why-getting-people-to-follow-restrictions-is-harder-the-second- time-around-141287.
8. Suemo, J. (2018). "How to Monitor Employee Behavior and What Benefits Are There?" WorkTime, January 18. https://www.worktime.com/how-to-monitor-employee-behavior- and-what-benefits-are-there.
9. Gatollari, M. (2020). "Elon Musk Helps Mitigate Creepiness of Neuralink With Pig Demonstration." Distractify, August 29. www.distractify.com/p/elon-musk-neurolink.
10. Warwick, K. (2012). "The Future of Artificial Intelligence and Cybernetics." In *There's a Future: Visions for a Better World*. Madrid: BBVA, 2012.
11. Nawrat, Z. (2020). "MIS AI – Artificial Intelligence Application in Minimally Invasive Surgery." *Mini-invasive Surgery* 4: 28. http://dx.doi.org/10.20517/2574-1225.2020.08.
12. Plisko, J.D., Flora, C., and Cusick, C. (2015). "Waste Prevention and Management in Hospitals." Proceedings of The Thirtieth International Conference on Solid Waste Technology and Management, Philadelphia, PA, March. https://recycle.com/wp-content/uploads/2016/06/ Waste-Prevention-and-Management-in-Hospitals-Final.pdf.
13. Nichols, G. (2020). "Big Backing to Pair Doctors with AI-Assist Technology." ZDNet, July 16. www.zdnet.com/article/big-backing-pair-doctors-ai-assist-technology/.

14. Hashimoto, D.A., Rosman, G., Rus, D., and Meireles, O.R. (2019). "Artificial Intelligence in Surgery: Promises and Perils." *Annals of Surgery* 268, no. 2: 70–76.
15. Groves, P., Kayyali, B., Knott, D., and Kuiken, S.V. (2016). "The 'Big Data' Revolution in Healthcare: Accelerating Value and Innovation." https://www.mckinsey.com/industries/healthcare-systems-and-services/our-insights/the-big-data-revolution-in-us-health-care.
16. Lohr, S. (2021). "What Ever Happened to IBM's Watson?" *New York Times*, July 16 (updated July 17). www.nytimes.com/2021/07/16/technology/what-happened-ibm-watson.html.
17. Xu, J., Ge, H., Zhou, X., and Yang, D. (2005). "Tissue Engineering Scheming by Artificial Intelligence." *International Journal of Artificial Organs* 28, no. 1: 74–78. doi: 10.1177/039139880502800112.
18. Biswal, B., Yada, P., Nayak, S.K., and Moharana, A. "Artificial Intelligence in the Advancement of Regenerative Medicine & Tissue Engineering." Department of Biotechnology and Medical Engineering, NIT Rourkela. https://www.academia.edu/9636207/ARTIFICIAL_INTELLIGENCE_IN_THE_ADVANCEMENT_OF_REGENERATIVE_MEDICINE_and_TISSUE_ENGINEERING (accessed December 1, 2021).
19. Warwick, K. (2004). *I, Cyborg*. Urbana and Chicago: University of Illinois Press.
20. Dr. Z: The Wearable Report. (2021). "Cybernetics and Its Role in the Future of Healthcare." https://personalmedicalsolutions.com/cybernetics-and-its-role-in-the-future-of-healthcare.
21. Pirogov Russian National Research Medical University. "30.05.03 Medical Cybernetics." pirogov-university.com/academics/programmes-and-degrees/undergraduate/medical-cybernetics/ (accessed December 1, 2021).
22. Wakefield, J. (2020). "Artificial Intelligence-Created Medicine to Be Used on Humans for First Time." BBC News, January 30. www.bbc.com/news/technology-51315462.
23. Kent, J. (2021). "Machine Learning Technique Could Accelerate Drug Discovery." Health Analytics, March 17. https://healthitanalytics.com/news/machine-learning-technique-could-accelerate-drug-discovery.
24. McFarland, A. (2021). "AI Quickens Process of Stem Cell Therapy." Unite.AI, June 26. www.unite.ai/ai-quickens-process-of-stem-cell-therapy.
25. Dembrower, K., et al. (2020). "Effect of Artificial Intelligence-Based Triaging of Breast Cancer Screening Mammograms on Cancer Detection and Radiologist Workload: A Retrospective Simulation Study." *Lancet Digital Health* 2 (9): e468–474.
26. Hardaway, R.M., 3rd. (1978). "Viet Nam Wound Analysis." *Journal of Trauma* 18 (9): 635–643.
27. Thomas, M. (2019). "Artificial Intelligence Helping Paramedics." *Quinte News*, June 27. www.quintenews.com/2019/06/27/210196.
28. Black, R. (2021). "Hack of Health IT System Has Had 'Catastrophic' Impact, Says HSE Chief." Yahoo! News, May 20. https://uk.news.yahoo.com/hack-health-system-had-catastrophic-141248631.html.
29. Landi, H. (2020). "Number of Patient Records Breached Nearly Triples in 2019." Fierce Healthcare, February 20. www.fiercehealthcare.com/tech/number-patient-records-breached-2019-almost-tripled-from-2018-as-healthcare-faces-new-threats.

6

Education

6.1 INTRODUCTION

There is already general acceptance that the increased use of AI and advanced analytics can drive efficiency, streamline tasks, and reduce administration. The events of the pandemic have acted as a catalyst in the transformation of the education industry, continuing to move it from an entirely physical classroom-based approach to being equally, or perhaps more of, an online activity. The focus of this chapter is therefore specifically on the topic of AI in education, which not only considers the technologies that are involved, but how they affect student behavior as well as the business models of universities. This part of the book also considers talent enhancement and talent management within businesses as part of the training process of professionals.

Key contributing factors to the progress of AI in the classroom include the potential for:

- Greater customization, which includes customized reading materials and customized feedback
- Use of technology to measure student performance and provide actionable insight
- Increased use of virtual learning environments, including collaboration platforms, games, and simulation, which provide immersive learning
- An increased ability to combine and converge different educational models (such as learner models, pedagogical models, and domain models).[1]

The use of technology in the education sector is not new, as capabilities such as smartboards have to a great degree already replaced traditional blackboards and whiteboards. In what is commonly known as edtech, or sometimes edutech, the use of technology has become increasingly common in education. Edtech as a topic need not be limited to young people, although the key drivers of education are to some degree dependent on different age groups and the demands of each. Effective use of AI will result in new educational formats and lead to new collaboration platforms. Additionally, there is recognition that exposing students to the type of technology that they will encounter in their working lives is becoming critical.

While online education is still able to meet many basic learning needs, social interaction remains a key part of learning, and both children and adults consider education to be in part social function. This relates to soft skill development, which will become an increasingly crucial capability going forward as automation replaces routine tasks in the workplace.

Younger people's key drivers are to further their personal knowledge and perhaps eventually go on to further or higher education. The specific knowledge they gain is critical in a changing and increasingly competitive job market. For the older age group, education may involve retraining in skills or competencies. At the far end of the age spectrum, the "University of the Third Age" aims not only to continue to stimulate the brain cells in old age but also to create interest and provide new experiences.

Education of the young is not provided purely for the sake of personal development but also plays a major part in the economic development of nations. In what might be described as global talent wars, countries vie to attract the best thinkers, and almost all major universities offer MBA courses to help create leaders of the future. Educational migration, as students travel from one continent to another, is evidence of them trying not only to gain the best knowledge but also to broaden their experience. This approach benefits not only the students but also the universities, which find themselves with motivated and dedicated students, and this flow of prospective talent has major financial implications as well. Universities, especially those that are less established or are situated in the provinces, are becoming increasingly dependent on foreign income.

The mood of many universities is that of opting for methodologies that not only improve the quality of education but also provide students with a good experience (experiential learning). The pandemic has not only increased demand for further education but has also fast-tracked the need for customized learning using AI-infused approaches.

According to a 2018 report, the use of AI in the US education market had been expected to increase by 47.5% between 2017 and 2021,[2] with an expected continued trend between 2021 and 2025 of a compound annual growth rate (CAGR) of 49.22%. These figures are based on detailed analysis of end users, emerging educational models, and forecasts by key edtech vendors.

6.2   LEARNING FOR THE FUTURE

In his book *Re-Imagine!*, Tom Peters makes the point that young people are still taught in an industrialized way that is more appropriate to a century ago.[3] The age of data and AI necessarily forces us to think differently not only about the future but also about the role that education plays in that future. Peters suggests that learning and education should become key enablers that prepare our young people for a future that will be uncertain, creative, innovative, and increasingly AI-infused. If a pessimistic view is taken that AI will remove jobs in the workplace going forward, people will need other things to do. Creativity will inevitably form a core of that alternative future, which might be one in which citizens will have a higher amount of disposable time.

TABLE 6.1   Job Growth by 2030[6]

Type of Job	% Change by 2030
Technical professions	+25 to +30
Care professionals	+20 to +30
Building and construction	−5 to +35
Managers and executives	+5 to +15
Educators	+3 to +9
Creative roles	+6 to +8
Other jobs (unpredictable work; i.e., repairers)	−3 to +8
Customer-facing jobs	−3 to +1
Office support	−23 to −20
Other predictable jobs (production workers)	−30 to −25

According to McKinsey, advances in technology will cause major disruptions in the workforce. They predict that automation could replace up to 50% of existing jobs in the United States alone.[4] At the same time, the fastest-growing occupations will increasingly require a higher level of cognitive skills in areas such as problem solving, critical thinking, and creativity, with 30 to 40% of jobs likely to require explicit social-emotional skills or soft skills.[5] Automation of the workplace will also generate a shift in the need of education, and some work types will change in terms of growth or reduce in size (Table 6.1).

Despite these developments, budgetary cuts in education are less likely to hit scientific studies such as mathematics and science. Budgetary allowances in these areas may even be increased, with the pressure most likely being on what are usually considered to be the softer skills such as music and art, which, ironically, are the areas with the greatest creativity flows. According to McKinsey, the future in the classroom will require distinct, integrated approaches where it is critical that social-emotional or soft skills are woven into the learning program. Jennifer Rexford, Princeton University's head of computer science, reinforces that point, saying:

If you flip the question around and ask, "What is AI not good at?"—in other words, "What are humans good at? What's left for us to do?"—two things that are harder for the machine to do are exhibit creativity and social skills and perceptiveness.[7]

Education today increasingly forms the bridge between the old world and the new one, using available technologies as a catalyst for that transformation and resulting in new educational models that build for an AI future. Even so, it is important not to forget that while the classroom can be a steppingstone to what might be described as grander jobs, this type of future is not for everyone. Traditional forms of education have in the past prepared students for jobs such as administration and manufacturing, but these are exactly the sort of jobs that will be taken over by computers and robots in the foreseeable future.

Changes in education as part of our future means that the pivotal role of teachers needs also to be considered. They have needed to move away from their traditional teaching role, however this might be described, to that of being motivators and as experts who understand and can apply new approaches to education. Technology-based tools and capabilities are increasingly likely to elevate the role of the teacher rather than undermine it. In many cases, teachers have needed to acquire many of the same skills as business leaders, especially as one of their roles is to encourage their students in the same way that a business leader needs to motivate their team.

Many schools and colleges still see technology as a subject to be learned separately rather than integral to science or other specific topics. Take for example the small issue of researching a history question. Where once the student might have spent time with an encyclopedia and research information, now all the information is instantly at hand with a search engine. There are even different interpretations of history, depending on the source. The student may not even need to type in the question with the keyboard, but rather simply verbally ask Cortana or whichever system is available.

Similarly, how relevant is a math lesson when computers can do the work for us? When this author studied engineering at university, it was important to be able to calculate manually to be sure that the computer-generated answer was likely to be correct, or at least in the right order of magnitude. Perhaps that was a recognition at that time of the degree of distrust in computer systems. Nowadays, it is seldom necessary to do a manual check of an algorithm to make sure that the answer being churned out is right. The exception is in some industries (such as insurance) where "black box" calculations have been used and outputs might need to be double-checked. Perhaps an intuitive sense of correctness exists, but this isn't always going to be the case. Students have increasingly come to accept the infallibility of data analytics and AI, and as a result unquestionably accept the output of algorithms. What then is the future of education in an AI-infused, nonquestioning world?

6.3   TEACHING IN THE FUTURE

At the heart of the future of education is innovation, which comes in three forms:

1. That which simplifies teaching expertise
2. That which leads to greater efficiency and effectiveness in the teaching process
3. That which automates the teaching experience

Princeton University's Jennifer Rexford suggests that the way AI will revolutionize the classroom requires a greater understanding about how people learn, especially in a virtual environment. Princeton's project was to scan volunteer students in an MRI machine as they watched video lectures to see how their behavior correlated with concentration and absorption levels.

From the data collected researchers were able to establish how many times a student rewatched a portion of a video lecture or if they slowed it down to watch it more closely. From this type of approach, lecturers were able to understand where the lesson hadn't been explained well, where the student was having difficulty, or a combination

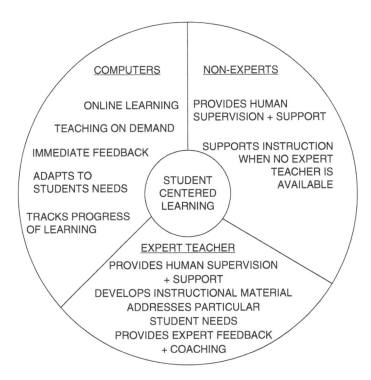

FIGURE 6.1 New Models of Teaching
Source: Adapted from T. Arnett, "Teaching in the Machine Age: How Innovation Can Make Bad Teachers Good and Good Teachers Better," Clayton Christensen Institute for Disruptive Innovation, December 7, 2016.

of the two. It also helped the personalization of student learning "so that they can learn at a more efficient pace than they can in today's one-size-fits-all classrooms."[8]

New methods of teaching are being adopted, such as Carnegie Learning, which carries the tagline "Shaping the Future of Learning," which uses AI for education and formative assessment, principally in mathematics but increasingly in literacy, world languages, and applied science.[9] New hybrid models of teaching are also emerging that combine teaching by computers, teaching by nonexperts, and teaching by expert teachers (Figure 6.1).

6.3.1 The Use of AI for Predicting Exam Success

One of the key potential areas for the use of AI in education is that of choosing the right students for particular courses and the prediction of their likely success. Particular concerns include:

- The high dropout rate of universities; for example, 36% of students drop out in the first year.
- Levels of graduate unemployment, which ranges from 9% to 30%.

- Visa rejections for overseas students at 7%.
- Inefficiency in the university admissions process, with over £6 million in man-hour costs per year in the UK alone.
- Inadequate insight into student outcomes, creating both financial strain and weakening the competitive position of individual universities.[10]

As one example, one particular solution provider, Zilter, describes itself as the world's first software as a service (SaaS) system. It helps universities to predict and enhance students' outcomes during recruiting, and also automates the admissions process. The system claims to help universities improve their profitability as a result of greater operational efficiencies, as well as empowering them to make more insightful and speedy decisions (claimed to be in less than 20 minutes compared to three to four weeks for traditional approaches). Their process comprises four key elements:

1. A scoring model, a little like a credit score.
2. A quantitative assessment, for example the minimum grades required by the university.
3. The predicted outcome, which includes the likelihood of completion, grades, and visa success.
4. Automation of the process, including scheduling of interviews, personal statements, and offer of admission.

6.4 AI AND LANGUAGE IN THE CLASSROOM

Verbal communication is a key part of learning and teaching, even if nonverbal communication is still recognized as being an important contributor to the process. Earlier in this book the use of conversational robots was considered in improving the care of the elderly, and in this section, the use of language in the context of AI will again be examined, but this time in the framework of learning and education.

6.4.1 Automated Essay Scoring

There has been very considerable progress in the development of what is known as computational linguistics. The key elements of computational linguistics comprise:

- Phonology/phonetics: The branch of linguistics that studies how humans produce and perceive sound (or, in the case of sign language, how signs are produced and perceived).
- Morphology: The study of words and how they are formed, and their relationship to other words.
- Lexicon: The vocabulary of a language, person, or branch of knowledge.
- Syntax: The arrangement of words and phrases in a well-formed sentence.
- Semantics: The branch of linguistics and logic concerned with meaning.
- Pragmatics: In linguistics, the study of how context contributes to meaning.
- Reasoning: The extension of the understanding of a word (from a dictionary, for instance) by applying the user's personal knowledge and attitudes.

One of the key elements of educational AI is automatic language processing, which is already used for spell-checking and translation but can also be used for automatic essay scoring and checking for plagiarism. Ellis "Bo" Page (1924–2005) is generally recognized as the father of automated essay scoring (AES), which is a type of program for educational assessment, and nowadays there is proprietary software available such as Intelligent Essay Assessor (IEA), Electronic Essay Rater (E-rater), and Mark-IT.

6.4.2 Removing Communication Barriers

Where language and disability differences once presented a barrier to learning, this is becoming less so. Microsoft's Presentation Translator, for example, allows students to have access to AI-powered speech recognition and translation, which in turn allows them to hear a presentation in their own language or using subtitles.[11] Systems like this also assist the deaf or hard of hearing.

For the visually impaired, Microsoft's Seeing AI app narrates the world to a student, removing limitations of impaired or even nonexistent vision. Taking a simple photo with their smartphone even uses audible beeps to help the user guide and align the camera, and Seeing AI delivers a simple "read aloud" capability.

6.5 ROBOTS IN THE CLASSROOM

Using robots in the classroom is also becoming more prevalent, even if the robots used are not necessarily humanoid in nature. This section considers different types of robotic applications in the classroom environment.

Avatars: Although avatars are often used in gaming, the broader meaning of the term is that of a character or embodiment of an online user. Swiss robotic expert Avatarion is a solution that allows absent children to have a quasi-physical presence in class.[12] It does this through using a cloud-based capability that links an absent child to a physical robot in the class. If a child raises their hand, then the robot raises its hand. The child uses a tablet device to control the robot's movements and its speech, to send images to classmates, and to answer questions by raising the robot's hand and speaking through a connected microphone and speaker. This approach is not a mandate for a child to avoid school but rather it provides children who might have been hospitalized for a lengthy period to continue their education.

Robotic tutors: Robotic tutors are currently being used for primary school children who might be in a weak emotional state.[13] One system, called MONICA, integrates educational software called Scratch with any commercially available robot. The approach is that the child is analyzed to determine their emotional cognitive state, usually through using analyzing keyboard strokes and mouse actions. The system then distinguishes the child into three key categories – concentrating, distracted, or inactive. Afterward, robotic systems help with some form of customized intervention such as voice or gestures in order to provide encouragement.

Scientists in Spain have also created a robotic capability, called ARTIE (Affective Robot Tutor Integrated Environment),[14] which interacts with educational software for primary school children, taking into account the idiosyncrasies and personality of the student. In effect, the robot takes the part of a robotic classroom assistant that takes into account the student's emotional state and provides them with appropriate support.

Evidence appears to show that robots have a positive impact on the learning process, helping students get better test scores and increasing their interest in learning more than books or other audiovisual systems do. It is also suggested that robots can improve the child's learning in an educational process known as constructivism, which is in effect learning by doing.[15] Elsewhere, Singapore also uses reading robots in kindergarten/preschool, assisting with mathematics and helping shy children become more comfortable.

Chatbots as Tutors: Chatbots with the capability to answer questions from advanced students as well as basic ones are increasingly being used in the education sector. An IBM solution was used at Georgia Tech's online master of science in computer science program, the chatbot based on IBM's advanced Watson capability. The chatbot, known as Jill Watson, was used to handle the high number of forum posts by students. Many students failed to recognize that Jill Watson was in fact a chatbot, although some did suspect it, considering the nature of the course.[16]

There are multiple other chatbot-like offerings such as Duolingo, a US-based language learning website and mobile app coupled with language proficiency testing. The company usefully offers a freemium model of pricing. A different type of solution rests with My Tutor, an online platform that is a sort of matchmaker for students and tutors. This system can not only deal with many different subjects and levels, it is also not constrained by geographical location, allowing international tutoring if appropriate.

6.6 THE SHORTAGE OF TECH TALENT

One area of particular concern in the context of education is the shortage of AI engineers. There is already a challenge in terms of the educational system being able to supply enough trained experts. Chinese tech giant Tencent suggests that there are just 300,000 AI researchers and practitioners worldwide but the market demand is for millions of roles.[17] The inevitable impact of this imbalance between supply and demand will be increasing the salaries of skilled and experienced experts, and even in some cases making their expertise unaffordable.

This issue presents particular challenges for the public sector, which has to compete with the private sector for talent at a time when there are less funds available to the public sector to spend. After graduation those with only a few years of experience can expect to earn base salaries of between US$300,000 and US$500,000 per year. One natural way forward is to increase the quantity of training courses and to make them more accessible in order to grow numbers of skilled people, but educational organizations might sense that with such large salaries available for trained people, it is entirely in order to pitch the cost of training at a commensurately high level as well.

The risk is that the provision of talent in adequate numbers will not happen quickly enough, and this could be a stumbling block to progress. New low-cost educational models will have to emerge that accelerate the number of people with appropriate skills. Elsewhere, others are already thinking about reworking the model and moving away from an approach that requires experts to be able to code and program, but rather use AI as a platform. This would mirror what has already happened in the business intelligence sector, such as in the creation of reports and dashboards, which has become much more user friendly. As a result, AI experts might become more business oriented than technical, and understand how to apply advanced technology to solve business problems rather than be the masters of the technology itself.

6.7 CASE STUDIES IN EDUCATION

By way of example, the Tacoma Public School District has already used AI-powered analytics to improve their student graduation rates from 55% to 82.6% over the course of six years. This was not an exercise in technology in isolation; rather, the school set out to measure the whole child.

They based the program on four goals, which were to:

1. Help students achieve academic excellence.
2. Create partnerships between parents, community, and staff in educating children.
3. Focus on early assessment and intervention to ensure academic success.
4. Create and maintain safe learning environments.

By pooling all available institutional data about the students in a cloud, along with accessing additional data from government departments and social media, they were able to use machine learning and AI to gain deep insights into their students. From this they were also able to identify in real time any at-risk students who required immediate intervention and support.[18]

Elsewhere, the Catholic Education of Western Australian (CEWA) implemented a LEADing Lights project, which was a cloud-first approach to delivering personalized and AI-informed education to the 78,000 students across 163 geographically dispersed schools. Similar to Tacoma, CEWA collected data points from a range of sources and from these were able to provide insights for teachers to use early intervention with students who needed it.[19]

6.8 CONCLUSION

As the use of AI has expanded in many sectors it is perhaps surprising that the use of AI in an education environment still remains relatively low, although the number of opportunities for further use in the near future remains high. According to researchers

Technavio, edtech is an area that is especially set to dramatically grow, with Africa and APAC identified as regions most likely to have the highest CAGR at over 30%.[20]

Increasing developments in AI and robotics also mean that many automated systems and even robots could potentially be used in the classroom without preprogramming and with limited or perhaps even no supervision. As a result, key implications of the use of AI and advanced analytics in education might include:[21]

- The transformation of classroom time to focus on personalized and customized learning, not only for those with learning difficulties but also in mainstream education.
- Teaching assistance, where routine and relatively straightforward tasks such as essay marking and grading could be carried out automatically.
- Improved international cooperation and collaboration in terms of learning content written in other languages, the ability to effectively teamwork, and for students to be able to improve ways of exploring their future career path.
- Improving teacher training, albeit recognizing that many of the skills needed by teachers going forward may be somewhat different to those of today.
- The ability of students to contextualize their learning, including real-time updating of content in topics that are themselves already advancing quickly, such as learning technical subjects like AI.
- The provision of immersive and multi-sensory experiences through AI and augmented reality systems that provide experiential learning for students.
- The ability to develop social skills through the use of collaborative platforms.
- The reduction and ultimate removal of barriers to learning as a result of language, location, or physical ability, and by providing greater inclusivity.

All this will lead to a reinvention of the concept of classrooms or, where they still exist in some sort of traditional form, the reinvention of teaching as a profession as one that interacts with students both more expertly and more remotely, providing a more customized and individual learning experience.

6.9 NOTES

1. Technavio. (2021). "Artificial Intelligence Market in the Education Sector in US by End-user and Education Model – Forecast and Analysis 2021–2025." June. https://www.technavio .com/report/artificial-intelligence-market-in-the-education-sector-industry-analysis.
2. Technavio. (2018). "Artificial Intelligence Market in the US Education Sector 2018–2022 | 48% CAGR Projection Through 2022." February 5. https://www.businesswire.com/news/ home/20200205005348/en/Artificial-Intelligence-Market-in-the-US-Education-Sector-2018- 2022-48-CAGR-Projection-Through-2022-Technavio.
3. Peters, T. (2003). *Re-Imagine! Business Excellence in a Disruptive Age*. London: Dorling Kindersley Publishing.
4. Manyika, J., Chui, M., Miremadi, M., Bughin, J., George, K., Willmott, P., and Dewhurst, M. (2017). "Harnessing Automation for a Future That Works." McKinsey Global Institute, January 12. https://www.mckinsey.com/featured-insights/digital-disruption/harnessing-auto mation-for-a-future-that-works.

5. Manyika, J., Lund, S., Chui, M., Bughin, J., Woetzel, J. Batra, P., Ko, R., and Sanghvi, S. (2017). "Jobs Lost, Jobs Gained: What the Future of Work Will Mean for Jobs, Skills, and Wages." McKinsey Global Institute, November 28. https://www.mckinsey.com/featured-insights/future-of-work/jobs-lost-jobs-gained-what-the-future-of-work-will-mean-for-jobs-skills-and-wages

6. Microsoft. (2018). "The Class of 2030 and Life-Ready Learning: The Technology Imperative." https://education.minecraft.net/wp-content/uploads/13679_EDU_Thought_Leadership _Summary_revisions_5.10.18.pdf (accessed November 1, 2021).

7. Rexford, J. (2018). "The Role of Education in AI (and vice versa) [video interview with Rik Kirkland]." McKinsey & Company, April 20.

8. Arnett, T. (2016). "Teaching in the Machine Age: How Innovation Can Make Bad Teachers Good and Good Teachers Better." Clayton Christensen Institute for Disruptive Innovation, December 7. https://www.christenseninstitute.org/publications/teaching-machine-age.

9. Carnegie Learning. www.carnegielearning.com (accessed November 1, 2021).

10. Zilter. www.zilter.io (accessed November 1, 2021).

11. McNeill, S. (2019). "Artificial Intelligence In The Classroom." Microsoft Education, January 11. https://edublog.microsoft.com/en-au/2019/01/artificial-intelligence-in-the-classroom/.

12. Avatarion Technology AG. www.avatarion.ch (accessed November 1, 2021).

13. Salter, I. (2016). "Robotic Tutors for Primary School Children." *Frontiers Science News*, November 4. https://blog.frontiersin.org/2016/11/04/robotic-tutors-for-primary-school-children.

14. Cuadrado, L. E., Riesco, A. M., and Lopez, F. (2016). "ARTIE: An Integrated Environment for the Development of Affective Robot Tutors." *Frontiers in Computational Neuroscience*, August 3. https://www.frontiersin.org/articles/10.3389/fncom.2016.00077/full.

15. "Constructivism (philosophy of education)." Wikipedia. en.wikipedia.org/wiki/Constructivism_ (philosophy_of_education) (accessed November 1, 2021).

16. Georgia Tech Professional Education. (2016). "Meet Jill Watson: Georgia Tech's First AI Teaching Assistant." November 10. https://pe.gatech.edu/blog/meet-jill-watson-georgia-techs-first-ai-teaching-assistant.

17. Vincent, J. (2017). "Tencent Says There Are Only 300,000 AI Engineers Worldwide, But Millions Are Needed." The Verge, December 5. https://www.theverge.com /2017/12/5/1673 7224/global-ai-talent-shortfall-tencent-report.

18. REY. (2016). "Microsoft Helps Tacoma Public Schools Use Data Analytics to Predict At-Risk Students." Harvard Business School, November 18. https://digital.hbs.edu /platform-rctom/submission/microsoft-helps-tacoma-public-schools-use-data-analytics-to-predict-at-risk-students/.

19. Fuller, E. (2017). "Cloud Based Learning Platform Sows Seeds of Students' Lifelong Learning." Microsoft News, October 30. https://news.microsoft.com/en-au/features/cloud-based-learning-platform-sows-seeds-students-lifelong-learning-2/.

20. Technavio, "Artificial Intelligence Market in the US Education Sector 2018–2022."

21. Nelson, K. (2018). "The Future of Artificial Intelligence in Education." TechWell Insights, July 31. https://www.techwell.com/techwell-insights/2018/07/future-artificial-intelligence-education.

Defense

7.1 INTRODUCTION

The emerging use of AI is creating significant implications for national security and defense, with many governments and organizations already looking at its application. As AI becomes more mainstream, the implication is that it could be used against countries by foreign actors. The issue of AI in defense is particularly interesting, insofar as if one country is using it, then others feel compelled to also use it in order to maintain some form of parity. It is an age-old model, recognized also in the use of nuclear deterrents.

One of the big challenges is how to develop appropriate AI for military purposes. While it seems that AI needs to be specially created for defense in the majority of instances, there are uses outside the defense sector where learning might also be taken and transferred. For example, in the area of logistics and supply chain, intelligent systems are critical to ensure that supplies are provided in the right place and at the right time. There are also potential parallels in cyberspace management as defense systems look to protect themselves against infiltration, whereas commercial entities are similarly keen to protect themselves against virus intrusion. Conversely, obsolete military technologies such as satellite imagery that has become dated and obsolete for that particular purpose often finds their way into commercial use.

The concept of "command and control" also bears similarities to the management of large corporations. Both have many moving parts in terms of operational behavior. The ability of a commercial executive team mirrors the defense team, as both seek to command and control the enterprise using sophisticated AI-infused systems, which have become increasingly critical, especially as the speed of change and its complexity quickens in pace. At the same time, there are also cost pressures and talent issues as defense, which is a particular part of the public sector, transforms to a different, more technological method of operating. Beyond this, the challenge of globalization means that countries have to be particularly careful in terms of from where they obtain these new, sophisticated capabilities.

This chapter first reviews those areas of defense and the military where AI is already being used, and later considers more carefully some of the ethical issues attaching to this part of the public sector.

7.2   USE CASES OF AI IN DEFENSE

The enormous breadth of a defense system ensures that there is likely to be a wide range of divergent technologies being used. The specific nature of defense means that there are seldom business drivers of the type that might be found in other public functions or in the private sector, but there is usually a defense framework or defense operating model that sets out the relationships across the organization and the relationship between the armed forces of a country and their government in terms of the level and type of expectations.[1]

Aligned to this, almost all parts of the operational service have a form of vision statement that sets out their ambition. In the case of the British Army, as one example, the vision statement is one that:

- Attracts, develops, and nurtures a twenty-first century workforce.
- Engages persistently to provide understanding and global influence for Britain while reducing external threats.
- Anticipates, adapts, and acts at speed to resolve crises at home and abroad across all domains.
- Innovates and digitalizes to transform the force and maximizes its integration with partners and allies.

It is the latter area that is of particular interest in the context of this book. The defense organization also has a series of enabling groups, one of which is called "Defence Digital" and that "provides both direction and coherence in the development and exploitation of digital technologies across the whole of Defence and acts as the primary delivery agent for Defence core digital systems and services." Also within the Governance Framework there is a "Defence Innovation and Technology Board" that contributes to top-level decisionmaking processes.[2] The scope of this particular Board includes tasks such as:

- Effective collaboration between human and technology-based decisionmaking processes.
- Digitalizing the battlefield, including the simulation of the future battlefield and the adoption of augmented reality and virtual reality.
- Delivering responsive cyber defenses, recognizing that commercial solutions are unlikely to meet the particular needs of defense.
- Providing an information-led wider business transformation, including the merging of in-house and commercially available data sets.

A typical digital defense implementation framework is shown by way of illustration of the complexity involved (Figure 7.1), although it is emphasized that other frameworks may exist.

This chapter aims to give some examples of the use of advanced technology and AI from across the world. All of the following examples are in the public domain as of 2021, but who would argue that other, more advanced, capabilities or prototypes don't already exist on a highly confidential basis?

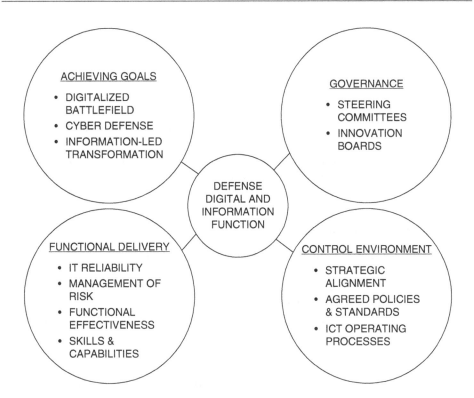

FIGURE 7.1   Typical Digital Defense Implementation Framework
Source: Adapted from UK Ministry of Defence, "How Defence Works," Version 6.0, September 2020, https://assets.publishing.service.gov.uk/government/uploads/system/uploads/attachment_data/file/920219/20200922-How_Defence_Works_V6.0_Sep_2020.pdf.

7.2.1   Intelligence, Surveillance, and Reconnaissance

AI has the ability to process very large (and growing) amounts of data in all its forms – structured and unstructured – and in multiple formats such as live streaming. In the case of the military, this might require rapid insight into the movement of vehicles, weapons, and people, in order to allow appropriate counter action to be taken. Multi-language translation ability is important, as well as the ability to identify conversation where there is a great deal of background noise. Integrated speech recognition provides an end-to-end speech solution. Recently, AI conversational startup Gnani.ai created a specific language surveillance capability for the Indian Armed Forces.[3]

Understanding the specific use of a building is also important. Military analysts use a technique called pattern of life analysis, which is a form of surveillance used to document and understand a subject's habits. In many cases, pattern of life analysis is undertaken in the private sector, with the subject's agreement, such as for employee monitoring, and it is being used more frequently in fraud investigations and criminal activity such as drug trafficking. Pattern of life tracking not only identifies normal behavior but also can identify abnormal behaviors, and is extremely effective when integrated with other forms of analysis such as timeline analysis and geospatial analysis.[4]

7.2.2 Logistics

The use of AI for predictive maintenance of military equipment is an approach that is commonly used already in the commercial sector. The US Air Force uses predictive maintenance to anticipate the need to either inspect or replace key aircraft components, and in using this capability they are able to improve reliability and reduce downtime.

Additionally, analysis of orders placed for replacement components ensures the effective and timely distribution of replacement parts. From an analysis based only on a sample of 10% of shipping requests, the US Army has saved over US$100 million by using this approach and they believe that, when fully adopted, the cost saving will be proportionately higher.

7.2.3 Cyberspace Operations

In the military context, an increasing dependence on technology with multiple points of potential weakness means that the need to maintain effective cyberspace defense is mission-critical. Without it, foreign agents could be able to rapidly disable existing military capabilities to their own advantage.

Commander of US Cyber Command Admiral Michael Rogers described reliance on human intelligence alone in cyberspace as "a losing strategy."[5] Currently, cyber tools look for particularly malicious code so hackers only need to modify a small part of that code to make it difficult to match. On the other hand, AI-enabled tools can search for malicious code in a much broader way, and in doing so are able to provide a much broader form of defense.

7.2.4 Information Operations and "Deep Fakes"

AI is increasingly being used to create realistic voice, image, and video; these imitations are known as "deep fakes." The impact of such false reality is that it can be used to mislead, which allows public opinion to be eroded, and it can even be used for the purposes of blackmail. The US-based Defense Advanced Research Process Agency (DARPA) has a project that enables them to "automatically detect manipulations, provide detailed information about how these manipulations were performed, and reason about the overall integrity of visual media."[6] In other words, in a process known as media forensics, their aim is to detect AI forgeries.

According to Cyber Law Chambers, an Indian-based cyber consultancy, Media Forensics also known as MediFor, comprises the use of "scientifically derived and proven methods towards the preservation, collection, validation, identification, analysis, interpretation, documentation and presentation of digital evidence derived from the digital sources for the purpose of facilitation or furthering the reconstruction of events found to be criminal, or helping to anticipate unauthorized actions shown to be disruptive to planned operations."[7]

7.2.5 Command and Control

Command and control, or, more precisely, multi-domain command and control (MDC2), centralizes the planning and execution of use of land-based, air-based, space-based, cyber-spaced, and marine-based services. It aims to fuse or converge data from all these sectors to provide a common operating picture. The intention is to provide a single view or version of the truth, that is, one that replaces the diverse and relatively fragmented information that is often provided in different formats and that leads to uncertainty and discrepancies. The aim is to use AI to resolve discrepancies from multiple data sets.

In some ways, this is a military operational comparison to the idea of "business intelligence," which is one of the foundational types of analytics in the analytical maturity curve of private organizations. Business intelligence also aims to provide a single version of the truth so that there is a consistent understanding of the organization across the many silos of business activity that might exist.

Beyond this, in a military context, command and control aims also to be able to provide an effective response where one or more communication links have been disrupted by the enemy. It also allows military organizations to establish alternative methods of communication and distribution of information where there has been operational disruption. The overwhelming ambition of command and control is to provide decision makers with real-time, accurate insights that allow them to implement actions in complex scenarios and to accelerate war-time decision making with greater certainty.

7.2.6 AI and Augmented Reality Soldiers

In 2021, Microsoft announced a massive contract of US$21.8 billion to equip soldiers with what is generically described as an augmentation system, providing "next-generation night vision and situational awareness capabilities to the Close Combat Force at the speed of relevance."[8] According to the report, the system incorporates "A head-mounted display used by soldiers for battle and training [that] will take advantage of sensors for night and thermal vision as well as engaging targets and making tactical decisions."

It is perhaps an early step in creating a superior infantryman who has enhanced fighting capabilities, and when converged with cybernetics as covered in an earlier chapter, the door is perhaps opened to the creation of military resources with extraordinary powers.

7.2.7 Semi-Autonomous and Autonomous Vehicles

The use of AI in semi-autonomous and autonomous vehicles such as aircraft, drones, land-based vehicles, and marine vehicles helps them "perceive the environment, recognize obstacles, fuse sensor data, plan navigation, and even communicate with other vehicles."[9] Typical examples include:

- In aircraft, the "Loyal Wingman" concept, where a manned plane is accompanied by an unmanned plane, with the latter being used for support services such as jamming of intrusive signals or carrying extra weapons.
- On the ground, the US Army's Multi-Utility Tactical Transport (MUTT) vehicle is used to follow land-based troops around and to carry equipment.

- Robotic Combat Vehicles (RCVs), which can be used for navigation, surveillance, and to deal with improvised explosive devices (IEDs). India's Defense and Research Organisation (DRDO) has an electric-powered remotely operated vehicle (ROV) called Daksh, which serves as bomb disposal units for the army and paramilitary forces.[10] An automated decision-making system sweeps the ground to look for mines by using a sensor to capture real-time images of the area of interest. The captured images are then fed to a computing unit and are digitally processed before being analyzed.[11]
- In the area of weapons disablement, COMRADES (Cooperative Multirobot Automated Detection System) is a multi-robot method for humanitarian demining, which is an attempt to reduce the social, economic, and environmental impact of mines. Another example is Minect.ai, which is an AI-based landmine detection system that detects landmines and other projectiles using neural networks. The device can process visual data streams from multiple sources, including drones, robots, and smartphones, in real time, to recognize and pinpoint the location of landmines.[12]
- The Anti-Submarine Warfare Continuous Trail Unmanned Vessel prototype "Sea Hunter" will be used to "autonomously navigate the open seas, swap out modular payloads, and coordinate missions with other unmanned vessels." In addition, the prototype will provide continuous submarine-hunting coverage for months at a time. After development costs, the return on investment is considerable, with an estimated cost of US$20,000 per day in comparison to the daily cost of a destroyer at US$700,000 per day.[13]
- The US military is also considering swarming devices, which range from larger to smaller devices. These swarms operate cooperatively to provide electronic attack, fire support, and communication networks for ground troops. Swarm devices act independently without centralized control, are able to communicate with each other, and are focused on a specific task. [14]
- The Lethal Autonomous Weapon (LAW) system is a type of weapon that acts without human intervention. It requires advanced algorithms and recognition systems in order to be able to identify the enemy, make a decision, and deploy a weapon. The United States is currently not using this capability, although legally, at present, there appear to be no restrictions in its use.

7.3 ETHICAL ISSUES

At the heart of many discussions regarding the use of AI in defense matters are significant ethical considerations. Notwithstanding wider considerations regarding warfare and defense generally, there are differences in thinking relative to the use of AI in defense systems. Some believe that AI will have only a minimal effect where AI is incorporated into existing systems, whereas others believe that it will have an evolutionary and dramatic impact involving the use of robotics. The question of the ethical use of AI in military use is different to that of when AI is involved in commercial use, due to issues of national competition and the security aspect of the usage. It's a problem that governments particularly need to consider in the area of funding and prioritization.

In their 2019 Congressional Report into Artificial Intelligence and National Security,[15] the US-based Congressional Research Service invited readers to think about key issues such as:

- The right balance between commercial and government funding for AI development.
- The impact of other defense reform initiatives on military AI development.
- How to manage and implement an effective oversight of AI development.
- How to balance the issues of artificial intelligence in autonomous systems with ethical considerations.
- What legislative or regulatory changes are involved.
- How to manage AI competition globally.

7.4 DRONES

In his 2015 book *Drone Theory*, author Gregoire Chamayou considered some of the issues relative to the use of drones.[16] While these devices are not directly AI-infused (although are likely to be in the future), there are some useful comparisons that can be made, especially as Chamayou draws out some important practical and ethical issues relative to semi-autonomous and autonomous devices.

A drone, he suggests, is comparable to some sort of "all-seeing eye" that allows military forces to optimize the quality and duration of surveillance, suggesting that:

- Drones can be on permanent or persistent watch.
- They can provide a wider perspective by having a wider visual viewpoint beyond that of humans. Drones are able to aggregate visual data and as a result can provide a better contextual picture. Chamayou compares this to the multiple facets in the eye of a fly.
- The system provides a permanent record or archive of what has been seen. This allows any visualization to be replayed multiple times and while initially focusing on one person, could be used in the future to investigate others in the vicinity. As a result the information drones collect, usually in an unstructured way, adds to a wider body of knowledge about a place or individual.
- Through the use of effective advanced analytics and AI, drones such as Predator and Reaper can be a key component in creating greater insight and operational intelligence. This might be in situations where the drones are used as a platform to incorporate information such as electronic communications from radios, cell phones, and other communication devices.
- Drones can help create a more detailed schematization of life, or pattern of life analysis (mentioned earlier), by combining visualizations with time and location metrics. In other words, the drone is able to capture the details of an individual, where they were, when they were there, and with whom. Overall it helps create a

much broader picture of an individual and provides information based on activity, which is the principle at the heart of countersurveillance. It also helps discover unusual activity that might lead the users to think that something suspicious was happening.

The main consideration is that drones and other surveillance devices generally operate on the principle of being able to detect anomalies that may be important in matters of security. Amid masses of other normal activities, systems such as these have the ability to pick out unusual actions that might be indicative in some way of being a threat. For example, if a bridge in an urban location suddenly empties of people then this perhaps may be as a result of local informal knowledge, such as a message being passed on outside of normal social media channels. Sudden action such as this could be indicative that a terrorist event such as a bombing might be likely to happen.

Surveillance of this nature also allows effective comparisons to be made. Predicting the future is dependent on understanding the past but this can be a very doubtful exercise, especially where there is considerable uncertainty, such as in the case of local cultural issues. The military aim is that by being able to predict the future accurately, it may be possible to take some sort of preemptive action, which may include the use of weaponry.

The names of some of these devices is revealing:

- *Argus* is named after a figure in Greek mythology with 100 eyes and was described as "the one who sees all." Argus drones are small, disc-shaped devices equipped with missile targeting systems.
- *Gorgon Stare* is named after the mythical Greek creature the Gorgon, whose gaze turned to stone those who caught its glare. Technically, the device has an array of nine cameras attached to a single drone, and is able to give an area-wide surveillance picture.

The wider topic of surveillance in the context of the actions of the State will be considered later in this book. It is difficult not to argue that in many places a surveillance society already exists to some degree. Drones provide an effective way of providing remote policing without the need to fix devices to walls and external buildings, as all that is required for these drone devices are the air and the sky. For those who might be under surveillance, it is a worrying and perhaps also a psychologically damaging place to be. Individuals hear the continual buzzing of the drone even if the device cannot be seen and, in a military context, are aware of the potentially devastating impact that the drone might have on their lives and community. Such permanent lethal surveillance is thought by some to comprise a form of psychic imprisonment, one not of walls or bars but virtual imprisonment by the endless circling of devices overhead.

For those operating the drones in a military context, it is an equally challenging but very different form of existence. The evolution of a new career now called drone pilot has resulted in individuals sitting in buildings many thousands of miles away from the point of impact of their weapons. They are obliged to make decisions that affect people that they have never seen in real life and are never likely to see. In an Associated Press article in 2008 it was suggested that "Long-distance warriors are suffering some of the same physiological stresses as their colleagues on the battlefield." Those who are actually on the front line do not see it that way and, with an element of contempt, often describe these drone pilots as "gaming warriors" who have a PlayStation mentality.[17]

There is already concern that military staff who may themselves be under contract from the private sector are already making life-and-death decisions with the same ethical consideration as someone shooting at targets in an electronic game or in an amusement arcade. An apparent lack of empathy by the pilot or controller of the remote device to the outcome of their decisions seems to be a worrying consequence of remote warfare. Perhaps this also ultimately might be a broader consequence of the development of autonomous or semi-autonomous technology. To what degree, if ever, will a programmer or AI developer feel some sort of vicarious responsibility for the injury and death of others?

This type of concern is not entirely new. Artillery gunners have traditionally hurled missiles great distances to try to injure or kill people that they have never seen or met. The dropping of the atomic bomb affected thousands of people that the crew of *Enola Gay* had never met, nor indeed the developers of the bomb itself. War has, in reality, already been a remote business for a long time.

7.5 CONCLUSION

Armed forces are not immune to defense cuts. As a result of economic pressures, these cuts are likely to occur not only at a time of heightened tensions in many parts of the world, which create additional pressures and create new complexities, but also at a time when there is a need for greater expenditure in areas of technology. In many cases, cost reductions result in lower headcounts but are often compensated for by improved operational efficiency through the use of better technology and as aging equipment is replaced.

What was once an arms war seems now to have become a technology war. In this new battle the weaponry of cyberattack in defense is every bit as threatening as it is in the private sector albeit with hugely different consequences. The concept of autonomous and semi-autonomous equipment also puts new pressures not only on ethical decisioning but also on humans who are expected to operate these devices while thousands of miles away from those suffering the consequences.

In terms of talent management, it is recognized that military personnel of tomorrow will be very different from those of yesterday or today. To what degree will these new mobile AI-infused experts need to have different skills and capabilities from those we presently know and understand? Will basic education for them still be sufficient as it is currently in many cases, or will they require a higher degree of education and technological capabilities to be able to use new complex systems?

At the other end of the talent spectrum, developers of new defense systems will increasingly require experts at a time when resources are limited. The idea of obtaining these skills on a contracted basis from the private sector should not be overlooked and in many cases the answer might rest in outsourcing. This approach might result in the public service of defense, ultimately comprising some form of public/private sector model, and one that mirrors other parts of the public sector.

7.6 NOTES

1. UK Ministry of Defence. (2020). "How Defence Works." September. Gov.UK. https:// assets.publishing.service.gov.uk/government/uploads/system/uploads/attachment_data/ file/920219/20200922-How_Defence_Works_V6.0_Sep_2020.pdf.
2. UK Ministry of Defence. (2019). "Defence Innovation Priorities." Gov.UK. https://www.gov .uk/government/publications/defence-innovation-priorities.
3. Choudhury, A. (2021). "5 AI Tools For Modern Warfare." *Analytics India*, March 29. analyticsindiamag.com/5-ai-tools-for-modern-warfare.
4. Williams, D. (2021). "Pattern of Life Analysis: How Timelines Uncover Hidden Behaviors." Cambridge Intelligence, February 3. https://cambridge-intelligence.com/pattern-of-life-analysis/.
5. Testimony of Michael Rogers, Senate Armed Services Committee, Hearing to Receive Testimony on Encryption and Cyber Matters, September 13, 2016. https://www.armed-services .senate.gov/imo/media/doc/16-68_09-13-16.pdf.
6. Turek, M. "Media Forensics (MediFor)." Defense Advanced Research Projects Agency. https://www.darpa.mil/program/media-forensics (accessed December 8, 2021).
7. Cyber Crime Chambers. "Media Forensics." cybercrimechambers.com/media-forensics.php (accessed December 8, 2021).
8. Agence France-Presse. (2021). "Microsoft Wins $22 Billion US Army Contract for Augmented Reality gear," April 1. https://news.abs-cbn.com/business/04/01/21/Microsoft-wins-22-billion-us-army-contract-for-augmented-reality-gear.
9. Canis, B. (2018). "Issues in Autonomous Vehicle Deployment." Congressional Research Service, Report R44940, May 17. https://sgp.fas.org/crs/misc/R44940.pdf.
10. Das, S. (2020). "AI Has Now Reached The Battlefield With Killer Robots, Automated Weapons & UAVs." *Analytics India*, January 8. https://analyticsindiamag.com/ai-has-now-reached-the-battlefield-with-killer-robots-automated-weapons-uavs.
11. Achkar, R. and Owayjan, M. (2012). "Implementation of a Vision System for a Landmine Detecting Robot Using Artificial Neural Network." *International Journal of Artificial Intelligence & Applications (IJAIA)* 3, no. 5 (September). 1210.7956.pdf (arxiv.org).
12. Choudhury, "5 AI Tools For Modern Warfare."
13. Turner, J. (2020). "Sea Hunter: Inside the US Navy's Autonomous Submarine Tracking Vessel." Naval Technology, January 30. https://www.naval-technology.com/features/sea-hunter-inside-us-navys-autonomous-submarine-tracking-vessel.
14. Baraniuk, C. (2021). "How Bees and Drones Team Up to Find Landmines." BBC News, March 30. https://www.bbc.co.uk/news/business-56344609.
15. Sayler, K.M. (2020). "Artificial Intelligence and National Security." Congressional Research Service Report R45178, November 10. https://crsreports.congress.gov/product/ details?prodcode=45178.
16. Chamayou, G. (2015). *Drone Theory*. London: Penguin.
17. Lindlaw, S. (2008). "Remote-Control Warriors Suffer Battle Stress at a Distance." Associated Press, August 8. http://archive.boston.com/news/nation/articles/2008/08/08/remote_ control_warriors_suffer_battle_stress_at_a_distance/.

Smarter Cities and Transportation

8.1 INTRODUCTION

In the context of smarter cities, one suitable starting-off point might be to consider what is meant by the term "city." This longstanding term reflects a place of large size with administrative boundaries, usually with sanitation and public spaces; the idea has been with us since at least the third or fourth millennium BCE. Cities were also places of power and by 1500–1600 CE some cities such as Venice had become city-states. In his book *The Republic*, the ancient Greek philosopher Plato also had a view of the "perfect city," which suggested divisions of labor and responsibilities that collectively created a "harmonious whole." In the context of today, perhaps the aim is to recreate a harmonious whole through the integrated use of data and analytics.

Cities are in a continuous state of change. With greater urbanization, that is, the movement of people from rural to urban settlements, the need for water and other municipal or public services such as education and policing have become even more essential. These have been considered in separate sections elsewhere in this book, but overall they reflect the interconnectivity of public services generally.

The focus for this particular chapter is that of the city infrastructure itself, and especially how it will be affected by the development of advanced technologies and AI. Additionally, with citizens needing to travel efficiently to their place of work, the topic of transportation both within and between cities and towns, as an integral function of the city, is included.

8.2 SMARTER CITIES

The concept of smarter cities has been around since the 1970s, when Los Angeles created what is thought to be the first city-orientated data cluster. The first smart city is generally accepted to be Amsterdam, which created the first digital city. The expression became more recognized in the mid-2000s, when both IBM and CISCO launched independent initiatives. By 2011 the inaugural Smart City World Congress was held in Barcelona; this has now become an annual event. In its broadest and most common meaning, "smart city" refers to the use of devices and sensors to collect data and, through the use of analytics, to help manage assets and the infrastructure effectively. Once imagined as being futuristic in some way, there are now already over 600 smart cities in operation around the world, collectively generating 60% of the world's GDP.[1]

This is as much an issue of urbanization as it is of technology, as people from rural locations move into the city. Urbanization often occurs not because of the superior nature of the city infrastructure but in many cases due to the relative lack of support of the rural environment. Rural transportation has been reduced outside the city and town and people live further away from hospitals, schools, and places of work than ever before. Even the concept of working from home, which is dependent on good connectivity, is undermined in rural locations by the relative paucity of the internet in terms of signal strength and speed.

With particular focus on smart cities (within which category might also be included smarter towns), and in the context of public services, the following issues are important examples of progress.

8.2.1 Smart Infrastructure

This is the ability to manage grid systems such as energy and utility to improve efficiency and operational effectiveness.

Smart infrastructure takes many forms, such as water flow and pollution measurement, both of which help to proactively manage public health issues. With infrastructure being so asset-intensive, the use of AI and advanced analytics in the form of predictive maintenance is critical to ensure that assets remain serviceable.

8.2.2 Smart Transportation

This is managed at multiple levels, typically:

- **Traffic management**, as AI ensures the free flow of traffic and avoidance of congestion. This helps reduce fumes, reduce travel times, and provides other traffic monitoring activities, such as traffic light control.
- **Public transportation**, which can be managed so that it operates in a more timely manner, encouraging citizen usage. Traffic lights are also aligned to bus journey flows.
- **Autonomous vehicles**, which will ultimately be able to integrate with these technologies to provide a more seamless traffic management experience.
- **Increased safety**; for example, trains and trams could have a systematic awareness of the train immediately in front of them and automatically hit the brakes to avoid collision.

8.2.3 Street Lighting

One key element of urbanization and effective communities is the provision of adequate and effective street lighting. The smarter cities concept ensures better use of energy through grid management and proactive management of the lighting infrastructure.

Additionally, data collection may correlate the presence and effectiveness of lighting with increased footfall, leading to better and more timely lighting at popular restaurants and public venues.

8.2.4 Water Utilities

Generally these are the provision of clean water and the collection and disposal of dirty or waste water. In their 2018 conference UK trade union Unison, which represents most employees in the water and wastewater sector, recognized the increasing impact of AI, robotics, and automation on their industry.[2] They reported that surveys of executives of those companies revealed that, in their view, the optimum solution was that of a convergence of skills between humans and machines to create "a more effective, engaged and meritocratic workforce." In their report Unison interestingly *redefined* the expression of "workforce" as being "both human employees and intelligence machines" and take the view that the future is most likely to be an operational combination of both rather than machines replacing humans.

The areas most identified as being likely to change as a result of AI in the water industry were:

- Contact center transformation, including the use of chatbots.
- Transportation, including self-driving tankers and tracks.
- Surveying, including the use of drones and remote imagery.
- Robots, especially in areas where work was likely to be hazardous.
- Human resource management, especially in the interview process with automated analysis of candidates who had submitted video or voice applications.

The overall concern of executives in this sector was that decisions to use AI and automated systems were likely to be based primarily on financial and economic grounds. They were worried, however, that robotic systems and AI did not have the requisite soft skills and body of experience to effectively undertake certain tasks, although these could potentially be created through effective programming and design. The trade union invited a two-pronged response to the problem, principally:

- Upskilling of current employees rather than redundancy of those with obsolete skills and their replacement with new, more suitable employees.
- An adjustment in payment, terms, and conditions of those involved with more routine work to reflect the likely reduced volume.

8.2.5 Emergency Services

The topic of emergency services is covered elsewhere in this book in terms of their nature, how they are best deployed, and the increasing effect of advanced technologies and AI.

Using remote imagery and integrated systems allows incidents to be identified and emergency services to be deployed more quickly and effectively. Greater insight into the nature and locations of incidents will also allow locating service bases more effectively.

8.2.6 Waste Collection and Disposal

Although this aspect has also already been partly covered under the healthcare section, the subject of waste collection and disposal is a critical part of public services. According to a 2017 US Environmental Protection Agency report, 4.5 pounds of rubbish is created per person, per day.[3]

In 2011 a Finnish company, ZenRobots, first created a capability for the automatic sorting of waste using AI. Automatic sorting is now being used by one South Korean city, Songdo, with sensoring technology, tracking RFID tags on refuse to sort waste and to bucket it appropriately.[4] The first step in terms of intelligent waste disposal in the urban environment is the use of intelligent or smart waste bins. These carry devices that measure the fullness of the bin and also allows waste collection services to optimize their collection route. Next-generation waste bins such as Bin-e identify, sort, and compact waste as it is discarded.[5]

Until all bins are automatic, sorting waste has to be mainly undertaken by hand, although automated sorting that relies on cameras and algorithms can increase sorting speed fourfold and, unlike humans, can work continuously.[6] Many of the problems of smart waste disposal rest with manufacturers, which often use a combination of recyclable and nonrecyclable materials in the same packaging, which makes waste more difficult to sort. Better packaging discipline, coupled with smarter ways of identifying and recycling rubbish, will go a long way toward reducing cost and improving the environment.

8.2.7 Maintenance of Public Places

Public places, such as parks and recreation areas, are an important part of the urban landscape. Their importance is likely to grow if, as some predict, the advent of increasing technology has a major impact on the workforce as many noncomplex jobs become automated and more citizens have more leisure time.

Although many gardening functions are immune from the impact of AI, the use of devices that measure moisture levels in the ground when coupled with automated systems for watering can ensure the longevity of plants and trees. Building sensors can also help to identify the optimum time for external building maintenance and, when combined with weather prediction, can support effective maintenance programs. Automated lawn mowing has been around for a while and is perhaps one of the most visible signs of simple robotic technology in this area.[7]

8.2.8 Humans as Devices

The possibility of humans also acting as contributors to the smart city infrastructure is a distinct possibility, even if it presents a slightly dystopian view of life. The prevalence of inbuilt sensors on mobile devices potentially permits each one of us to act as human devices that collect information overall for the data landscape.

In what we might describe as a form of data democracy, the flow of information could be bidirectional in that outputs are of benefit to everybody. For example, in the same way that citizens can check when the next bus is likely to arrive, the flip side is the idea that the bus company also knows that it has one or more customers waiting and can schedule its service accordingly.[8]

8.2.9 Data Challenges for Smart Cities

One issue is that of the sheer amount of data generated through a fully connected smart city and the amount of computing and analytical power needed to make it operate effectively. Overloading of data might simply result in the system grinding to a halt. The introduction in time of quantum computing will clearly help, although this may be decades ahead. There are also some serious security issues, with the number of devices and data entry points providing multiple opportunities for cybercrime breaking into the system.

It's not a clear-cut argument for change to everyone, and some even argue in favor of turning the clock back to a low-tech, nonconnected environment.[9] Shoshanna Saxe, assistant professor at the University of Toronto, suggests that smart cities "will be exceedingly complex to manage, with all sorts of unpredictable vulnerabilities." Tech products age fast and she asks what happens when the sensors fail. She also queries whether cities are likely to be able to afford expensive new teams of tech staff as well as keeping the ground workers they'll still need. She provides a reminder about the more practical issues of managing a city: "If smart data identifies a road that needs paving, it still needs people to show up with asphalt and a steamroller."[10]

Saxe adopts an interesting counterpoint to the argument for cities connected by technology, arguing for low-tech solutions to drainage, wastewater, agriculture, and pollution. Comparison is made with methods that have served indigenous people in the past for centuries without the need for technology, and she's not alone in her views. Julia Watson, of Columbia University, New York, is an urban designer who also calls for "rewilding" of cities, saying of a project she is engaged in at Shenzhen, China, "You can leapfrog and embed local intelligence, using a nature-based traditional . . . technology that's climate resilient, ecologically resilient and culturally resilient. And we can make beautiful urban spaces with them as well."[11]

One other European example is the use of public parks in Copenhagen to create temporary reservoirs when flooding occurs, using natural flood runoff. Local planners there call it a "green and blue" solution. Another argument is that walking or cycling are vastly superior to technologically-driven systems or car travel as they provide a carbon-free, pollution-free solution that creates exercise at the same time.

8.3 TRANSPORTATION

For a town or city to function efficiently requires comprehensive and optimized transportation systems. Citizens need to be able to travel to and from their place of work in a cost-effective and safe way. The experience of the 2020 pandemic and the move toward working from home did not undermine the broader need to continue to provide public transport but rather perhaps changed the way it was used, especially in terms of frequency, degree of usage, and alongside private means such as cars, other vehicles, and bicycles. Future comprehensive transportation systems need to be versatile to accommodate future change.

In this section, issues of traffic management and safety are considered. Then three different types of transportation are reviewed along with the possible impact of AI and advanced analytics on them.

8.3.1 Traffic Management

One undeniable element of the smarter city is that of effective traffic management, particularly the management of intersections and the adherence with traffic laws. Traffic management systems also provide data and information that give insight into driver behavior and support the drivers themselves in their personal decision making.

Key benefits of effective traffic management systems include:

- Real-time analysis of traffic conditions
- Increasing the effectiveness of traveling by road
- Integrating vehicle traffic with other public transport systems
- Reductions in pollution
- Issuing of penalties and effective collection of fines, when coupled with an e-billing system
- Use of speed sensors to warn drivers of violations
- Reduction of traffic incidents and freeing up of police time
- Association of traffic and pedestrian needs with smart urban lighting systems

The essential components of a traffic management system (TMS) include:

- A central control system that is integrated with multiple devices such as cameras, smart signaling, queuing systems, and locational awareness.
- Smart signaling that is active and responds to traffic conditions rather than working to a predefined program.
- Use of intelligent cameras and queuing systems.

It is also likely that effective traffic management systems will play an integral part in the operation of autonomous and semi-autonomous vehicles.[12]

Cycling provides a healthier alternative to car travel in many circumstances, and there are intelligent systems in place already that assist the cyclist, known as "smart cycling." These systems, which are specifically designed for the cyclist, differ from car systems, in that systems for cars are predominantly time- and distance-oriented whereas systems for cyclists need to take into account their behavioral and energy patterns.[13]

8.3.2 Road Safety

In addition to traffic management systems, a new concept, called "AI for road safety,"[14] has been introduced for a Thai company, Global Chemicals by FRONTIS, in conjunction with Microsoft. This idea arose as corporate drivers were obliged to use one of the most dangerous roads in Southeast Asia as they commuted from one factory to another. In order to identify driver behavior, the system adopted a combination of facial recognition within the vehicle itself coupled with GPS to detect speeding. In addition, data collection helped the company to understand the most efficient routes and to optimize fuel consumption.

If the driver shows signs of drowsiness through detection of facial behaviors or there is evidence of speeding through the use of GPS monitoring, an alarm is sent to the driver and, if needed, a replacement driver can be sent. Two particular issues that concerned the developers of the system included:

1. The bulkiness of the camera, which was too obtrusive, resulting in the driver focusing on the camera rather than the road.
2. The variability of facial expressions that reveal drowsiness – eyes closed, droopy eyes, or yawning, for example – and their relative importance.

8.3.3 Highway Maintenance

With greater pressure on the public purse, it becomes more important to manage assets effectively, including highway and road maintenance. Advanced analytics and AI are being used to:

- Objectively analyze road conditions
- Upload automated assessment and inspector notes
- Make more effective maintenance decisions
- Check and maintain road markings

Badly maintained road markings are a significant safety issue for drivers and cyclists and make it difficult for motorists to know where they can park or overtake and change lanes, and for cyclists to travel in safety. Effective use of imagery can help identify possible areas of risk and can assist local authorities in prioritizing services.

8.3.4 Autonomous Trams

There can be fewer experiences more dissatisfying that being in a car caught behind a bus that is belching diesel and causing congestion. If public transportation was better, that is, more efficient and affordable, then there is a chance that a car may not be the preferred means of transport in any event. That said, for many the car is a pleasure, a convenience, and a status symbol.

Increasingly, attention is being paid not only to trams as a means of urban transport but to the use of autonomous, AI-controlled tramway systems. Key potential benefits for the use of autonomous trams include:

- Reduction in fuel consumption
- Less tram downtime

- Improved tram efficiency
- Reductions in salary for drivers and assistants
- Improved customer service
- Reduction in road traffic accidents

The overall aim of the use of autonomous trams in the urban environment is to minimize their dependence on the human factor, according to Jack Wu of FITSCO, one of China's urban rail transit signal providers. In a joint pilot project that was demonstrated in Russia in 2019 between FITSCO and Russian-based company Cognitive Pilot, autonomous tram systems use visual recognition to detect red lights, people on the track, or a threat of collision. It comprises a combination of information about the location of the tram using satellite navigation, allowing precise location of the tram to 30 cm, wheel rotation sensors, radar, and video cameras. The system warns the driver, automatically reduces speed, and, if necessary, applies the brakes itself. During operation, the driver remains on the tram but as a safety controller only.[15]

In 2018, Siemens launched its version of a fully autonomous tram in Potsdam, west of Berlin in Germany.[16] The Combino tram is fitted with multiple radar, LIDAR (light from a laser), and camera sensors that detect every part of the tram's journey and its surroundings. The Potsdam transport company, ViP, manages 33 million customers a year and says that the intention is that these high-tech trains will not affect driver jobs. Rather, it says, drivers will be redeployed marshaling passengers on the platform and helping people with special requirements such as with a disability or with a pram. "Our main priority is safety," says Oliver Glasser, manager of ViP, "and secondly we think it'll improve efficiency."

So why is a driver needed, anyway? Automatic metros or "sky trains" often seen at airports seem already to be driverless, but the difference is that these are automatic as opposed to autonomous, and that they are performing in a closed environment. This means that there are no external events to disturb the normal operation. On the other hand, autonomous trains operate in an open or semi-open environment and they need to be able to cope with unknown situations.

In Germany, Thales has also been active in this space. With a background in other technologies such as defense, aerospace, and avionics, it is applying new methodologies such as a robot train, which they call Railbot. They recognize that there is a need to find a balance between safety and availability. A train that is stopping all the time as a result of false detects will impact adversely on usage. As a result, Thales understands that it is very important to have an effective visualization system, one that not only monitors what is in front of the train but also monitors what is happening in the immediate environment. A three-layer approach is adopted: detection, recognition, and identification. The nature of the obstacle is important, as the train's response will be different if the obstacle is a tree as opposed to a plastic bag. The system is required to "understand the intention of the object" before implementing a course of action, which may range from slowing down to stopping altogether. Thales recognizes that there are other safety advantages as well, in that a robotic system can detect in poor conditions or bad light.[17]

8.3.5 Autonomous Taxis

The concept of autonomous road vehicles is more widely understood, even though trials to date have been uncertain. A picture might exist in our minds of the autonomous vehicle user handing over control to the vehicle itself and doing some paperwork as part of the daily commute, or the idea that the driver might switch to some sort of autopilot when on major free-flowing roadways, leaving the tricky stuff like starting and stopping to the human who, with parking aids, for example, can effect a bump-free maneuver. The reality is that cars continue to increase in sophistication, and major companies such as Tesla and Volvo are already experimenting with these advanced technologies.

A natural extension of this idea, in the context of a smart city, is that of the concept of driverless taxis, similar to those that were approved for use in 2021 in Beijing, although the impact of the pandemic delayed its usage. The system, operated by Baidu, was intended to be China's first autonomous paid taxi service, although for the moment a safety driver was still to sit behind the wheel in case sudden intervention is needed. It's expected that the driver will need to remain there for a while yet, until regulatory and safety issues have been adequately resolved. However, developers hope that Chinese consumers, who have been quick to embrace digital concepts such as e-commerce and online payments, are likely to quickly get used to the sensation of traveling in a car without a driver.

It's a sophisticated model. Using the Apollo Go app, the user can locate a cab in the vicinity and, upon making contact, the passenger can unlock the vehicle using a QR code that verifies identification and the payment process. Upon boarding the vehicle, the passenger then pushes a "Start the Journey" button, but the taxi will only move when all the safety protocols have been complied with, such as fastened seat belts and closed doors. Although ultimately the plan is for there to be no safety driver on board, a 5G communication system allows human operators to remotely operate the vehicle in exceptional circumstances. "Introducing unmanned services is an indispensable stage for the commercialization of autonomous driving," says Yunpeng Wang, VP of autonomous driving at Baidu, whose original ambition, pre-Covid, had been to introduce 1,000 autonomous taxis over the next three years. "In the future, Baidu Apollo will launch driverless robotaxis in more cities enabling the public to access greener, low carbon and convenient travel services."[18]

8.4 RAILWAYS AND THE FUTURE OF RAIL

In terms of transportation, there are many who think that there is likely to be a massive shift toward the reuse of rail rather than flying and driving. Supporters cite key benefits of railway use:

- Higher speed than conventional trains
- More effective routing than planes, including intermediate stops
- Lower maintenance, especially with maglev (magnetic levitation) trains
- Greater availability and less susceptibility to adverse weather

Using railways requires governments to:

- Undertake a strategic overhaul of existing railway systems, especially in the context of "net zero."
- Recognize the future trends of the railway industry so as to "future-proof" any proposals, and to consider the impact of future innovation.
- Create a clear pipeline of activities and a system of continuous learning from existing projects.
- Be prepared to allocate adequate funding.

Examples of innovation in rail include Maglev and the Virgin Hyperloop. Maglev trains provide rail travel at impressive speeds that are comparable to flight, although the concept is also quite capable of more routine slower routes. Virgin Hyperloop is from a US technology company seeking to transform rail travel using a variant of the vacuum train, by using a maglev-type concept but in a vacuum tube, as most of the energy drag of a maglev device is from wind resistance. Virgin's ambition is to move freight and passengers at airline speeds but for a fraction of the cost of flights.[19]

8.4.1   Net Zero in Rail

The concept of net zero, aka zero net carbon emissions, is high on many agendas, including that of transportation.

While there are different rail models on a country-by-country basis, different governments nevertheless tend still to have common objectives. These were encapsulated at a recent International Railway Summit conference entitled "Achieving Net-Zero Mobility by 2050."[20] Speakers there identified three key goals:

1. **Net zero:** A zero-carbon footprint that comprises the elimination of diesel and a movement toward a net-zero culture. According to European Commission transport commissioner Adina Vălean, "My objective . . . is to see rail become the driving force it once was. This traditional transport mode, enabler of the Industrial Revolution, could now play a central role in yet another fundamental transformation, one that will lead us to a sustainable and emission-free transport system."
2. **The development of sustainable mobility:** Recognition that technologies including digitalization, automation, 5G, and AI will create sustainable mobility, which is a way of moving around that does not damage the environment and takes care of city space. According to UIC, the worldwide railway organization, Director-General François Davenne said "[Developing resilience and a sense of urgency] is absolutely crucial for us because we think that the railway should become the backbone of sustainable mobility."
3. **Technology-driven:** Recognition that technology will not only provide railways with increased capacity but will allow operators to run train networks with greater energy efficiency, less noise emission, having high availability and able to use the same tickets across several modes of transportation, including across borders.

8.4.2 AI and Effective Rail Timetabling

The use of AI in more effective timetabling is high on the agenda. The Indian railway, for example, is a government-owned enterprise run by a separate ministry that is putting considerable focus on this area. The growth of India's population, plus the impact of urbanization and the desire for greater efficiency, has put even more pressure on a railway system comprising 70,000 km of track and that is already the fourth-largest in the world. The traditional response has been to build more track and put more cars on trains, but this comes at a high capital cost.

The Indian railway already runs on the SCADA (Supervisory Control And Data Acquisition) system, which is a control system involving computers, networked systems, and graphical interfaces that already generates a large amount of data. The aim is to improve the efficiency of the railways by using advanced analytics and AI to reduce waste in the system. This approach comprises:

- The use of predictive analytics to anticipate train delays, which is especially important given the knock-on effect.
- Predictive maintenance of line condition to anticipate the development of faults and help plan repair programs.
- Predictive maintenance of rolling stock, especially in regard to defects in the wheels.
- Scheduling of trains, which includes more effective timetabling of trains on lines (including single and bidirectional), rescheduling, and the scheduling of freight. The Indian problem differs from that in the United States, as the majority of freight in India travels by train, whereas in the United States the majority of freight travels by road.
- Crew management that includes long-term planning (rostering) and short-term planning (scheduling)
- Vehicle rotation planning to ensure that there is enough rolling stock in the right place, including locomotives, to run trains on time. This issue goes hand in hand with the crew management program.

Running the system effectively requires many layers of support and decision management. This can be done at both a macro and micro level, and there are many decisions that are made at a local level. Local decisions historically have tended to be made by humans using supervised learning, and there is an approach of continuous conflict resolution. Traditionally this has been done through the effective use of signaling (red, green) but a more sophisticated approach would be that of reducing train speeds, which also has an impact on energy consumption.

Beyond these challenges are the major ones of safety and passenger experience. The ability to respond to a major incident is critical, especially in India, where such large distances are involved, but this may relate to other areas as well. The problem of cybersecurity in such a large network also cannot be overstated. The passenger experience goes beyond matters of capacity, including those of ticket verification as well as those that are more fundamental, such as adequate washroom facilities.

In an invitation to the technology industry, Harshad Khadilkar of Tata Consultancy Services makes an argument for an ambitious AI-based solution that not only is able to integrate all the issues just mentioned but that also has:

■ The ability to handle variable and large scales.
■ The ability to use transfer learning across multiple problem areas without the hands-on involvement of a data scientist.
■ Explainable algorithms, rather than black box technology, which are especially important where issues of safety are concerned.
■ Compliance with existing (and probably future) rules and procedures.[21]

8.5 AIR TRAVEL

In the context of the public sector, air travel is included, especially by virtue of the fact that many airline companies are state-owned enterprises as well as an effective means of transportation. The State ownership of businesses is covered in Chapter 10. The practice of State ownership of airlines is already common practice in many countries, especially flag carrier airlines that are registered within a sovereign state and often enjoying preferential rights and privileges for international business. Typical airlines include Emirates (Dubai), Finnair (Finland), and LOT (Poland), for example.

We often think in terms of unmanned flight as comprising drones or other unmanned aerial devices, but these are usually remotely controlled and are not autonomous in their true nature. Today many planes are so complex as to be virtually autonomous, or close to being capable of being developed. The use of robotic assistants such as ALIAS (Aircrew Labor In-Cockpit Automation System)[22] are being tested in planes and helicopters, especially in the area of human/system interaction.

The use of autonomous systems within flight has an impact in the training and required competencies of pilots, and Table 8.1 considers what might be their required competencies, based on the International Air Transport Association's Training and Qualification Initiative.[23]

Pilots are an expensive commodity, with the cost of training being as much as US$100,000, and with some pilots earning a salary in excess of US$700,000.[25] The US Bureau of Labor Statistics places the average salary of a US commercial pilot at US$186,700 in 2020.[26] With the use of AI and advanced analytics increasingly challenging existing business models, alternatives to the human cost of piloting a plane start to look commercially attractive. The reality, however, is how confident passengers would feel if there was nobody in control sitting at the front of the plane, or perhaps not even in the plane but rather somewhere completely different.

Elsewhere, on the ground, the use of analytics and AI is increasingly playing a part in what is the most hazardous part of the flight, that of taking off and landing. With regard to air traffic control, there is increasingly a move toward virtual management, even if some degree of human intervention remains. For example, in 2021 London City became the world's first major international airport without a manned control tower

TABLE 8.1   Future Competencies for Pilots[24]

Existing Required Competencies	Additional Competencies Required Going Forward
Ability to effectively manage manual and automatic flight systems (i.e. fly the aircraft)	Ability to operate as human backup to mainly automated and robotic systems, from either within or outside the aircraft.
Ability to demonstrate leadership and team building	Capable of regaining or retaining control or perceived control (in the eyes of the passengers), even if acting in a virtual capacity and not actually within the aircraft itself.
Ability to have situational awareness, solve problems, and be an effective decision maker	Ability to have appropriate experience, obtained through regular training and scenario modeling in simulated conditions, and to be able to apply mitigating actions where there are problems.
Ability to correctly apply procedures	Ability to co-work with robotics pilots so that both of them comply with greater levels of regulations, including ethical protocols that will inevitably need to be created.

as eagle-eyed, locally based controllers are replaced with a mast with sensors and cameras.[27] London City now captures 360-degree information "in a level of detail greater than the human eye," which is relayed to a national control center in Swanage over 130 miles away. The intention overall is to use the UK's pool of over 2,000 controllers to manage movement in multiple airports, using virtual images. In doing so the costs of managing air traffic will be reduced by 20–30%.

Trials for these technologies are under way in Australia, Hungary, France, Ireland, Germany, Switzerland, France, and the United States. The pioneers of this approach were in Scandinavia, where remote airports with only a flight or two per day could not justify full-time air traffic controllers. The first use of virtual control was at Örnsköldsvik Airport in April 2015, followed by Sundsvall in 2016. Takeup since then appears to have been rapid, despite the view that this is a technology initially designed for small airports only. As Steve Anderson, Head of Airport Transformation at NATS, puts it:

> *Yes, there are clear benefits for smaller airfields, absolutely. Economies of scale, the ability to control multiple airports from one location, that's all true, but I think it's a total misconception that digital towers are only suitable for airports of low complexity and low ATM volume. Frankly, that's just lazy thinking.*[28]

While virtual air traffic control is still dependent on humans, these humans are located some distance away from the point of action, and their services are heavily supported by technology. It seems quite possible for intelligent systems that interact directly with aircraft to perform with increasingly less human intervention.

8.6   CONCLUSION

The concept of the smart city coupled with more effective transportation with a zero-carbon footprint is not a pipedream nor is it an exercise in research. Rather, it has real and important consequences, especially in an era of greater urbanization, which is recognized to be one of the major megatrends of change.

A data-driven city infrastructure brings multiple complexities, not least because of the interaction between multiple services. With the advent of 5G and the proliferation of even more devices, sophisticated and intelligence systems will be essential to maintain control and order.

At the same time, there is likely to be continued pressure on urban budgets. Already, citizens have a level of expectation as to what standards of service they are entitled to receive from the public sector. Not only do citizens expect police and emergency services, but they also expect their bins to be emptied on time, and other services to be readily available and to run smoothly. How all these will be managed and prioritized going forward will become a major issue.

8.7   NOTES

1. Maddox, T. (2016). "Smart Cities: 6 Essential Technologies." TechRepublic, August 1. https://www.techrepublic.com/article/smart-cities-6-essential-technologies.
2. Unison. (2018). "Automation, Artificial Intelligence and Robotics in the Water Industry." Motion 2018 Water, Environment & Transport Conference, February 27. https://www.unison.org.uk/motions/2018/water-environment-transport/automation-artificial-intelligence-and-robotics-in-the-water-industry/.
3. United States Environmental Protection Agency. (2020). "National Overview: Facts and Figures on Materials, Wastes and Recycling." https://www.epa.gov/facts-and-figures-about-materials-waste-and-recycling/national-overview-facts-and-figures-materials (accessed November 1, 2021).
4. Joshi, N. (2018). "4 Ways AI Can Revolutionize Waste Management." Allerin, October 3. https://www.allerin.com/blog/4-ways-ai-can-revolutionize-waste-management.
5. Bin-e. "Smart Waste Bin." https://www.bine.world.
6. Keymakr. (2021). "How Artificial Intelligence Is Transforming Waste Management." May 8. https://keymakr.com/blog/how-ai-is-transforming-waste-management/.
7. HL Services. (2021). "AI and Automation in Grounds Maintenance." https://www.hlservices.co.uk/ai-and-automation-in-grounds-maintenance (accessed October 1, 2021).
8. Doctorow, C. (2020). "The Case for . . . Cities That Aren't Dystopian Surveillance States." *The Guardian*, January 17. https://www.theguardian.com/cities/2020/jan/17/the-case-for-cities-where-youre-the-sensor-not-the-thing-being-sensed.
9. Fleming, Amy. (2020). "The Case for . . . Making Low-Tech 'Dumb' Cities Instead of 'Smart' Ones." *The Guardian*, January 15. https://www.theguardian.com/cities/2020/jan/15/the-case-for-making-low-tech-dumb-cities-instead-of-smart-ones.
10. Saxe, S. (2019). "I'm an Engineer, and I'm Not Buying Into 'Smart' Cities." *New York Times*, July 16. https://www.nytimes.com/2019/07/16/opinion/smart-cities.html.
11. Fleming, "The Case for . . ."

12. SoulPage IT Solutions. (2020, January 8). "Smart Traffic Monitoring And Management System." soulpageit.com/smart-traffic-monitoring-and-management-system/.

13. Panozzo, N. (2017). "Smarter Cycling Series: Big Data and Artificial Intelligence Are Transforming Bicycle Navigation." European Cycling Federation, August 16. https://ecf.com/news-and-events/news/smarter-cycling-series-big-data-and-artificial-intelligence-are-transforming-1.

14. Microsoft Asia News Center. (2019, March 4). "Artificial Intelligence and Road Safety: A New Eye on the Highway." https://news.microsoft.com/apac/features/artificial-intelligence-and-road-safety-a-new-eye-on-the-highway/.

15. Mehmet, S. (2020). "Joint Venture Tests Autonomous Tram Control in AI-Based Trial." Intelligent Transport, April 23. https://www.intelligenttransport.com/transport-news/98288/joint-venture-tests-autonomous-tram-control-in-ai-based-trial/.

16. Connolly, K. (2018). "Germany Launches World's First Autonomous Tram in Potsdam." *The Guardian*, September 23. https://www.theguardian.com/world/2018/sep/23/potsdam-inside-the-worlds-first-autonomous-tram.

17. Thales Group. (2019). "Artificial Intelligence for the Autonomous Trams." February 15. http://www.thalesgroup.com/en/germany/news/artificial-intelligence-autonomous-trams.

18. Intelligent Transport. (2021). "Baidu Launches Autonomous Robotaxi Service in Beijing." May 4. https://www.intelligenttransport.com/transport-news/123764/beijing-robotaxis/.

19. Virgin Hyperloop. https://virginhyperloop.com.

20. Macola, I. G. (2021). "Net-Zero Rail Mobility by 2050: Three Lessons from the IRS." Railway Technology, March 8. https://www.railway-technology.com/features/net-zero-mobility-2050-three-lesson-from-irs/.

21. Khadilkar, H. (2020). "Artificial Intelligence for Indian Railways." AI4Bharat. https://ai4bharat.org/articles/railways.

22. Anderson, S. (2017). "Control without Boundaries – The Rise of the Digital Remote Tower." Airport Review, June 13. https://www.internationalairportreview.com/article/35229/nats-digital-tower/?msclkid=f766da49b12f11ec8c167ee726dafaaf.

23. Robeck, V. (2012). "IATA Training and Qualification Initiative (ITQI) – A Total System Approach to Training." ALPA Conference, July 12. http://pilottrainingconference.alpa.org/LinkClick.aspx?fileticket=DaltKtZceh8%3d&tabid=6957&msclkid=342a8890b11f11ecb0018d6687356c13.

24. Boobier, T. (2018). *Advanced Analytics and AI: Impact, Implementation, and the Future of Work*. Chichester, UK: Wiley.

25. Epic Flight Academy. (2021). "Airline Pilot Salary." https://epicflightacademy.com/airline-pilot-salary/.

26. US Bureau of Labor Statistics. (2021). "Occupational Employment and Wages, May 2021: 53-2011 Airline Pilots, Copilots, and Flight Engineers." https://www.bls.gov/oes/current/oes532011.htm.

27. NATS. (2021). "London City Is First Major Airport Controlled by Remote Digital Tower." April 30. https://www.nats.aero/news/london-city-is-first-major-airport-controlled-by-remote-digital-tower/.

28. Anderson, "Control without Boundaries."

Housing and the Environment

9.1 INTRODUCTION

One of the major areas of interest in the public sector is social housing, also known as public housing, which is a key element of the benefit system. The term social or public housing is commonly used to describe a range of affordable housing, rental subsidies, and regulation models around the world. (In the context of this chapter the expression social housing will be used throughout.)

The management of social housing is not without its difficulties in terms of allocation, maintenance, and even fraud. In some areas the provision of new housing is controversial, as the increased demand for more property requires new building programs, but often building is undertaken in areas that have been avoided for natural reasons, such as being located in an area prone to flooding.

Although the topic of healthcare and looking after the elderly has been covered earlier in this book, there are obvious synergies. Aging demographics are leading more and more frequently to a greater need for home-based care. Effective management of social housing plays a key part in providing a holistic care solution.

Ultimately these are matters of balancing demand with supply, anticipating future needs, providing affordable housing, and also providing a safe, secure, and ultimately healthy environment at a time when there is economic uncertainty and greater focus on climate change and the impact of natural disasters. These are common challenges in many parts of the world, yet differences in practices and cultures often lead to solutions with different outcomes. This chapter considers some of these aspects within the context of the era of data and the benefits of better analytics and AI.

9.2 AI IN SOCIAL HOUSING

In their 2019 UK report "A Perfect Storm: Risk Perspectives from Social Housing Senior Leaders," commissioned by Zurich Municipal Insurance, social housing leaders suggested that the housing crisis remains "arguably Britain's biggest domestic policy challenge."[1] There is a recognizable shortfall of available property and the aim of the UK

Government in particular is to plug that shortfall by setting ambitious targets for new housebuilding. It is commonly understood that there is a growing urgent need to provide good quality affordable housing not only to young people but to provide care and support for the elderly.

The answer, it seems, may not only be one of urbanizing the problem, in other words, to move old people currently living in small communities into towns and cities but also to provide greater support to people in remote rural locations. Key issues to consider by social housing providers are how to:

- Serve the most vulnerable.
- Create sustainable communities.
- Fill the gaps left behind by local authorities as a result of other budgetary cuts.
- Transform social housing providers as an entity.
- Protect owner-tenants should there be a housing crash, and manage how that might affect shared ownership schemes.
- Better understand the impact of cost-cutting strategies, one example being the Grenfell Tower tragedy in London in 2017. This was the worst residential fire in London since World War II, where the building specification was found to be reduced and safety compromised to obtain cost savings.
- Interact better with their social customers who expect a standard of service comparable to that which they receive in the private sector.
- Manage social housing provider data in an improved way and create actionable outcomes.

Like almost all organizations, the social housing sector is going through digital transformation, including that of how users and providers communicate with each other. As stated by one UK Housing CEO, "Over 90% of our customer transactions are over the phone – this isn't sustainable." Key drivers for better technological interaction include:

- Using AI to reduce operational costs
- Replacing telephone calls with an online response
- Providing other added-value services such as online information

Already social housing providers are using chatbots as the first interaction with their customer, as this allows effective routing while maintaining human interaction as a backup option.

Cyberattack also remains a concern. For example, how do social housing companies, which often operate at the limit of their budget, manage issues such as GDPR, and especially how do they make financial provision for the potential size of penalties in the event of failure? Outsourcing their technology platform as one option places the management of data outside the organization, but there are intrinsic risks in that approach as well.

Stakeholder management is also a problem, especially relating to board members of social housing organizations who may not fully understand the key technological issues.

9.2.1   Risk Management in Social Housing

In a follow-up article on the risks of using AI in the social housing sector,[2] Zurich Municipal also asked whether social housing providers have a clear strategy regarding:

- Financial risks
- Ethical risks
- Cultural risks
- Data risks

They make the point that much of the information they collect, especially in a social housing context, is extremely personal or sensitive. Zurich Municipal invited social housing providers to consider four key questions:

1. "Does risk feature in your digital strategy?
2. Who is accountable for digital risks in the organization, including cyber risk?
3. Are your risk and governance frameworks future-proof, including compliance?
4. Who has oversight on ethics and morality?"

One issue that Zurich Municipal are particularly concerned about is whether the solution for social housing is digital by default rather than by choice. They make the point that customers, especially the more elderly, who may not be familiar with technology, should have a choice as to how they interact with social housing organizations. A 2018 YouGov survey indicated that nearly half of the public dislike dealing only with machines and not having humans involved in decisions that affect them.[3] Zurich Municipal also pointed to the concern of reduced human accountability, which might replace ethical and perhaps also empathetic decisions with straightforward algorithmic logic.

9.2.2   Transforming the Tenant Experience

One of the real challenges is that at least 30% of social housing tenants do not have digital access.[4] The use of AI and advanced analytics potentially allows social landlords to transform the experience not only by improving the quality of occupation but also by making social housing more pleasant to stay in. Typically this may be through:

- **Improving security:** Having smart keys allows tenants to leave their homes safely and allows access by third parties only for agreed reactive or proactive maintenance. In effect, the tenant provides the visitor with virtual keys that are accessed through their smartphone or a similar device.
- **The virtual maintenance worker:** The use of devices and analytical schedules allows landlords not only to react to problems but also to anticipate the need for repairs. Identifying the problem remotely reduces or removes the burden on the tenant to describe what exactly the issue is. As a result, the maintenance function becomes more efficient and ultimately costs less.

- **Condensation and dampness sensors:** Damp, mold, and condensation are frequent issues reported by many tenants. A report suggested that as many as 12% of social housing tenants have reported a dampness or mold problem. This is seldom a problem that occurs by itself but rather is a result of other maintenance problems. The use of remote moisture sensors may help to identify these problems at an early stage, when they are capable of being readily resolved. The overall impact of this approach would be to reduce the cost of mold treatment by replacing it with the cost of early intervention, usually involving dehumidifiers.[5]
- **Preventing water escape:** The use of smart leak detectors can automatically shut off stopcocks at the water main, preventing water flow and reducing damage. This will reduce not only the cost of repair but also the cost of relocating a tenant.

Overall, the use of smarter technology not only improves the quality of social housing stock but also reduces the cost of maintenance for social landlords. As a result, they can make investments in their property with more certainty and confidence.

9.2.3   Case Study – Housemark Pilot

In 2017, Housemark, a UK-based membership organization, owned partly by the Chartered Institute of Housing and the National Housing Association, reported on a pilot with software company Illumr into the use of AI in social housing.[6] Illumr was originally developed at the University of Birmingham, UK and now works across fields such as systems engineering, cognitive neuroscience, ETL (extract, transform, load) language, and human computer interaction. The National Housing Association comprises housing associations, local authorities, and not-for-profit landlords, and this pilot used data from 75,000 properties owned by seven social landlords.

The piloted software offered a capability called augmented cognition and used systems to self-organize data into 3D clusters to reveal new patterns. In effect, this cluster approach attracts data points with similar characteristics and repels those data points with different characteristics. Other data can then be overlaid to create additional correlations. This type of approach using data self-organization not only removes bias but also avoids the traditional approach of creating a hypothesis and then seeing if the data supports this. It is also said to avoid overfitting, which is when an analysis of data results in the creation of an algorithm that isn't flexible enough to cope with data outliers in the information. The developers took the view that many of the existing data management tools cannot cope adequately with differing and increasing types of data as they miss small signals, and as a result the process of augmented cognition can find new insights not previously seen.

The pilot focused on seven landlords, with a particular interest on three areas: responsive repairs, rent arrears, and antisocial behavior. Four key data sets were analyzed:

- Characteristics of the property, including weekly rent, block height, stock type, number of bedrooms, type of dwelling, and year built.
- Void and empty days, number of terminations.

- People data, including lead tenant characteristics, age, and ethnicity.
- Type of repair (e.g., plumbing or electrical) needed.

From the findings of the limited case study, the developers found:

- There was a correlation between the numbers of responsive repairs needed to a property, tenancy termination, and rent arrears. This was more pronounced for younger tenants and seemed to disappear for larger properties.
- Antisocial behavior was more associated with the probability of tenancy termination and the amounts of repair needed.
- Responsive repairs were linked to the size and age of the property, as expected, but there was a higher number of repairs among younger people, especially in urban environments.
- Market rental properties (where rents are at market rates rather than subsidized) have double the amount of rent arrears compared to other properties.
- In many cases there were geographical clusters revealing groups of behavior, and "good" or "bad" neighborhoods.

Users of the pilot indicated that they found it useful for creating a strategy of sustainable tenancy (i.e., less churn among their tenants), and that the findings provided landlords with "evidence, not hunch." One downside of the pilot was that, with such limited amounts of data, it was difficult to create actionable insights. Overall, the pilot developers concluded that:

- New actionable insight can be discovered, but not always.
- Clean data was important.
- Housemark as an organization provided a safe place for data to be stored, in this particular instance.

Beyond this, they also detected a new trend emerging, that of the data manager or head of data role in social housing organizations.

9.2.4 Social Housing Fraud

The issue of fraud in social housing is a major consideration, and usually occurs at three levels:

1. Eligibility for provision of social housing.
2. In property repairs, which in many cases are carried out as part of a framework agreement by an external contractor.
3. Unlawful subletting, where an authorized tenant sublets to one (or more) unauthorized occupants.

According to a Freedom of Information request by *The Guardian*, over half of UK local authorities already use an algorithm-based solution to allocate social housing, many of them without notifying the public on their usage.[7] There are concerns, though, with one (unnamed) council admitting that the algorithm was only 25% correct, mainly as a result of poor data entry. According to one UK-based not-for-profit group, Algorithm Watch:

> *There will never be a way to objectively define who should be first in line for affordable housing. Transparent algorithms can help, but so can professional caseworkers who take the time to discuss with the applicants.*[8]

The issue of repairs in social housing constitutes a very different area of potential fraudulent behavior. With repairs and maintenance often being carried out under a framework or term contract, and work being paid for according to agreed schedules of cost, the pressure is on major social landlords to get value for money. However, aggressive procurement processes coupled with weak supervision open the door to opportunism on the part of the repairer. This can happen in multiple ways, such as being paid for work not done, high levels of wastage with parts reused on private work, and incorrect coding of repairs. Effective use of AI and reporting can identify key trends and ensure improved auditing.

The challenge of preventing unlawful subletting currently mainly relies on manual audit and inspection, but AI-infused systems, including facial and voice recognition, could be used to check on tenant identity.[9]

9.2.5 Tenant Viewpoint

In her article "What Does It Mean for Residents and Communities?," Bev Wright of telecommunications business O2 considered how improved connectivity is a key enabler for transformation of the social housing community and for tenants.[10] O2 has worked with Digital Birmingham and its Social Housing Digital Champions to run digital workshops in social housing communities. The use of 5G communication will:

- Improve the efficiency of homes, with 5G automated systems and services making the property more effective and responsive to the use of AI.
- Provide benefits for the elderly and infirm through the use of sensors that detect movement, and alert caregivers and relatives of danger and unexpected behavior.
- Reduce loneliness by providing more effective video communications such as Zoom and Skype.
- Drive predictive maintenance, including the ability to anticipate when repairs are likely to be needed.

The downside of consistent progress is that of universal access and how social housing organizations cope with the problem of digital exclusion. This links not only to social affordability but also to the rural community. One way in which the UK social housing sector has addressed this is through the We Are Digital or WAD program. WAD focuses on digital and financial inclusion training, which has included the provision of targeted one-to-one training for housing association tenants in their own homes (e.g., at Arcon Housing Association), with training tailored to the individual based on their own personal skills. This provides more online access to services that assist with employment and other benefits, such as cheaper utilities.

9.2.6 AI as a Virtual Housing Assistant

One question that might reasonably be asked is whether your next housing officer could be virtual. The role of the housing officer can differ from organization to organization, but principally comprises the functions of:

- Ensuring rent is paid.
- Managing tenant inquiries.
- Organizing property maintenance and emergency repairs.
- Interviewing prospective tenants.
- Dealing with neighborhood disturbances.

Dealing with social housing tenants can be demanding, and tenants often compare the services they receive from social landlords to that which they receive in the private sector. With more accurate profiling of tenants, AI could be used to:

- Provide a much more tailored approach to specific tenant needs.
- Make more informed and timely decisions about repairs and maintenance if coupled with sensors and devices.
- Improve the living standard and environment of tenants.
- Manage arrears and courts cases, ensuring that correct legal processes have been followed, leaving the housing officer to deal with the more personal element of the situation.
- Add value to the customer's experience, for example by suggesting appropriate energy tariffs.
- Manage rent arrears by creating a form of "propensity to pay" score similar to a credit score, and provide defaulted tenants with a manageable payment plan.

9.2.7 Chatbots in Social Housing

Enabled by 5G technology but perhaps not entirely dependent on it, the use of chatbots and virtual agents such as those from Fuzzlab[11] can help tenants to access information and help by:

- Offering the opportunity for self-service.
- Reducing call volumes, therefore reducing call waiting times.
- Freeing up contact center staff to deal with the highest-priority customers.

One of the key principles of Fuzzlab's solution is that it provides tenants with a quick and simple response. According to their website, "Tenants want more than a simple answer to their questions. A virtual agent that understands what people are

TABLE 9.1   Virtual Housing Assistant Capabilities

Nature of Inquiry	Typical Chatbot Functions
Inquiries	Assist registration for housing
	Complete applications
	Answer queries about existing applications
	Automate decision making
	Apply to swap or buy property
Maintenance	Support intelligent repair diagnosis
	Configure for repair type
	Improve prioritization
	Query job status
Rent management	Check a balance
	Make a payment
	Check arrears
	Request a refund
	Set up or amend direct debits
Everything else	Update contact details
	Request aids and adaptations
	Report antisocial behavior
	Identify a tenant's housing officer
	Record complaints and compliments

asking for, and helps them complete their transaction, is four times more efficient at reducing call volumes." Typical inquiries and functions for a social housing chatbot are shown in Table 9.1.

Beyond functions that can be directly accessed by tenants, an effective chatbot solution can also provide:

- Seamless transaction from virtual agent to live chat.
- The ability for a human to monitor a chatbot and jump in if appropriate.
- The capability to update any of the standard chatbot replies in real time.
- Data analysis to see what tenants are asking and if their requests are being fulfilled.

9.3   AI AND THE ENVIRONMENT

In the context of the public sector, environmental issues comprise the interest of the government in safeguarding the natural environment, supporting the agricultural industry, and maintaining a thriving rural economy.[12] In specific AI terms, recent developments have triggered considerable debate about the application and relevance of AI and new technologies in this sector. One of the major focuses is that of global warming, and AI is likely to play a major part in energy management, which is ironic in that AI is often in a cloud-based environment, which in itself is a major consumer of power.

Using smart grids in cities can help regulate power supplies across urban networks. Smart grids use information techniques to deliver exactly the amount of power needed to a network, unlike conventional grids that can be wasteful due to uneven power distribution. Traffic management may also play a key part including solutions such as route optimization, auto sharing, and eco-algorithms, all of which help reduce the carbon footprint. Additionally, controlling energy emissions from industry can be undertaken using advanced systems that detect leaks, identify hazards, and ensure compliance with local government regulations. One area that is also receiving considerable attention is that of agriculture, which is dealt with in the next chapter.

According to EcoMENA,[13] this use of advanced technologies is also having a big impact on the Middle East, where the United Arab Emirates, Saudi Arabia, and Qatar are also already showing commitment to digital transformation. Although their current focus is on healthcare and employment, the expected level of future investment in the EMEA (Europe, the Middle East, and Africa) area (likely to be about 15% of their GDP) will result in these countries using AI to meet their own environmental needs. These needs especially relate to their surrounding waters to prevent overfishing and contamination as well as more effective aquaculture techniques, innovations in sea farming, and better utilization and protection of freshwater resources.

9.4   MANAGEMENT OF NATURAL DISASTERS

9.4.1   Flooding and Flood Management

Flooding is the most common natural disaster on the planet, affecting the lives of hundreds of millions around the globe at a total cost of US$10 billion in damage annually. Additionally there are between 6,000 and 18,000 deaths per year, 20% being in India. The insurance costs of the floods in 2007 in England, which were the most expensive in the world that year, totaled over £3bn from 185,000 claims. The major flooding of New Orleans in 2005 as a result of Hurricane Katrina and the flooding of New York in 2014 appear to dwarf the UK event, but in reality there is no competition involved here, as each event is locally significant in its own right.

Flooding is also one of the more predictable weather events. It is one that lends itself to greater and deeper analysis with the application of AI, and is of major interest to those managing both the public and private purse. In addition to human distress, flooding places major pressure on local economies as a result of commercial disruption.

Flood prediction principally comprises key elements such as:

- Forecasting of river levels in periods of excessive rainfall and understanding how a river reaching certain levels will affect the floodplain and how many properties and people will be affected.
- Modeling work, principally by using high-quality elevation maps and physics-based models to predict water flow across digital terrains. The use of satellite imagery allows mapping to be done in areas that are relatively data poor.
- Vulnerability modeling to understand details such as the height of the property above ground level, its construction, and previous record of flooding.

The modeling work, known as inundation modeling, has a high degree of computational complexity, especially where very large areas of terrain are involved and where a high degree of resolution is needed for these areas. There are additional challenges, such as the nature of accurately modeling the river bed itself (known as bathymetry) and coping with missing or incomplete data.

Work by Google as part of their AI for Social Good project, in collaboration with the Indian Central Water Commission, led to a pilot for more accurate flood forecasting in the Patna region of India in 2018. This was subsequently expanded to the Ganga and Brahmaputra rivers, which are two of the most flood-affected rivers in the world.[14] In addition to the prediction program, the Indian system sends alerts through direct messaging or other push notification, or by using interactive flood maps. Effective insight allows governments to immediately implement rescue solutions and relief effects with greater operational efficiency.

The alert system comprises a very simple three-level system: "some flood risk"/"greater flood risk"/"greatest flood risk." Both accuracy and reliability are especially important, as incorrect warnings or vague information can do more harm than good.[15]

9.4.2 Flood Defense

Flood defense is an issue where there is tremendous pressure on public expenses. Governments are faced with the choice of taking no action and then ultimately needing to respond to catastrophes or, alternatively, taking action by way of major expenditure on capital projects that might only provide relatively temporary relief.

One of the key methods of description is that of the concept of the 100-year flood, which is a flood that has a 1% chance of occurring in any given year. However, this is only a statistical description of a particular flood event happening, and flooding can occur in the same properties or area in consecutive years. At best, all public authorities can hope is to understand the propensity of a property or area to flood at some time in the future and to plan accordingly. The impact of climate change, which is leading to more frequent flash flooding and potential increases in sea level, places additional emphasis on the need for an effective flood management and defense strategy.

There are naturally joint interests between the public and private sectors in managing risk, in the latter case particularly concerning insurers. In the UK, Flood Re is an insurance arrangement, which replaced the Statement of Principles agreed between the government and insurance companies. It ensures that flood insurance coverage remains available to domestic properties deemed to be at significant risk of flooding. In effect, the UK Government ultimately underwrites the risk taken by domestic insurers, as without domestic insurance the property would be unsellable at full market price. It is estimated that in the UK this covers the most at risk properties, representing 2% of the housing stock, or 250,000 homes.[16] Promises by the UK Government in 2021 to improve flood defense spending to unprecedented levels are important but, in the wider context, could be no better than a proverbial finger in the dike. The continued impact of climate change will mean that for many people, in many countries, the problem of flooding and its consequences are likely to exist for the foreseeable future.[17]

9.4.3 Earthquakes, Windstorms, and Forest Fires

In taking a global perspective, other weather events such as earthquakes, windstorms, tornados, tsunamis, forest fires and other natural catastrophes need to be taken into consideration.

All of these natural incidents have a major impact on the public service response. In some cases, where, for example, there is a greater likelihood of a particular event occurring, plans can be put in place not only to anticipate the impact and the required public sector reaction needed, but also to manage the effectiveness of the response. Meteorological analytics already is sufficiently advanced as to be able to predict the likelihood of a major storm, and earth tremor monitoring can also give a clue as to the location and severity of ground destabilization. The reality is that there is always likely to be a degree of unpredictability in natural weather events and, as a result, the public sector needs to remain on call to manage that uncertainty, even with reduced resources.

There is a certain paradox, as emergency relief for natural events is increasingly dependent on the armed services to provide relief support. However, as has been noted elsewhere in this book, there is a growing tendency to transform the armed services to one with lower headcount but higher technical capability. That is to say, there are fewer abled-bodied people available "on the ground," which means that it is even more critical that they be able to mobilize more effectively in terms of location and speed. The ability to anticipate natural catastrophic events with a higher degree of accuracy is a key enabler of that process.

9.5 CONCLUSION

The use of AI is a critical enabling capability in the seemingly diverse issues of social housing, and separately of managing the environment. The reality is that both are interlinked, as one solution might be to build new affordable homes in locations that might be less physically vulnerable to the impact of climate change.

Used effectively and especially taking the matter of inclusivity into account, the quality of life for social tenants also seems capable of improvement through the use of AI and advanced technology. By the same measure, social landlords may be able to manage their properties more safely with greater efficiency and with less risk. In such an environment, more properties might be made available and this could assist in contributing to existing supply-and-demand imbalances.

The reality, though, is that technology in itself is unlikely to provide the panacea to solve the social housing problem in its entirety. Ultimately, it may be that new models of rental and ownership may need to be created, which is principally a political and financial issue. It is already recognized that the future in an AI-infused world is not simply a digitalized version of today's analog environment, but rather that new business and operating models will need to emerge. Innovation in social housing should not be confined to the use of more devices connected by 5G technology; rather, it should take a wider viewpoint.

Similarly, the use of AI is not going to prevent natural weather disasters from occurring but it will be important in guiding the response to them. Effective prediction can lead to earlier and more accurate warnings and better mitigating action where practically possible. AI also has the potential to improve collaboration and provide a unifying force of emergency services that integrates both professional and voluntary services. Even so, its effectiveness may ultimately be dependent in part on communication channels remaining open and power supplies remaining intact in the worst of situations, which may not itself be a certainty.

9.6 NOTES

1. Zurich Municipal. (2019). "A Perfect Storm: Risk Perspectives from Social Housing Senior Leaders." March. https://www.zurich.co.uk/news-and-insight/-/media/News-and-Insight/Documents/Useful-documents/ZM_Housing_CEO_report.pdf.
2. Zurich Municipal. (2019). "What Are the Risks of Using AI in Social Housing?" November 5. https://www.zurich.co.uk/news-and-insight/what-are-the-risks-of-using-ai-in-social-housing.
3. Dsouza, R. (2018). "Global: More People Worried Than Not About Artificial Intelligence." YouGov, November 18. https://today.yougov.com/topics/technology/articles-reports/2021/11/18/global-more-people-worried-not-about-artificial-in.
4. Capita. (2018). "Smarter Property Management: When the Internet of Things Meets Smart Asset Management." https://www.capita.com/sites/g/files/nginej291/files/2021-08/Capita-SmarterProperty%20THOUGHT%20LEADERSHIP%20HOUSING.pdf
5. CIT (Consultancy, Investigation and Training). (2019). "CIT Shares Research into Damp and Mould in Social Housing." Local Authority Building and Maintenance (LABM), January 23. https://labmonline.co.uk/features/foia-research-damp-mould-social-housing/.
6. illumr | Augmented Cognition | See your way to better decisions. https://illumr.com.
7. Marsh, S. and McIntyre, N. (2020). "Nearly Half of Councils in Great Britain Use Algorithms to Help Make Claims Decisions." *The Guardian*, October 28. https://www.theguardian.com/society/2020/oct/28/nearly-half-of-councils-in-great-britain-use-algorithms-to-help-make-claims-decisions.
8. Ibid.
9. National Fraud Authority. "The Guide to Tackling Housing Tenancy Fraud." https://assets.publishing.service.gov.uk/government/uploads/system/uploads/attachment_data/file/118463/tackling-social-housing-fraud.pdf
10. Wright, B. (2020). "Digital Transformation in the Housing Sector: What Does It Mean for Residents and Communities?" O2 (blog), January 23. https://businessblog.o2.co.uk/2020/01/23/digital-transformation-in-the-housing-sector-what-does-it-mean-for-residents-and-communities/.
11. Fuzzlab. (2021). "Virtual Assistants for Social Housing." www.fuzzlab.co.uk (accessed December 1, 2021).
12. Gov.UK. Department for Environment Food & Rural Affairs. https://www.gov.uk/government/organisations/department-for-environment-food-rural-affairs (accessed December 1, 2021).
13. Muraleedharan, S. (2021). "Role of Artificial Intelligence in Environmental Sustainability." EcoMENA, January 30. https://www.ecomena.org/artificial-intelligence-environmental-sustainability/.
14. Moltzau, A. (2020). "Improvements in Flood Forecasting." Towards Data Science, September 15. https://towardsdatascience.com/improvements-in-flood-forecasting-aa0d4c1d9ddc.

15. Matias, Y. (2019). "Tracking Our Progress on Flood Forecasting." Google Blog, September 19. https://blog.google/technology/ai/tracking-our-progress-on-flood-forecasting/

16. Flood Re. A flood re-insurance scheme. https://www.floodre.co.uk/about-us/.

17. Carrington, D. "Record Funding for Flood Defences in England as Climate Crisis Worsens Risks." *The Guardian*, July 29. https://www.theguardian.com/environment/2021/jul/29/record-funding-for-flood-defences-in-england-as-climate-crisis-worsens-risks?CMP=Share_AndroidApp_Other.

10

Employment, Industry, and Agriculture

10.1 INTRODUCTION

While the impact of AI on each of these subjects is likely to be considerable, this chapter focuses on its impact on employment, industry, and agriculture specifically from a public sector point of view. Employment is the first topic for consideration. Earlier, under the topic of education, the problem of supply and demand in the tech sector was reviewed and how this might provide a barrier to progress. As a result, the provision of additional training should be high on the agenda of many governments, but this relates to all levels, including those seeking reemployment.

The chapter then considers the topic of industry in its broadest meaning while recognizing that there are many different types of industry with multiple different processes and characteristics. As a starting point, it explores the role of governments in supporting the industrial sector and, following this, within the context of public services, the area of the state-owned enterprise. State-owned enterprises (SOEs) are in effect a hybrid of the public and private sectors.

Finally the topic of agriculture is examined, again not to cover the impact of AI on the agricultural industry per se but rather how AI is influencing matters of agricultural policy.

10.2 EMPLOYMENT

There are different views on the impact of AI on industries and professions. One generally accepted approach is that there will, in effect, be a catenary effect (that is, in the shape of a hanging chain or cable that hangs under its own weight, supported equally at each end), with those whose skills place them at either end of the catenary least affected, and those in the middle affected to some degree or another (Figure 10.1). Additionally it is thought that those employed in roles that are most capable of being automated are especially likely to find themselves most vulnerable. An earlier chapter also deals with unemployment processes in greater detail under the heading of Personal Social Services.

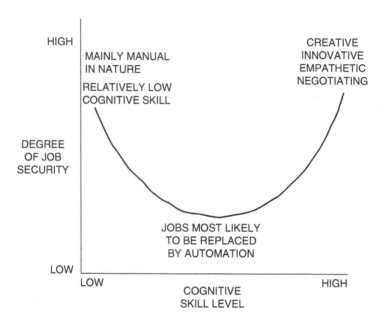

FIGURE 10.1   Susceptibility of Job Losses to AI.

Pessimists say that unemployment levels will rise as a result of AI. This will have a knock-on effect not only on taxation but also in respect of the need for benefits and other forms of welfare. On the other hand, optimists would suggest that with people having additional time on their hands, there will be an expansion of the leisure industry, whose growth will accommodate all those displaced by automation. Table 10.1 suggests pros and cons of unemployment, but it's rather a bipartisan approach to what is likely to be a complex evolution in the workplace, and people are bound to be affected in many different ways. For some, regrettably, retraining is unlikely to be an option and they will need to face the problem of continued unemployment, or at best reeemployment in a form that differs from what they have experienced in the past.

10.2.1 Unemployment

Governments recognize that long-term unemployment is damaging to individuals and also to communities. It affects mental and physical health, and holds back economic growth. There are many challenges in an environment where there are high levels of employment. The major one is that of the management of inequality that is often found as a by-product of the labor market. Inequalities can be found across sectors, between wages and level of earnings, in access to work generally, and in organized and unorganized sectors of work.

At a public policy level, solutions may be found in:

■ Macro policies
■ Sector policies
■ Social policies, including health and education

TABLE 10.1 Different Approaches to Unemployment

Type of Benefit	Optimists (might say)	Pessimists (might say)
Personal benefit	More leisure time	Potentially less and fragmented income
	Better work–life balance and improved well-being	Challenges of managing self-employed status, and more complex tax returns
Financial considerations	More time to balance income against expenditure (better financial planning)	More uncertain pensions, leading to long-term uncertainty in lifestyle
	Greater flexibility in terms of type of job and potential for portfolio working	Difference between urban and rural opportunities
	Growth and evolution of leisure industry	Working in a relatively poorly paid leisure sector
Creative considerations	Greater scope for entrepreneurism, and opportunity to use own initiative	Not everyone is entrepreneurial in nature
	Opportunity for flexible (free) learning	Less scope for company-sponsored learning
	Less constraint by corporate rules	Risk taking may have greater personal consequences
National considerations	Losses to individual pension and tax contributions offset by greater company taxes	Reduced personal taxes collected by government
	Shadow market exists already, and systems can be put in place to capture more information	Growth in "shadow market" economy
	Analytical measure only, and of little real relevance as can be estimated	Reduced measured contribution to GDP

Public policies need to address issues of inadequate social protection and gender inequality and guard against the risk of corruption. A more equal or egalitarian society can be created through public policy that especially focuses on health, education, an improved social infrastructure, and ultimately by affirmative, or positive, action on the part of governments. However, the problem is more acute in countries such as India due to issues such as scale and degree of development.

There is no shortage of economists who have argued the case for greater equality. Thomas Piketty's 2009 book *Capital in the Twenty-First Century* convinced many that inequality is embedded in economic policy and makes the point that inequality is "neither economic nor technological. Rather, it is ideological and political."[1] If that point is accepted, then the introduction of AI may not be the sole cause of any unemployment problem, but by the same measure, it may not provide a solution to the problem, either.

10.3 AI AND INDUSTRY

From mobile devices to transportation, from leisure to manufacturing, there are few who truly dispute that AI in all its guises will not have a transformative effect, even if the question of when this might happen is open to discussion. During the course of this book many different types of services have been reviewed as far as where they fall within the overall spectrum of the public sector, and in earlier books the author has discussed the specific impact of AI on jobs and professions. The industrial sector is equally broad and there are multiple functions and professions within it and, as a result, there can be no real question that it will be heavily affected:

- Routine and repetitive jobs will be replaced by robots.
- There will be an impact on the need to travel.
- Process changes will emerge.
- The nature of social interaction will change, especially as the workplace plays such a large part in that human function.
- There could be impacts on healthcare and well-being, especially if there are fewer participants using company-funded private services.

The threat, if that is the right word to use, is summed up in this expression, paraphrasing Robert Cannon, who is an internet lawyer:

If it is difficult to explain or describe the particular value that a human brings to a job, then that job is likely to disappear.

The other side of that particular coin is that new jobs and functions will emerge that almost certainly will be a hybrid of the old and the new, that is, new professions will be created that are a hybrid of existing professional skills and the application of new technologies.

The scientist Stephen Hawking also had a view on this, saying:

If machines provide everything that we need, the outcome will depend on how things are distributed. Everyone can enjoy a life of luxurious leisure if the machine produced wealth is shared, or most people can end up miserably poor if the machine-owners lobby against wealth distribution. So far the trend seems to be towards the second option, with technology driving ever-increasing inequality.[2]

Governments are increasingly responding to the challenge by creating new AI university courses, mainly at the Master's level, through the development of new dedicated centers.[3] In the UK, the Turing AI Fellowships initiative is aimed at attracting and maintaining the best talent in artificial intelligence. Turing AI Fellows[4] are appointed in UK universities for a period of five years, and are tasked with pioneering unique and exciting areas of research in the field of AI. Although a positive step, critics might suggest that this reinforces the idea that AI is an academic rather than practical issue that will directly affect the nature of work.

Unfortunately, not all the workforce are of a type to benefit from this type of evolution as they fall outside the so-called professional classes, and for these employees the so-called jewels of academic life seem almost impossible to achieve or to benefit from. The challenge for that part of the workforce is likely to be very different.

10.3.1 State-Owned Enterprises

A state-owned enterprise or SOE is a business entity in which the government has significant control through total, substantial, or significant minority ownership. It is a term that is subject to differing interpretations but is usually categorized as one that:

- Has public policy objectives
- Is distinct from other organizations because of its approach to profitability
- Often has preferred access to government loans
- Is able to lobby for regulations that drive out private competition

In many cases SOEs have monopolistic or near-monopolistic status, such as Indian railways, for example. Because of this monopoly status they have the advantage of being able to capture scale efficiencies, but they are often viewed as being less efficient due to political interest and interference. Government interest in particular sectors often competes with and sometimes inhibits foreign investment.

The background of SOEs rests in the massive nationalization that took place after World War II. In Eastern Europe, countries followed the Soviet model, whereas in Western Europe countries saw nationalization as a way of rebuilding economies that had been badly affected by the war years. Nowadays there are many examples of SOEs, ranging from rail and power supplies to oil and gas. They even extend to financial companies such as Freddie Mac (Federal Home Loan Mortgage Corporation) and Ginnie Mae (Government National Mortgage Association) in the United States.

In their report "OECD Corporate Governance of State-Owned Enterprises," the Organisation for Economic Co-operation and Development (OECD) provide guidelines that help countries operate SOEs in a competitive, efficient, and transparent way.[5] In 2019, they also approved a set of principles for AI that both complemented existing guidelines and aimed at being sufficiently flexible to cope with the future.[6] The OECD identified these principles as being that:

- AI should be beneficial to people and the planet.
- AI systems should be designed in a way that respects the rule of law, human rights, democratic values, and diversity.
- There should be transparency in the operation of AI systems.
- Systems should be continually monitored and there needs to be ongoing risk assessment.
- There needs to be accountability.

In effect, these principles would seem to be little different from those discussed elsewhere in the public sector. Beyond this, the OECD suggested that governments:

- Facilitate investment to create trustworthy AI.
- Foster AI ecosystems that share knowledge.
- Ensure a policy environment that encourages adoption.

- Empower people with skills for AI "in a fair transition."
- Cooperate across borders and sectors.

It is worth looking at how these approaches, or complementary ones, have been adopted in different territories, for example, China, South Africa, the UK, and the United States.

10.3.2 China Model

In China, SOEs have been a kingpin in that country's transformation towards becoming a manufacturing powerhouse with considerable political influence. According to the World Economic Forum (WEF), 85% of the 109 Chinese corporations featured in the Fortune 500 are state-owned.[7] Despite this, the Chinese SOE sector is often thought to be "clunky." WEF suggests that many of these firms "would not survive in an innovation-driven market environment without the perks they currently enjoy." As the Chinese government continues to support innovation, especially in the technology sector, AI will almost certainly be increasingly infused into SOEs in order to improve their efficiency.

Many already look to the China model as being unique in that it comprises a particular combination of nationalism and liberalism. There are differences of opinion and some suggest that this is a specialist model that would work only in China.[8] It is important not to get too overwhelmed by this discussion about China per se, especially as the interest in this book is the application and usage of AI in the public sector, as opposed to the working of one particular country that has a set of unique dynamics.[9] Nevertheless, the interlock between the attitude of the state and the acceptance and endorsement of AI by SOE organizations cannot be overlooked.

10.3.3 South African Model

SOEs also play a very large part in the South African economy, especially in electricity, transport, and telecoms. Their journey has been much more difficult and especially linked to financial troubles and government bailouts.

The use of AI in South Africa is at a very different level of maturity compared to that in China. There is a sense that the country is still in catch-up mode. There also remains perhaps a dominant concern about the impact of AI on employment levels, in a country where there are still high levels of unemployment.[10]

10.3.4 UK Model

The so-called Thatcher years of 1979–1990 were, for the UK, a major period of privatization as it moved away from the SOE model. Although there are some notable exceptions, such as the British Broadcasting Company (BBC), there remain relatively few SOEs and statutory corporations in the UK.

The BBC as a case study is going through their own unique transformation as they respond to the consumption of news and entertainment through a whole new set of devices. For them, the use of AI is a component in the transformation of their offering from a linear service to an on-demand, AI-infused solution. Their particular issue is that, as well as dealing with organizational complexity, they do not have a monopolistic position but rather they are competing with other broadcasters and social media channels. Some say that the crux of the BBC's particular challenge is that they are an age-old SOE that is trying to take on the attributes of a startup.[11]

10.3.5 SOEs in the United States

In the United States, the federal government owns companies that provide work in the public sector but, unlike federal agencies or commissions, these companies are independent agencies and are politically independent. They often comprise organizations that were set up by external agencies but subsequently were nationalized through acquisition by the federal government due to tax debt default or sometimes, as in the case of the Alaska Railroad and Amtrak, to ensure that services are continued. Additionally there are other levels of SOEs in the United States, comprising state ownership of organizations with particular local interest, or tribal/indigenous ownership of organizations that might benefit their tribal causes.

Overall there does not seem to be any obvious specific strategy for the use of AI in SOEs in the United States, other than its use being embraced in wider initiatives to encourage the use of AI in industry. In Chapter 8, which dealt with smarter cities and transportation, the use of AI in the Indian railway network was mentioned. Following that theme, the US National Railroad Passenger Corporation, known as Amtrak, is also a proponent of advanced systems. Founded in 1971 and employing 20,000 people, Amtrak carries over 30 million passengers per year and deals with 375,000 visits to its website each day. It uses a virtual assistant chatbot called Ask Julie to support its customer service, and it reports that its use has led to a 30% increase in bookings.[12]

10.4 AGRICULTURE

The agricultural market is already being transformed through the use of remote devices, typically driverless tractors, milking robots, and automated harvesting machines. Specialist robotic systems include seeding robots, mowing robots, and pruning robots. Monitoring of soil can help with understanding crop yield, and to identify and predict factors that affect the yield. Additionally, technology is being used such as by agricultural tech startup PEAT, which has developed a deep learning solution that identifies nutritional defects in soil.[13] Algorithms are also used in connection with remote imagery to predict weather, analyze crop sustainability, and evaluate crops for vulnerability to pest and drought.

There is, however, considerable scope for further activity in the AI space typically:

- Greater accuracy into understanding the best time for planting and fertilizer treatment to ensure increased yield, taking into account climate and weather, harvesting and baling, and soil fertility.

- Management of crop "stress" as a result of environmental change, using sensors and applying intervening techniques in a timely and cost-effective manner.
- Alignment of growth with market demand and supply chain availability and capacity.
- Automation of farm activities that replace manual labor, including robotic harvesting.
- Pest and disease management.
- Automatic irrigation, including "just-in-time" water intervention.
- Measurement and management of crop quality, including inventory and risk management.

10.4.1   The Role of AI in Agricultural Policy

AI has already been used for the determination of agricultural policy in order to forecast financial outcomes, which a study indicates has a better outcome than normal statistical methods.[14] Machine learning techniques are used to extract the most appropriate economic variables from data relating to multiple agricultural commodities from different countries, and from this it has been possible to establish the most appropriate policy that should be adopted.

Agricultural policies in the world are classified into five groups:[15]

1. Countries that do not have a specific agricultural policy, so their macroeconomic policy (that is, general economic factors such as interest rates and employment levels) is more important than individual sectoral considerations.
2. Countries that have long-term protectionism policies for the agricultural sector, including the provision of aid.
3. Countries with agriculture-oriented laws.
4. Countries with directing laws for agriculture that do not regulate specific aspects but provide guidance.
5. Countries with short-term agricultural policies that are sometimes not aligned to a wider macroeconomic policy.

Against this picture of fragmentation, the world continues to be faced with a forthcoming food shortage. Global demand for food is likely to double within 50 years as the population of the world increases from 6 billion today to 9 billion by 2040, and as a result many hopes are being placed on digitalization and AI. Livestock farming accounts for three-quarters of the world's agricultural land, including pasture and fodder creation, yet at the same time livestock farming is a major contributor to greenhouse gases. When added to fossil-fuel-intensive machines and the decomposition of nutrients, there is a major push to create a more sustainable, environmentally friendly agricultural industry.

It is a complex picture. Expert systems in the United States have been applied to determine the use of water and land in agriculture, agricultural production, the impact of climate, and what comprises the most effective public policy to adopt in the agricultural sector.[16]

The role of government is to establish key policy initiatives, such as they do in education. This can be done not only through legislation but also through the encouragement of new, efficient techniques. However, this is not straightforward, as "digital literacy" remains a problem in terms of implementation of new technologies and methods, especially in developing nations. This problem is sometimes described as the "digital divide." Digitalization also requires cross-border cooperation for the easy and friction-free movement of foodstuffs. Future movement of foodstuffs will almost certainly be managed through the use of blockchain, which will be a key part of the food supply chain. Such initiatives not only require product and technology innovation but also public investment. Experts are concerned that those countries that are further advanced in the use of technology may use that advantage to obtain disproportionate benefit.[17]

10.4.2   The Role of AI in Environmental Issues

Already, 25% of potential farming land suffers from environmental degradation. For example, in India 75% of water is contaminated by industrial and agricultural waste. In many cases the focus is on improved efficiency and productivity in agriculture, but it is important that this not be done in an environmental vacuum and that consideration is given to the impact of new technologies and processes on the environment.

The reality is that the ambition of net zero, in this case zero fossil fuels, is unlikely to be achieved by the use of technology or digitalization alone; an integrated approach is essential. Experts suggest that the best response to meeting the agricultural supply challenge, as well as providing both environmental and climate protection, is to link these aspects together, coupled with appropriate governance. In agriculture, in 2017 Microsoft launched a new project, AI for Earth, to help with the prediction of climate change where there were bottlenecks due to the lack of algorithms in order to help with the challenges related to climate change, agriculture, water, and biodiversity.

10.5   CONCLUSION

The intention of this chapter was not to consider the impact of AI on all industries, as this is covered in an earlier book by the author, but rather to view the three elements of industry, agriculture, and employment particularly through the lens of the public sector. At first sight the three may look to comprise an unusual fit but they are collated in this way to reflect the current grouping used by UK Government (as opposed to being at the discretion of the author).

Even so, they have at least two key things in common. First, the grouping reinforces the connection between employment and industry, both in terms of the private sector and, more relevantly, public sector industries that are described as state-owned enterprises or SOEs.

Second, the particular nature of SOEs is that they are influenced by a different set of imperatives when compared to the private sector. The emphasis is less on profitability than on providing an essential service to the end user. That is not to say that SOEs are oblivious to the matter of financial control, but there seems to be less pressure on this as a pressing demand. Their emphasis is probably one of not incurring a financial loss rather than achieving a profit. At a professional level, those in charge of SOEs may equally be more concerned that they not take unnecessary risks that prejudice their careers, as opposed to being keen to engage with cutting-edge technologies and innovations.

That is not to say that AI innovations are unlikely to find their way into SOEs, as evidenced by Amtrak's use of chatbots, but perhaps this is due primarily to the broader degree of acceptance of these ideas in North America compared to in other places. Perhaps in time there will be a sort of leveling out process, especially as systems that are developed in the private sector find public sector applications. There is potentially an employment issue to consider as well. SOEs are not beyond shedding staff when they are taking financial losses, but this is often a decision of last resort.

The connection between industry and employment relates to the need to provide industry with adequate skills and competencies to undertake the AI revolution. This is also partly covered in Chapter 6, Education, recognizing the need for training and education to narrow the gap between demand and supply. Additionally, this chapter provides a reminder that the idea that impact of AI will be negative in terms of employment may be incorrect, as the true issue might rather rest with matters of political or economic policy.

Finally, continuing the theme of policy, the closing section on agriculture provides some insight into the use of AI in the creation of a framework for sustainable provision of food, against an increasingly deepening problem area. It demonstrates the use of AI and other advanced systems to help meet the current and likely future needs as a result of climate change. Already there are areas of research that use AI to carry out more accurate predictions, such as Climate Change AI,[18] but AI research as a general topic, even government-sponsored, remains outside the scope of this publication.

10.6 NOTES

1. Munson, James. (2020). "Autonomous Equality: A Review of Thomas Piketty." New Politics, May 3. https://newpol.org/autonomous-equality-a-review-of-thomas-piketty/.
2. Kaufman, A. (2017). "Stephen Hawking Says We Should Really Be Scared of Capitalism, Not Robots." *Huffington Post*, updated January 5. http://www.huffingtonpost.com/entry /stephen-hawking-capitalism-robots_us_5616c20ce4b0dbb8000d9f15.
3. Gov.UK. (2019). "Next Generation of Artificial Intelligence Talent to Be Trained at UK Universities." Press release, February 21. https://www.gov.uk /government/news/next-gene-ration-of-artificial-intelligence-talent-to-be-trained-at-uk-universities.
4. Gov.UK. (2021). "Turing Artificial Intelligence Fellowships." Updated March 30, 2022. https://www.gov.uk /government/publications/turing-artificial-intelligence-fellowships/turing-artificial-intelligence-fellowships.
5. Organisation for Economic Co-operation and Development (OECD). (2015). *OECD Guide-lines on Corporate Governance of State-Owned Enterprises, 2015 Edition*. Paris: OECD Pub-lishing https://doi.org/10.1787/9789264244160-en.

6. Organisation for Economic Co-operation and Development (OECD). (2019). "Recommendation of the Council on Artificial Intelligence." OECD Legal Instruments. https://legalinstruments.oecd.org/api/print?ids=648&lang=en (accessed December 1, 2021).

7. Guluzade, A. (2019). "The Role of China's State-Owned Companies Explained." World Economic Forum (WEF), May 7. https://www.weforum.org /agenda/2019/05/why-chinas-state-owned-companies-still-have-a-key-role-to-play/.

8. Breslin, S. (2011). "The 'China Model' and the Global Crisis: From Friedrich List to a Chinese Mode of Governance." The Royal Institute of International Affairs. http://www.eu-asiacentre.eu/documents/uploads/pub_17_breslin_in_ia.pdf (accessed December 1, 2021).

9. Scissors, D. (2011). "The China Models." The Daily Signal, September 6. https://www.dailysignal.com/2011/09/06/the-china-models/.

10. Edwards, C. (2018). "The Development of AI in South Africa." *The South African*, November 20. https://www.thesouthafrican.com/news/the-development-of-ai-in-south-africa/.

11. BBC. (2021). "Lead Architect – Innovation." Job advertisement, now closed. BBC Careers (accessed December 1, 2021).

12. Verint. (2020). "Helping a Railroad Service Conduct Business." https://www.verint.com /wp-content/uploads/CS_Amtrak_US_Final_0720.pdf (accessed December 1, 2021).

13. Progressive Environmental and Agricultural Technologies. (2021). "Empowering Farmers Around the Globe to Ensure Their Profitability." PEAT Technology. https://peat.technology (accessed December 1, 2021).

14. Sánchez, R. J. M., Rodríguez, J.P., and Espitia, H. E. (2020). "Review of Artificial Intelligence Applied in Decision-Making Processes in Agricultural Public Policy." MDPI, October 29. https://mdpi-res.com/d_attachment/processes/processes-08-01374/article_deploy /processes-08-01374.pdf.

15. Machado, A. (2002). *De la Estructura Agraria al Sistema Agroindustrial*. Universidad Nacional De Colombia Sede Bogotá.

16. Batarseh, F., and Yang, R. (2017). *Federal Data Science: Transforming Government and Agricultural Policy Using Artificial Intelligence*. London: Academic Press.

17. Garske, B., Bau, A., and Ekardt, F. (2021). "Digitalization and AI in European Agriculture: A Strategy for Achieving Climate and Biodiversity Targets?" *Sustainability* 13, 4652.

18. Climate Change AI. "Climate Change AI is a global initiative to catalyze impactful work at the intersection of climate change and machine learning." https://www.climatechangeai.org (accessed December 1, 2021).

The Role of the State

11.1 INTRODUCTION

Sometimes I feel like, somebody's watching me.

—Rockwell
(pop artist), 1983

Throughout this book, consideration has been given to the collection of data and its analysis, which ultimately leads to actionable outcomes. In the case of the public sector, the overall intention is to provide a service that is maintained at the current level or perhaps even improved, but at lower cost. This surely must be one of the main targets of the State, regardless of country. The effective use of data can not only enhance but perhaps also remodel existing traditionally based processes, and in so doing remove latent inefficiencies. But for many, the growing degree of data capture by the state from an increased number of devices, and how the data is stored, is a worry. Because of this, it is essential that the topic of data capture and management be considered in the context of the role of the State, and the digitalization of public services.

11.2 WHAT IS THE ROLE OF THE STATE?

The role of the State is a matter that has concerned thinkers since the days of Plato (c. 428–347 BCE). He suggested that the ideal State is one in which a system exists in which the different needs of the citizens are best satisfied in a model where everybody works together, albeit recognizing their different roles within society. Thinking has changed over time, with the pendulum swinging between different approaches:

- Highly interventionist, such as mercantilist economics, which aims to build a strong and steady economy by managing imports and exports to maintain a healthy balance of trade.

- Minimal government intervention, such as physiocratic economics, whose followers believe that the wealth of nations is derived solely from productive work, and classical views, which focus on self-regulation of the economic marketplace.

A philosophical discussion on this topic is not intended here, but rather this book seeks to make the point that all citizens are entitled to safety and security. This includes their protection from fraud, coercion, and attack from foreign powers. Additionally, citizens have the right to be protected from the acts of others, or, perhaps more controversially, from their own acts or omissions. Furthermore, the State should also protect the individual against external events such as unemployment, inadequate healthcare, inequality, and ineffective redistribution (including redistribution of wealth). It does this through a series of measures such as regulation, provision of safety standards, and in other legitimate ways, even if how it brings about these protections is also the subject of political debate and often disagreement.

Why might an individual object to such important protections? Mark Thoma, professor of economics at the University of Oregon,[1] suggested that objections might arise to measures proposed if:

- The proposals are ineffective.
- The measures are unaffordable.
- The measures encourage irresponsible behavior.
- The measures restrict individual autonomy to an unacceptable degree.

In the context of the data, analytics, and AI discussion, it might be reasonably argued that the collection of individual data from citizens on either a willing or unwilling basis forms a legitimate use of the powers of the State. If that is accepted to be the case – and there are some who might disagree – this opens the door to a notion of some form of State that has an absolute insight into the behavior of the individual and that this in some way constitutes some form of loss of liberty or personal freedom. This might reasonably be described as a surveillance state, although some might make comparisons to Orwell's Big Brother (which comprised the use of hidden devices behind mirrors to monitor every citizen). Nowadays the term is representative of government control and intervention in the personal lives of individuals.

Many are also concerned not only about their personal privacy but also that the data might be monetized in some way by being sold to third parties without the permission of the individual. The individual might well be willing to provide information about themselves, but how can they then be sure that it will be used for the purpose intended? In the eyes of many, the directives given by governments in terms of what could and could not be done to control the spread of the Covid pandemic were also an indicator of an emerging surveillance state, as data and analytics were used to inform policy and decision making.

It is against this background that this chapter looks into the topic of data collection and management by the State, as part of its legitimate function to provide protection to the individual citizen. In doing so, the term *surveillance* is used; although this term might have negative connotations, these are not implied in this discussion. Considering the watchful eye of the State as a supportive guardian places this particular term in a more positive light. Context is important, especially as the opposite of surveillance can be defined as indifference.[2]

11.3 WHAT IS SURVEILLANCE?

In the setting of this book, it might be helpful to consider what is meant by *surveillance*. Many readers will already have a notion of its definition being that of being looked over or supervised in some way, but others might consider it to be some form of spying. The word is French in origin, from the Latin *super* (over) and *vigilantia* (watchfulness), dating back to the late eighteenth century, when France's first Comité de Surveillance was set up in 1792 in order to check up on suspicious strangers during that period of French history, a time that came to be known as the Reign of Terror. Surveillance takes many forms, occurring in CCTV and video recording, facial recognition, telecommunication interception, and even the traditional form of covert human spying, which remains a surveillance function. Contemporary surveillance now includes the systematic use of devices, data collection, and analysis. In many cases it comprises an infrastructure or ecosystem of different but usually overlapping information-seeking activities that might either coincide with or complement each other.

There are already worries that the amount of information being collected and analyzed will inevitably lead us into a surveillance society. In a 2004 interview, the UK Information Commissioner Richard Thomas expressed his anxiety "that we don't sleepwalk into a surveillance society," saying that surveillance was "traditionally associated with totalitarian regimes but some of the risks can arise within a more democratic framework."[3]

There are two broadly different kinds of surveillance:

1. Mass surveillance, which collects broad-based information about a large group of people. This is often known as passive or undirected surveillance.
2. Targeted surveillance, which is surveillance targeted at particular individuals or groups and that can be carried out covertly or overtly. Targeted surveillance is usually connected with a specific operation or project. Intrusive surveillance can be targeted at an individual and may even include the interception of communications.

Additionally, the term is associated with personal surveillance, and comprises the collection of information and data about a specific individual. Sometimes known as *data-veillance*, this can relate to the collection of data aimed at a better understanding or even manipulation of an individual's behavior. This may comprise:

- **Data matching:** This is an approach where different databases are compared in order to find common trends. One example of this is the comparison of unemployment benefit with employment records to identify benefit fraud. Another is the comparison of DNA samples taken from the scene of a crime with a national DNA database in order to identify possible criminal activity.

- **Data profiling:** This is where analytical tools are used to detect certain trends in a group of people, such as a propensity to buy a particular good or service or perhaps even take part in a criminal activity. The same tools are then used by public sector services to identify individuals or groups who might be in need of special focus. Issues of bias can arise, especially if the data set on which an algorithm is distorted in some way.
- **Data sharing:** This is a difficult area, as it relates to issues such as to what degree should social services share personal data with the police, for example, as part of a criminal investigation. Data sharing gives rise to complex difficult legal and ethical considerations.

11.4 REASONS FOR SURVEILLANCE

Stepping back, surveillance has many components and is carried out to understand key elements of information, obtain specific insights, and can lead to establishing public policy. Governments typically might need to focus on important considerations, such as:

- Management of the population
- Control of movement
- Social impact of restrictions
- Economic impact as a result of changes of behavior
- Political impact of governmental decisions

Many of these issues will be recognizable from the pandemic, where decisions were, at least notionally, data driven. Where a need for increased surveillance (or additional data collection and analysis) arises, citizens usually need to understand that there is a genuine reason for its being done. They also need to be reassured that the reasons data is collected are both legitimate and in the public good. If this benefit isn't explicit, then at the very least the public needs to be confident that the data will be securely stored.

On the whole, the idea of data surveillance is not a new idea to the general public even if it masquerades under different names, such as supermarket membership or some form of points card. Surveillance is already prevalent in the commercial world, such as in the way supermarkets collect information about their customers and their shopping habits, so that targeted offers can be made to an individual in a well-timed and relevant way. Banks track spending patterns so that a timely offer of a loan can be made, and online retailers use predictive models to prompt the user to spend their money. Streamed online entertainment companies regularly suggest the next program or game that a user might wish to download and watch. The more widespread adoption of customer relationship management (CRM) has become a key tenet in how private sector organizations deal with and relate to their end users, and many of its principles have drifted into the public sector.

In the public sector itself, citizens are already familiar with databases that identify those who are most at risk or in need of benefits. Our ability to drive on the roads safely comprises a subtle and ongoing collaboration between different agencies.

There are compliance conditions, but in meeting those requirements, drivers on the road are reassured that all the vehicles they are likely to encounter are safe to drive and that both they and other drivers can safely and legally be in control. The essence of all this is that the citizen needs to recognize that one of the key reasons for data collection, analysis, and storage is that it is ultimately for public safety. If that is accepted to be the case, then this should not prevent the sharing of data between public and private services where there is a common aim, as long as there are adequate and effective safeguards.

At a time where new business models are being created with an ebb and flow between insourcing and outsourcing, the likelihood of data crossing from public to private sector, and vice versa, increases. It also opens the door to greater risk of breaches of cybersecurity. Sharing of data can also happen within organizations, especially as the concept of e-government and "transformational government" is primarily concerned with sharing information across different departments. It's an approach that has been called the "database state," but comes in for particular criticism where there has been a loss of data or security breach, as everyone involved is considered at fault, regardless of culpability.

The issue of "need" is critical. Data surveillance needs to have a clear purpose and be collected with a clear focus as opposed to being obtained randomly. Collectors of personal data need to be sensitive about the gathering, storage, and use of personal information. Citizens need to be confident that the information will not be held for different reasons, such as marketing or some other form of management. This is often easier said than done, as personal consent is often buried in the small print or tied into other terms and conditions of usage so as to be almost invisible. There is an alternative viewpoint in that correlations *might* exist that might not be immediately apparent but that data and sophisticated algorithms might ultimately expose. One example of such a correlation from the insurance sector (but that may also apply to social or public housing) is when an arsonist sets fire to their own home, they almost always remove their pets from the premises beforehand. Behaviors like this might be perhaps obvious in hindsight but they are not always apparent beforehand, and may be revealed by data collection.

11.5 SURVEILLANCE CAPITALISM

Surveillance capitalism is the expression coined to represent the commodification of personal data; in other words, the recognition that personal data has a value and can be commoditized or monetized. Overall it comprises a combination of surveillance and experience, and collectively feeds predictive models that can affect our behavior. Some argue that it is also a mechanism for wealthy online companies to grow even wealthier.

With leading web companies making as much as two-thirds of their income from digital advertising, new sales models have been created that place more focus on the digital insight of users; in other words, a better understanding of their data profile. These companies increasingly use gaming approaches to affect the way individuals interact with online systems, with a behavioral management approach primarily influenced by Skinner, of "Skinner's rats" fame, whose behaviorist theory was based on how reward and punishment affect response.

Data scientists at Google also recognized that more data would emerge if they expanded collection into other areas of people's lives. Through this approach, Google is now thought to be one of the pioneering organizations in establishing public rights to what was once thought of as private information.[4] Their process came to be known as the dispossession cycle, which principally comprises four key elements, which occur in this order:

1. **Incursion:** This equates to deliberate, uninvited intrusion into our lives to collect data.
2. **Habitualization:** This is all about staying in that space for as long as possible.
3. **Adaptation:** This is a response to public outrage by promising modified practice.
4. **Redirection:** The redirection of public focus while continuing to do exactly the same thing.

There are sometimes unexpected consequences, typically described as the law of unintended consequences, which relates to outcomes that are neither foreseen nor intended. When Facebook decided that they had ownership of all content created on their site regardless of origin and that there were to be profits made from selling data-driven outcomes, it was unlikely that they thought that Cambridge Analytica would ultimately use Facebook-derived data to influence major political events, including the 2016 US presidential election and the UK Brexit vote. Domestic surveillance as a subject also remains topical with devices such as Amazon's Echo existing in the home as a device but with the potential for collecting mass amounts of personal and domestic information.[5]

In a paper, "Surveillance Capitalism: The Hidden Costs of the Digital Revolution,"[6] three differing perspectives are offered:

1. **The delusion of technological hope:** This suggests that technology provides the salvation of the future, with systems being so intuitive that we cannot resist using them.
2. **The Hook Model:** This takes the view that social media has the potential to take over everything else in our lives, if we let it, and as we become addicted to social media, we become exploited by the sophisticated algorithms it uses.
3. **The cost of exploitation:** This relates to the idea of a trade-off, where "netizens" trade contentment in the form of benefits against the idea of sharing their personal information.

Perhaps some may argue that this book might also fall into the *first* category of delusion of technological hope as far as the public sector is concerned, as it suggests that public services will not only ultimately be transformed by data, analytics, and AI but also that the technology will be both compelling and irresistible. In terms of the *third* perspective, which considers exploitation, how can individuals realistically fight mega corporations with a powerful and commercially driven agenda? But if there is no resistance to that commercial momentum, what ultimately will be given away in terms of individual freedom, responsibility, and self-determination?

In the context of public services and the surveillance state, it becomes important also to recognize the likely future techniques that the State might choose to use in improving its data collection and analysis, regardless of its intention. There is a clear record of private sector initiatives finding their way into the public sector and there is no reason why the approach to data, analytics, and AI may be different. Recruitment of private sector leaders to the public sector will exacerbate that progress. There should be little doubt that surveillance capitalism demands more ethical and critical thinking. National governments can step in and offer direction and regulation, but the reality is that this particular issue transcends national boundaries. Perhaps at the end of the day it is for the mega data corporations to self-regulate in some way – but history also tells us that self-regulation is seldom effective.

11.6 SURVEILLANCE IN COVID "TRACK AND TRACE"

In the case of the Covid pandemic, many will be aware of surveillance in the form of contact and "track and trace," which is a form of location tracking and proactive intervention. In many cases, citizens were prepared to share details of their personal whereabouts using personal devices such as smartphones. Overall, "Track and Trace" (or whatever its local variation was, e.g., "TousAntiCovid" in France) was an example of people being prepared to concede personal information, including their location, as part of the common good, and where there was a benefit to be had not only to them as individuals but also to society as a whole. People came to realize that not only was this a very blunt and therefore potentially misleading instrument but also that the example shown in some cases by certain political leaders disappointingly did not match those standards required of the wider population.

It is a fine balance between obtaining insight and infringing on personal freedoms. In India, the Kerala State Government was prepared to defy national government as they felt that the track and trace app impacted on civil liberties. In that particular case they considered infringements in terms of traveling, for example, to be disproportionate to the issue. Globally, however, this was not a generally held viewpoint as, conversely, in Singapore the "Trace Together" solution was much more widely accepted by the public.

Public trust in government is critical to the effective working of a digital system, and is normally measured in a political sense by how well the government keeps their commitments. This trust was lost in Mexico when the government there called for mandatory participation of social isolation and mask wearing without any form of democratic process. Even the Mexican Data Protection Commissioner tweeted his objection and, as a result, the government back-pedaled to make the scheme voluntary, regardless of the merits of the situation. Elsewhere, Israel used the Shin Bat security agency (which is usually used to track Palestinian terrorists) to operate a track and trace approach, but this process was one without Parliamentary approval and without transparency.

Trust and justice are interrelated and both are similar in that they operate on a large as well as a small scale. Being trustworthy might be defined as whether someone keeps their word. Justice treats an individual in the way that is fair, and this correlates to a standard of rightness. There is a link also to culture and to local traditions. True justice accommodates those who are disadvantaged and, as a result, the identification and management of bias has become increasingly critical.

Effective and comprehensive surveillance and management of the population of this kind may require a high degree of individual cooperation. It is possible, however, to speculate on how a broader, connected state system might work when it adopts a more integrated technological approach. For example, drones could be used to observe those who are required to self-quarantine. Similarly, it would be possible to identify the location of individuals by using personal tracking devices such as wearables, similar perhaps (despite being an unfortunate comparison) to the way that criminals are often tagged when released into the general community.

Going forward, surveillance may not always be either visible or obvious (as in the case of wall-mounted cameras or drones), nor specifically noticed by the individual (as in the case of location tracking built into a personal device, for example), but is almost certain to exist in one form or another.

Perhaps there is a need for less sentiment and sensitivity about surveillance. The reality is that the data is mainly not identifying an individual but in many cases is no more than a digital profile of that individual. In a surveillance state, individuals no longer comprise flesh and blood but rather comprise sets of digital data. Individuals or groups are identified not as humans but rather by their digital characteristics, stop being citizens and are rather netizens who comprise invisible data analyzed by unaccountable algorithms.

If that is the case, then what is a digital citizen, and if we are no longer individuals, what else is left? If such a creature exists that is mainly digital in nature, then what is the role of government in defining their status and how can they maintain the integrity of their people? Beyond all this, what data ghosts will be left behind when we are gone as individuals? In the same way that many of us seek to learn about our ancestors, the citizens of today and tomorrow will almost certainly leave a much clearer and traceable footprint. What will that footprint tell our descendants about who and how we were?

11.7   DATA JUSTICE AND INDEPENDENT OVERSIGHT

The essence of the concept of data justice is that we need to be treated as individuals rather than as pieces of aggregated data. Data gives insight and can also reveal social inequalities such as poverty, but gaps in the data can also provide misleading results. In many cases there may be issues regarding the unsuitability of data collection, the analysis, and the algorithms being used.

All these provide new levels of insight, but it is increasingly believed that there need to be genuinely independent bodies involved. These issues should not be solely in the domain of the technical expert but should also involve other civil society groups. The reality is that computer scientists see their work as mainly technical, but there can also be important ethical considerations that, if poorly handled, can significantly affect life chances and choices available. If surveillance is going to happen, then there are important questions that need to be asked, especially about how to mediate.

Linnet Taylor, associate professor at the Tilburg Institute for Law, Technology, and Society (TILT), focuses on the use of new sources of digital data in governance and research around issues of human and economic development. She talks a lot about data justice, describing it as "the way that people are visibly represented and treated as part of the production of digital data."

In her 2017 paper "What Is Data Justice?,"[7] Taylor reflected on the political and practical way that people are seen and treated by the State and private sector as a result of the increasing amount of data generated by the use of devices. She pointed out that while there had been technical advances in the way that data was stored and analyzed, insufficient attention has been given to the way in which it has been connected to a wider social agenda. In other words, we have only addressed one part of the discussion insofar as we had not yet created adequate awareness and mechanisms to respond to the social implications.

Taylor describes the need for greater awareness as a new rule of law that she calls data justice. It comprises the issue of fairness in the way people are treated as a result of the digital visibility, their representation, and how they are treated in a digital world. Put a different way, she seeks to create ethical paths, and proposes three key pillars of justice:

1. **Visibility or invisibility:** This deals with the issues of privacy and representation, but also reflects on the issues of data of those at the social margins, the aggregation of data, and the extent to which data might be considered to be a public good.
2. **Engagement or disengagement with technology:** This considers not only the proliferation of data-producing technologies but also the freedom of the public to engage, or not to engage, with data markets. She compares the current situation to a postcolonial situation, and states that we are split into hierarchies: those who collect and use the data, and those who provide it but are unable to control its usage.
3. **Antidiscrimination:** This comprises two elements: (1) the freedom to not be discriminated against by the data and (2) the issue of bias. She recognizes the need to ensure that issues of bias are not systematically included within algorithms even unconsciously, a seemingly recurring theme.

These three pillars aim to combine both positive and negative rights. Their intention overall is to challenge the existing rights of data security and protection, even for those that many believe are already adequate in the current climate. It's a big topic that has been compared to a "periodic table" of issues. Two examples are the freedom not to engage with the data market and the freedom not to be represented in commercial databases. The concept of data justice is perhaps comparable to that of the Luddite Movement, whose aim was not only to create a new political framework but more importantly to create new workers' rights in the context of new industrial technology.

One of the major issues is the matter of how to balance the need of the individual to be included in the data with the wider public need. Taylor asks, "What are the implications of letting people opt out of data collection? Where does legitimate observation end and illegitimate surveillance begin?" Her overriding aim is "to make sense of life in datafied societies," and by way of conclusion, she suggests the need for a new structural framework especially focusing on governance that:

- Takes into account "responsible data usage"
- Includes "accountable data usage"

11.8   A CONTRARY VIEW

There is a contrary view to all this. Philosophers have suggested that the need to be "an individual" is just a fad or notion, principally brought on by the eighteenth-century approach to enlightenment, which sought to break the human shackles of the constraints of religion.[8] Individualism at that time was represented by a romantic approach to the uniqueness of the individual coupled with the spirit of entrepreneurism. These ideas were represented by some degree of elitism as evidenced by artists and writers but were further stimulated by the youth culture of the mid-1960s that paradoxically represented a movement of mass individualism.

Even now that spirit of individualism remains in many places and people. Entrepreneurism is alive and well; "You can be anything you want to be" is the mantra. This approach has its foundation in two specific theories:

1. The Darwinian approach, which argues for the survival of the fittest, and that individualism is the greatest expression of identifying the fittest.
2. The concept of neoliberalism in economics, which argues that markets, like individuals, should be free to take advantage of the competitive environment.

Perhaps these were, and to some degree still are, just expressions of their time. The free market overall has led to greater and widening inequality. Our individualism is measured not only by self-awareness but rather by how we compare to others in the social environment and how we measure ourselves against them. Beyond this, our individual nature is apparently best expressed in the groups we belong to, the networked games we participate in, and the social networks in which we participate. Even the digital groups we belong to are transient in that our membership in them is optional and we can more or less join or leave whenever we like. It is as if, digitally, we have shifted away from individualism into some sort of twenty-second-century digital tribal behavior that best represents our own personal preferences.

Perhaps we are beginning to recognize that we cannot ever be fully free, as total freedom comes at a price and there are few who can either afford that price or are prepared to accept the consequences of total freedom. We are prepared to have limited freedom in return for digital participation. If that is the case, then we are by default part of an arrangement where we are willing to provide a digital footprint and, in doing so, have implicitly consented to being surveyed, monitored, and manipulated.

11.9 THE ETHICS OF SURVEILLANCE

The question also remains as to whether it is ethical to have a surveillance state. The issue of ethics in both technology and particularly in AI has raised a great deal of attention and the theme has popped up in various parts of this book. "Techno-ethics" is a specific area of research that invites scholars to consider both the connection between technology and ethics and how these relate to life and society.

Ethics as a topic is a branch of philosophy that considers the rightness and wrongness of behavior, and looks into issues such as right and wrong, good and evil, and what constitutes justice and crime. It is often interchangeable with morality, and an ethical framework can be set by culture, traditions, and even religion. Scientists believe that the concept of an ethical or moralistic framework exists in all social animals as a way of either survival or reproduction.

The matter of ethics can exist at either an individual or a group level. It is said that an individual's ethics or moral beliefs might also modify with age and experience. At a group level, ethics or morals constitute a shared set of concepts of beliefs that may even be codified or written into some law. This seems to suggest that as AI systems improve and reach the same level of intelligence as humans (a process known as singularity), then perhaps a set of ethics could even be coded into an automatic system. If that were to happen, then the door begins to swing open on controversial issues such as autonomous systems that are involved in life-or-death decisions. These need not necessarily be only in the area of healthcare but may be relevant in the wider use of autonomous vehicles, which is very definitely on the near horizon.

The reality is that many people already live in a state of surveillance, if not in a surveillance state, through the retailers and financial organizations they deal with. Both Amazon and Walmart, for example, are profoundly surveillant, and during the pandemic a great deal of debt and security was especially subject to scrutiny by financial services. Specifically in the context of surveillance, citizens need to take a view as to why this is being done and ultimately for whose benefit. History is littered with references to excessive surveillance in totalitarian states, which created a framework of fear rather than of safety, with little obvious benefit for the individual. Naturally there are some who are concerned that an AI-infused surveillance state might reinvent that particular totalitarian scenario but updated for modern times.

If citizens can be convinced that surveillance is being conducted for their own benefit on grounds of safety and security, they are more likely to be accepting of the process. On the other hand, they may be less happy if surveillance is being undertaken solely for the benefit of the State. In reality it is unlikely to be one or the other, but most probably a combination of both. Governance is critical, but in its absence, and where gaps emerge in respect of oversight and management of benefits, people start to make up their own ideas. It is at that point that conspiracy theories begin to circulate.

Surveillance can also expose hidden social and economic inequalities, and it forces interaction and discussion between different disciplines such as those of data scientists and social scientists. As more data is collected, it is likely that greater insights will be discovered. With advances in the development of AI, the use of neural networks will develop the capacity to create previously unseen links or patterns from data, with the computer itself designing the algorithm. Beyond this, additional data and insights could result in the overall public sector being reorganized, perhaps with greater emphasis on preventing inequalities.

The ethics of surveillance are different from the ethics of AI, although there are naturally some crossovers. The UK House of Lords addressed the matter of AI ethics in their report "AI in the UK: Ready, Willing and Able?"[9] In that report, they recommended five key ethical principles:

1. Artificial intelligence should be developed for the common good and benefit of humanity.
2. Artificial intelligence should operate on principles of intelligibility and fairness.
3. Artificial intelligence should not be used to diminish the data rights or privacy of individuals.
4. All citizens should have the right to be educated to enable them to flourish mentally, emotionally, and economically alongside artificial intelligence.
5. The autonomous power to hurt, destroy, or deceive human beings should never be vested in artificial intelligence.

By comparison, in their 2013 Code of Practice for Surveillance Cameras,[10] the UK Government created a framework for camera use on the basis that it was:

- In pursuit of a legitimate aim.
- Necessary to meet a pressing need.
- Proportionate.
- Effective.
- Compliant with any relevant legal obligations (which at that time comprised the Data Protection Act 1998, the Regulation of Investigatory Powers Act 2000, and the Protection of Freedoms Act 2012).

The aim of the code was "to ensure that individuals and wider communities have confidence that surveillance cameras are deployed to protect and support them, rather than spy on them," and to address issues of "abuse or misuse of surveillance by the state in public places." Additionally, the Government created the role of Surveillance Camera Commissioner to encourage compliance with the code but without enforcing responsibilities.

11.10 NUDGING THE CITIZEN

Organizations such as ACEVO (the Association of Chief Executives of Voluntary Organisations) are calling for more effective operation of the public sector, but believe that to do this properly would constitute remaking the State. Their approach is based on three key elements:

1. Re-establishing the purpose of public services.
2. Increasing the amount spent by governments on preventive actions.
3. Having a "community-first" approach to the provision of public services.[11]

Their proposals particularly target prevention as being a critical area, which they believe will have a beneficial impact on the public purse even if any return on investment is sometimes difficult to measure. At its heart must inevitably be the use of data and analytics to track performance of initiatives and their impact on behaviors both of groups and individuals. If these behaviors are capable of being tracked and measured, then they are also capable of being modified.

The behavioral scientist Burrhus Frederic (B. F.) Skinner argued that the "classical" approach to the way that individuals are conditioned, which is by learning through association to create a new learning response, was not truly representative of complex human nature. He argued for a new approach, which he called "operant conditioning." It was a concept he trialed on rats, the now-famous Skinner's rats experiment, which identified how reinforcement and punishment can modify behavior. Skinner identified three forms of operant (or "response") behavior:

1. **Neutral:** That is, where the response obtained through an action does not affect a behavioral outcome.
2. **Reinforcement:** Where the response obtained can reinforce that behavior in either a positive or negative way, and increase the probability of that behavior being repeated.
3. **Punishment:** Responses that weaken behavior and reduce the likelihood of an action being repeated.

The reality is that Skinner's experiments were carried out in controlled conditions, yet give an important clue that human behavior can be affected by an environmental response to their actions.[12] In a digital world, that environment is most likely to be created through the use of social media.

In 1948 Skinner added the skills of being a novelist to those of being a behavioral scientist. His book *Walden Two* was written well before science-based methods for altering people's behaviors came into existence. It was considered controversial, as it dealt with characters who relinquish their free will in favor of what Skinner called external environmental variables. It's a form of behavioral manipulation but in the course of the story the characters create a sort of utopia. The story has been subject to a lot of criticism, with one critic suggesting (in 1999, almost 50 years after the book was originally written), "We find at the end of *Walden Two* that Frazier [a founding member of Walden Two] . . . has sole control over the political system and its policies. It is he who regulates food, work, education, and sleep, and who sets the moral and economic agenda."[13]

Today, while there may not be a single individual who regulates our life, conspiracy theories aside there are nevertheless organizations that seek to influence and manipulate our decisions by nudging us in whatever direction they consider to be "correct." In the UK, what was once a government department more commonly known as the Nudge Unit has now spun off as a part of the UK Government–owner enterprise called the Behavioural Insights Team. They provide services ranging from healthcare to humanitarian aid, economic growth to early-years' schooling, social capital to consumers, and claim to work in 31 countries, with 750 projects under their belt.[14]

The concept of nudge theory is that through behavioral science it is possible to "help" people improve their thinking and decisions, manage all kinds of changes, and identify and change existing influences. The idea has been around since 2008, based on the book by Professor Richard Thaler called *Nudge: Improving Decisions About Health, Wealth, and Happiness*.[15] Thaler received the Nobel Prize in 2017 for his work in behavioral science. The overall approach is not about enforcement but rather offering people a different thinking environment (or "choice architecture") and providing them with different choices so that they make decisions that are more likely to be useful and positive. The model adopts a four-stage approach:[16]

1. Establish what behavior needs to change.
2. Establish what current behavior is.
3. Determine which nudges (or relatively simple policy shifts) need to be adopted, which may be perceptional, motivational, or in terms of ability (ease of process).
4. Testing and evaluation.

The thinking behind behavioral manipulation has been questioned as being an infringement of human liberties. John Stuart Mill (1806–1873) is best known for creating Mill's Harm Principle, which holds that the actions of individuals should only be limited to prevent harm to other individuals. He argued the topic in his book *On Liberty*: "The only purpose for which power can be rightfully exercised over any member of a civilized community, against his will, is to prevent harm to others." Expanding that viewpoint, almost everybody knows what is in their best interests and should have a (manipulation-free) opportunity to make that decision. In her paper "Fifty Shades of Manipulation," Cass R. Sunstein comments that manipulation comes in many forms and to different degrees and that is why it is so difficult to police.[17] One problem is that a manipulator coerces an individual to make a decision against their free will, by using tools and methods, but it presupposes that the manipulator has better knowledge than the individual, which is not always the case.

In their 1961 paper "The Manipulation of Human Behaviour," Biderman and Zimmer also suggested that we have a deep-seated and perhaps nonrational concern about being manipulated, stemming back to a "loss of the autonomy that is believed to be fundamental to the conception of the self."[18] These worries express themselves in myth, dreams, drama, and literature, as evidenced by books such as *1984* and *Brave New World*. Perhaps it is the same paranoia about manipulation that people have about surveillance and, ultimately, about AI.

11.11 CONCLUSION

This is a chapter that spans the topic of surveillance from the end of the eighteenth century to some other time in the future. The topic has its foundation in considering the role of the State, which is fundamentally there to protect the citizen, but "protection" can take many forms. If you were a suspicious-looking foreigner in France 300 years ago, there was a reasonable chance that any uncertainty about you might ultimately result in a place in one of their already overfilled gaols. On the other hand, the impact of the pandemic has not only brought many of us into a world of greater scrutiny but also has highlighted existing concerns and potential problems.

Surveillance has perhaps also taken on a different meaning in a more complex world and as different databases and flows of information converge to create a total digital impression of who we are, what we like, and what might be our propensity to take certain actions. Taken at a macro level, this aggregated information can paint a picture of entire societies and has the potential to provide new and unforeseen insights that help to form public policy. Effective use of data might even help to reorganize the public sector in some way. Taken at a micro level, aggregated data might help predict potentially threatening behaviors at an individual level, but there are major ethical issues in terms of bias, and also who sets the rules in terms of what is threatening or not.

If through the use of data and analysis it is possible to gain better insight into public behavior, then it needs to be recognized that behavior can also be nudged into a particular direction. How this is managed is vitally important. Already, savvy politicians are prepared to use this approach as part of the election armory, and it is on record that the UK population, for example, was nudged into Brexit.

There are, however, risks, especially relative to the use of the data and ultimately its privacy, and as a result protection and governance become key requisites to ensure that public trust is maintained. Not everyone will be happy with what is proposed and will state their concerns regarding loss of freedom and the need for liberty, but in so doing might fail to remember that issues of individualism and entrepreneurship are relatively recent phenomena. Any future system that eventually emerges will need not only to operate at significant scale but also to accommodate those who are less willing to support and contribute to the arrangement. Data justice remains critical, in whichever way it is implemented, and by whom.

A surveillance state might appear menacing but ultimately is there to protect both the individual and people as a whole. This protection may be that of safety and security but might also comprise national stability. The "AI genie" is already out of the bottle, never to be put back, but through effective governance it can be tamed and controlled. We also already live in an environment of observation and scrutiny that will almost certainly expand as more devices are used in a 5G or later in a 6G world. It's critical that humans can flourish despite the multifaceted use of data that may not be to everyone's liking. How this might happen, where there might be mistrust and potential risk of misuse, is likely to be one of the great challenges going forward.

11.12 NOTES

1. Thoma, Mark. (2010). "What Is the Role of the State?" *Economist's View*, September 8. https://economistsview.typepad.com/economistsview/2010/09/what-is-the-role-of-the-state.html.
2. "What is the opposite of surveillance?" https://www.wordhippo.com.

3. House of Lords, Select Committee on the Constitution. (2009). "Surveillance: Citizens and the State." London: The Stationery Office. Crown copyright. https://publications.parliament .uk/pa/ld200809/ldselect/ldconst/18/1804.htm (accessed December 12, 2021).

4. Ross, A. (2019) "How Big Tech Built the Iron Cage." *New Yorker*, April 1. https://www .newyorker.com/culture/cultural-comment/building-the-digital-iron-cage.

5. Su, J. (2019). "Why Amazon Alexa Is Always Listening To Your Conversations: Analysis." *Forbes*, May 16. https://www.forbes.com/sites/jeanbaptiste/2019/05/16/why-amazon-alexa-is-always-listening-to-your-conversations-analysis/?sh=4edd03ea2378.

6. Ebsworth, J., Johns, S., and Dodson, M. (2021). "Surveillance Capitalism: The Hidden Costs of the Digital Revolution." *Cambridge Papers* 30 (2). https://f.hubspotusercontent20.net/ hubfs/6674075/P_CP_Jun21_8pp_web_compressed.pdf?hsCtaTracking=1f9d3a45-da2c-4d89-b79e-92f311c018bf%7Cc47f4503-5006-4a1e-84cc-84ae928e85e4.

7. Taylor, L. (2017). "What Is Data Justice? The Case for Connecting Digital Rights and Freedoms Globally." *Big Data & Society* 4 (2): 1–14. https://doi.org/10.1177/2053951717736335.

8. Foy, M. (2017). "Is The Age Of Individualism Coming To An End? *Philosophy Now*, Issue 120. https://philosophynow.org/issues/120/Is_The_Age_Of_Individualism_Coming_To_An_ End.

9. See Gaskell, A. (2018). "Automation, Ethics And Accountability of AI Systems." *Forbes*, April 18. https://www.forbes.com/sites/adigaskell/2018/04/18/automation-ethics-and-account-ability-of-ai-systems/?sh=314737f3bc43.

10. Home Office. (2013). "Surveillance Camera Code of Practice." London: The Stationery Office. Crown copyright. https://assets.publishing.service.gov.uk/government/uploads/system/uploads/ attachment_data/file/1055736/SurveillanceCameraCodePractice.pdf (accessed December 12, 2021).

11. ACEVO. (2019). "Remaking the State: Research Report." acevo.org.uk (accessed December 12, 2021).

12. McLeod, S. (2018). "What Is Operant Conditioning and How Does It Work?" https://www .simplypsychology.org/operant-conditioning.html#:~:text=Skinner%27s%20study%20of %20behavior%20in%20rats%20was%20conducted,to%20press%20a%20lever%20because %20they%20wanted%20food (accessed December 12, 2021).

13. Gamble, H. L., Jr. (1999). "Walden Two, Postmodern Utopia, and the Problems of Power, Choice, and the Rule of Law." *Texas Studies in Literature and Language* 41 (1): p. 3. Retrieved September 19, 2009 from accessmylibrary.com.

14. The Behavioural Insights Team. "About us." https://www.bi.team (accessed December 12, 2021).

15. Thaler, R., and Sunstein, C. (2008). *Nudge: Improving Decisions About Health, Wealth, and Happiness.* Yale University Press (Reprinted Penguin).

16. Sari, J. (2020). "Nudge Theory." https://www.toolshero.com/psychology/nudge-theory/ (accessed August 5, 2021).

17. Sunstein, C. (2015). "Fifty Shades of Manipulation." Digital Access to Scholarship at Harvard. harvard.edu (accessed December 12, 2021).

18. Biderman, A., and Zimmer, H. (1961). *The Manipulation of Human Behavior.* New York: John Wiley & Sons, xii, 323.

Risk and Cybercrime

12.1 INTRODUCTION

As a public sector infused with advanced analytics and AI is considered, it is important to recognize that there is a degree of uncertainty in the way forward. That uncertainty is described as *risk*.

In this chapter the meaning of risk will be considered, including typical types of risk, specifically operational and reputational risk, and what internal strategies need to be adopted to counter those events. Additionally, the question of risk as a result of cybercrime will be looked at, as it is one of the areas of greatest concern in the current business environment. Finally, the impact of using AI to mitigate or remove those risks will be reviewed.

12.2 THE NATURE OF RISK

When the issue of risk is considered, we almost immediately consider the downsides. What will risk events mean for organizations or for individuals? In the context of the public sector whose services are so entwined onto the fabric of society, what will these risks even mean for society and the way we live? As a starting point, the term *risk* needs to be understood. Risk is commonly described as being the threat of loss, damage, injury, liability or other event that might occur as a result of an internal or external action, and which might otherwise be avoided by taking preventative action.

Loss can also extend to loss of value or financial risk, which in many cases may relate to financial transactions, but in the case of public services may relate to payments to other parties, such as through benefits. It might also include investment risk and blackmail by propagators of ransomware.

Risks are all around and can be generally categorized as being generic, specific, or relating to the individual sector or type of organization (Table 12.1).

In their paper "AI for Public Services,"[1] Zurich Insurance identifies key questions that organizations need to ask themselves:

- Does risk management fit into the digital strategy?
- Who is accountable for risk within the organization?
- Has the implementation program been adequately risk assessed?

TABLE 12.1 Types of Risk

Type of Risk	Type of Failure
Risk from people	Risks that emerge from internal or external fraud, loss of key staff, training failures, poor supervision, employee fraud, reputational damage
Risk from failed processes	Failed payment process, poor procurement, weak project management, incorrect reporting, strategic failure
Systemic risk	Technology or system failure; failure of a system, failed implementation of a new system, cybercrime, inadequate resources to manage existing systems
External events	Major weather event, political risk, regulatory change, terrorist attack, economic downturn
Major projects	Risks associated with a specific project, typically a change in requirements, slippage in the timeframe, inadequate funding, failure to deliver

- What is the process for ongoing risk management?
- Are risk and governance frameworks future proof?
- Has there been a GDPR/DPA compliance assessment?
- Who has oversight on ethics and morality?

Specifically from an insurance point of view relative to third-party providers such as technology companies, they also ask:

- What checks have been made on the liability insurance of software companies?
- What risks have been retained or transferred to third parties?
- What is the scope of insurance coverage?

12.2.1 Management of Risk

Organizations increasingly adopt a three-stage approach to the management of risk (Table 12.2).

The trend is to move toward an environment of risk-adjusted decision making, whereby every decision made by the executive or senior management takes into account the risk appetite of the organization. Risk appetite is the propensity of an organization to make certain decisions that carry a degree of risk or uncertainty. The risk appetite of an organization may differ from function to function and from department to department, and is often influenced by the leader or manager of that department. Risk appetites are generally categorized as:

- **Averse:** Avoidance of risk and uncertainty is an organizational imperative.
- **Minimal:** Adoption by the organization of an ultra-safe approach to risk and recognition that this will limit their rewards.

TABLE 12.2 Three-Stage Approach to Risk Management

Key Stage	Description of Activities
Key building blocks	Create a risk-orientated culture
	Establish clear roles and responsibilities
	Establish effective communication
	Build risk management capabilities including training
Routine processes	Identify risks
	Identify those who own the risk
	Assess the risk, when balanced against the risk appetite of the organization
	Consider contingency arrangements
	Review and monitor
	Reporting of risk
Periodic activities	Consider the risk environment
	Learn lessons
	Review by peers
	Use data and analytics
	Report to key stakeholders, including at the board level

- **Cautious:** Preference for safe options with limited risk and limited reward.
- **Open:** Willingness to be open minded and to balance risk against the reward opportunity.
- **Hungry:** Eagerness to innovate despite risks, in the knowledge that greater rewards may follow.

Some organizations pride themselves on their attitude to risk by constantly encouraging innovative processes and procedures. One reflection of this is the approach of "agility" or "agile working," which seems to positively encourage innovation to take place in a controlled-risk environment. Innovation is by its nature risky, as it encourages relatively uncertain behaviors that seek to create revolutionary products or services. As a result, it is not a trait one immediately associates with the public sector.

Having an effective risk-informed decision-making process is most likely a by-product of effective integration between the risk and finance functions. Decisions can be made more quickly and easily in smaller organizations where there is a lower level of complexity, typically in organizations with shorter management chains of command. In larger organizations the risk department often still see themselves as a separate function with a degree of independence. However, they are often vexed by the issue of needing to be both poacher and gamekeeper simultaneously as they guard against risks and adverse events occurring, yet at the same time seek ways to support and give advice on business decisions. In fact, this duality can often extend to the way that members of the risk department describe the remainder of the organization as "the business," as if the risk department itself is not part of that same business.

The challenge for the risk department is that they need to ask themselves: "Are we helping things happen, or are we stopping things from happening?" In reality, while this might almost promote a Dr. Jekyll and Mr. Hyde syndrome, these are not necessarily mutually exclusive. This can be done by not only offering insight into complex matters but also ensuring that considerations regarding risk are embedded into business decisions.

12.2.2 Three Lines of Risk Defense

Traditionally organizations manage operational risk through what is called the three lines of defense:

1. Risk management at the operational level, that is, the point of delivery. This is called the first line of defense.
2. The risk and control function, in effect a series of controls and compliance processes. This is known as the second line of defense.
3. The internal audit function, known as the third line.

Although this approach is well established and provides a comprehensive, coordinated approach to risk management, a new model of risk management is also emerging called the Three Lines Model, which places greater emphasis on roles, responsibilities, and interactions, and aims to both protect and enhance the value of organizations.

12.3 ROLES AND RESPONSIBILITIES IN THE PUBLIC SECTOR

A key element of risk management is understanding roles and responsibilities. Table 12.3 sets out an indicative framework for such duties particularly relevant to the public sector, recognizing, however, that different organizations may vary in terms of their structure and responsibilities depending on size. Specific job titles will also change from country to country.

12.4 EXAMPLES OF RISK

There are many different types of risk that can affect organizations. The following section considers some of the key ones, primarily:

- Technology risk
- Data security
- Employee error
- Failure of systems and processes
- Reputational risk
- External risk

TABLE 12.3 Risk Roles and Responsibilities in the Public Sector[2]

Roles	Responsibilities
Ministers	Create new policy that is aligned to agreed political imperatives
	Understand the high-level risk that relates to those imperatives
Board membership	Provide effective leadership, direction, support, and guidance to the organization
	Ensure that the policies and priorities of the Minister are implemented
	Support the Accounting Officer in their understanding of the risk appetite of the organization
	Assume key stakeholder responsibility for the assessment and management of risk
Finance and accounting officers	Understand and describe the risk appetite in the context of change
	Ensure the effective management of risk
	Ensure that the risk management function carries out its role effectively
The governance, audit, and risk assurance committee	Review and sign off on the completeness of risk management
Managers (first line of defense)	Actively identify and manage risks on a day-to-day basis
	Escalate new risks quickly as appropriate
The risk management function (second line of defense)	Facilitate the management and oversight of risk
	Define risk management practices and operating framework
Internal audit (part of the third line of defense)	Provide independent and objective assurance on the effectiveness of the risk management arrangements
	Share best practices

12.4.1 Technology and System Failure

Technology and system failure is usually associated with data security and cyberattack but can also apply to the failure to effectively implement new systems. This is relevant especially as the focus of this overall text is to consider the impact of new advanced analytics and AI systems on the public sector. A report into the failure of implementing a new UK National Health Service computing system, which was abandoned in 2013, defined failure as:

- Going over budget
- Having a significant delay, sometimes measured in years
- Not doing what was intended in terms of the contracted specification
- Not fitting into the organizational structure or work practices[3]

The intent is not to be critical but rather to learn. In the case of the NHS system, the prime causes of system failure were described as being "problems in project management, engineering principles, organizational change, and change management." Specific other topics mentioned in the report that seem to be recurring themes include "accountability, professionalism, formal training, research, good communications, leadership, risk management, and ownership."

In their report, investigators identify three principal distinct periods of failure:

1. *Pre-Implementation*
   a. Lack of research, risk management, and long-term commitment
   b. The "acceptability" of failures
   c. Lack of user buy-in and ownership
   d. Inappropriate use of technology
2. *During Implementation*
   a. Poor communication
   b. Absence of a powerful guiding coalition
   c. Insufficient change management
   d. Lack of short-term wins
3. *Post-Implementation*
   a. Declaring victory too soon
   b. Failure to learn from previous mistakes

Risks of failure of this type are unlikely to be specific to one public sector entity nor indeed to any particular geography but rather could be viewed as being potentially applicable anywhere across the public sector as a whole. As this book is essentially about the use of new systems that will potentially transform the public sector, it remains especially critical to heed the lessons of the past.

12.4.2 Data Security and Privacy

Matters of data security and privacy arise in many different areas of the public sector and are perhaps most relevant to the social and health sectors. It is worth taking a moment to step back and consider some of the broader issues, especially bearing in mind some of their ethical implications. In their paper "Big Data Ethics," authors Neil Richards and Jonathan King say:

> *If we fail to balance the human values that we care about, like privacy, confidentiality, transparency, identity, and free choice, with the compelling uses of big data, our big data society risks abandoning these values for the sake of innovation and expediency.*[4]

It's an important viewpoint, but one that arguably must be balanced against issues such as public welfare, especially at a time when there is increased pressure on the public purse. The question is whether we are able to adequately satisfy the needs of the public in an increasingly complex society without having a data-driven approach. Some will inevitably argue that of course it is possible. After all, they might argue, weren't all these services provided in a pre-Information Age environment? It is reasonable, though, to question the effectiveness of past services in a less complicated society, or, at the very least, a different one.

Failure to safeguard personal data not only creates reputational risk issues in terms of trustworthiness of organizations but also attracts substantial financial penalties where breaches of security occur. These breaches may not always be systematic in nature but they can be deliberate, malicious, or even opportunistic by disgruntled or underpaid employees.

The introduction of the General Data Protection Regulation (GDPR) in 2018 has also led to three particular developments in the public sector, which differ from those in the private sector:[5]

1. Public sector organizations are obliged to appoint a data protection officer, although these can be shared with other public organizations if size and organizational structure are taken into account.
2. Public authorities are prevented from using the argument of "legitimate interest" as legal grounds for processing public data.
3. There are special issues under GDPR relative to the flow of data internationally between governments that normally need the consent of the citizen, unless there is a legally binding agreement between the countries.

12.4.3 Employee Error

Employee error is a key element of risk. Life is complex, and errors in behavior and decision-making often occur as a result of:

- Environmental factors such as physical, organizational, or personal issues
- Intrinsic factors such as the selection of individuals, training, or lack of experience
- Stress factors, which may be both personal and circumstantial

AI and robotic systems are increasingly being seen as the panacea for the avoidance of mistakes, especially in routine, volume, process-driven tasks. They lead to fewer mistakes, greater consistency of decision-making, and scale efficiencies. They also allow for reduced audit and, in doing so, help create a financial saving, which is an important consideration where there is a particular focus on return on investment. Not all employee error is innocent in nature and can also include employee deceit in the nature of expense, procurement, and payment fraud. Otherwise known as "economic crime," a PWC 2011 survey of the Australian public sector revealed:

- Government and state-owned enterprises suffered a higher level of fraud than in the private sector, with more than one-third of respondents saying that they had experienced economic crime in the previous 12 months.
- 69% of fraud was related to misappropriation of assets.
- Senior staff in government and state-owned enterprises were more likely to commit fraud than in any other industry.[6]

Additionally, the PWC report makes a series of interesting and useful observations:

- The likelihood of fraud increases where power is centralized, typically where an individual has the power to make decisions on procurement, contracting, and approval.
- Where standard policies are avoided due to what are described as "addressing urgent business needs."
- Power to mitigate fraud and corruption is not applied evenly and flawed processes and inadequate records can result in insufficient evidence being available with which to undertake a complete and proper investigation.

It would be entirely wrong to single out one country as being representative of the overall behavior of employees in the public sector globally, or to fail to recognize the age of the report, which is now over a decade old. At the same time, it is difficult to entirely ignore some more recent public sector decisions that were made as countries were faced with urgently sourcing massive quantities of protective equipment at the beginning of the pandemic.

12.4.4 Failure of Processes, Systems, and Policies

The nature of failed processes, systems, and policies is extremely varied throughout the public sector. They are also heavily linked to the issue of how a public sector organization is perceived and therefore how much it is trusted. At the heart of an AI-infused public sector is whether automation, in any of its forms, will simply digitalize existing processes or will open the door to new and innovative ones that meet the public need in an improved, more cost-efficient way.

In the private sector the idea of "business process reengineering" (BPR) is commonplace, but in the public sector is less common. Where this happens in the public sector usually requires some sort of burning platform for change. The pressure to improve efficiency in order to improve competitiveness, as is usually the case in the private sector, does not show itself in the same way in the public sector but may occur where there are other pressures on finance.

In many cases, process reengineering is a difficult task to undertake internally. Often, external organizations are used to review existing processes and systems, to make recommendations, and ultimately to play a part in their implementation. Inevitably this requires the cooperation of the public sector organization's own staff, but this cooperation cannot always be relied upon. At best any disagreement might be frictional; at worse, it might be a matter of conflict.[7] The issue perhaps at the end of the day is one of organizational benefit. If new processes are introduced that have no beneficial impact on cost, performance, or customer service then it might be reasonably asked, what is the point of BPR?

According to Davenport and Stoddard,[8] there are four critical components of BPR:

- An orientation to broaden cross-functional processes, or how work is done
- The need for radical change in process performance
- Increased use of information technology as an enabler as to how work is done
- Changes in organizational and individual arrangements as to how work is done in a reengineered way

Some level of BPR is almost certainly an essential prerequisite to AI transformation of public sector operations. Changes within public services seldom occur as a result of any Big Bang but rather on an incremental basis. This is acceptable if the public sector has the luxury of moving at its own pace and gently absorbing new ideas and technologies, but perhaps in the current climate it will need to be different as financial pressures create a new, stronger impetus for change. In terms then of what constitutes the operational risk in this category, perhaps the issue is not the BPR process itself but rather the speed and manner at which it needs to be implemented if there is pressure on the organization.

12.4.5 Reputational Risk

Some of the types of risk mentioned earlier in Table 12.1 might appear at face value to be of less concern to the public sector, such as reputational risk. In the commercial sector, where reliance is placed on the impact of brand as a key element of marketing, a loss of reputation can heavily impact the consumers' or customers' viewpoint of that organization. In the public sector, reputation is mainly influenced by issues such as trust, ethics, security, behavior, and management culture, and there are often also linkages to political leadership.

The rise of technology and use of social media are placing even greater pressure on governments and the public sector to manage their reputations. One way this is done is through the use of "codes of practice" that set down and codify what might be considered acceptable behaviors. These might also include what an employee posts as an individual on social media. In many cases, breach of a code of practice can ultimately lead to dismissal or even criminal proceedings, such as in the case of a breach of the Official Secrets Act in the UK. Some employees might think that such restraint is unreasonable, but organizations aim to use such penalties primarily as a deterrent to others. Their argument is that the public sector cannot ensure the safety, security, and welfare of not only its employees but also the general public unless there are rules of conduct in place.[9]

In terms of the impact of the introduction of AI to public sector organizations, reputational impact will relate to the:

- Degree of innovation within that organization; in other words, how the new technology is being used to the public benefit
- Capability to operationally transform successfully
- Ability to operate the new model, including staffing
- Quality and vision of leadership

The importance of the latter should not be understated, especially given the link between operational delivery and political fodder in the case of failure. For many senior public sector workers, failed transformation not only brings uncertainty but also considerable personal risk, especially if they have led an unwilling organization into a new technological area in which they have no personal experience. The topic of leadership will be considered in more detail in the next chapter.

In the 2012 article "Public Sector Organizations and Reputation Management: Five Problems,"[10] five key areas of reputational management are identified as particularly affecting the public sector:

1. **The political problem:** This recognizes that all public sector organizations are connected in one way or another to a political super-ordinate level. Generally speaking, political authorities decide the strategies and their administrative levels are tasked with their implementation. All public sector bodies therefore are, to some degree, instruments of elected bodies carrying out public policies and, as a result, it is difficult for them to have independent strategies.

2. **The consistency problem:** Organizations in the private sector with good reputations are usually consistent in their approach and are often bound together across the breadth of their business through a shared vision. The public sector taken as a whole cannot manage their reputation across its entirety due to the diversity of its operations. For example, some parts of the public sector such as social services provide money and services by way of benefit, whereas others such as taxation take money away from the citizen. This diversity and existence of multiple identities makes it more difficult to create a single public service brand that inspires trust and confidence among its citizens.

3. **The charisma problem:** The strongest brands in the private sector are those for which the user has an emotional attachment. Some describe this as charisma, a magnetism, or even a spiritual power. Effective brand management is a bidirectional process in that private sector companies are also able to choose their "followers" in terms of segmentation, whereas the public sector is unable to make that choice. Another reason the public sector is unlikely to be viewed as charismatic is that it is bureaucratic by nature and that the sector, on the whole, is continually tainted with the impact of negative news such as unemployment, crime, and poverty.

4. **The uniqueness problem:** Organizations constantly seek to be able to find success through differentiation, but public sector organizations generally struggle to find a unique identity. Even in the case of the health service, where patients often have a choice between private and public attention, the problem of state hospitals is that their value proposition is one of providing a normal service as opposed to doing something unique. If they differ too much from the norm, their reputation will be adversely affected, as the hospital needs to be considered to be universal, which itself demands a degree of conformity.

5. **The excellence problem:** As organizations pursue excellence, the reality is that in benchmarking between the public and private sectors for particular services, the public sector often finds itself down the league table. Excellence measured through ranking is a difficult topic as it requires sustainability and is usually resource hungry. In most cases private sector organizations are better funded than public ones.

This does not imply that public sector organizations should not try to achieve excellence and have great reputations, but these are issues that should not be underestimated. Even having a poor reputation should not detract from the legitimacy of a public service provided its raison d'être is not challenged. Beyond this, diversity of the public sector means that reputational management might need to differ from one part to another depending on function, autonomy, and degree of visibility.

12.4.6 External Risk

In the category of risk management, the outstanding one is external risk, which relates to risks or events that are external to the organization. These are often sector specific but can be generic insofar as they relate to weather conditions or political considerations.

The ability to tap into the indicators of external risk is increasing. Data that is either structured or unstructured can help all organizations, including those in the public sector, anticipate what risks might be reasonably expected and to act in a proactive way. Even so, the nature of the public sector seems, in many cases, to be reactive rather than proactive. A digital model demands that the public sector think ahead, especially in a data-driven and AI-infused environment, to ensure that it is ahead of the curve in terms of events.

The challenge then is one of creating systems that not only recognize the potential impact of external events but also set in motion a process involving internal and external resources in order to protect the public interest. One might imagine that an AI system could detect likely weather conditions, recognize the vulnerabilities involved such as people and property, and operationalize a set of solutions that might at best mitigate the ensuing problems or even avoid the consequences entirely. With the likelihood that extreme weather events will happen more frequently, it seems almost logical that the public sector will increasingly need to automate their response to such external events such as storm and flood.

12.5 CYBERCRIME IN THE PUBLIC SECTOR

Although business leaders might be tempted to focus on those projects that provide the greatest benefits, they overlook the very real challenge of cyber risk at their peril. The public sector is especially at risk for two key reasons:

1. Pressure on budgets is only likely to get worse. This may lead to issues of excessive workload on employees, leading to carelessness, reduced or inconsistent support, or a tendency in some cases to work with external third parties where adequate due diligence into cybersecurity has not been carried out.
2. The sensitive nature of the data that many public sector organizations hold, especially the case in respect to health and financial data but can also extend to matters such as the names and addresses of individuals, including the most vulnerable.

The problem is endemic. In 2019 nearly one-third of all UK public sector organizations faced a cyberattack. Of these, 20% suffered more than 1,000 different attacks.[11]

The 2017 WannaCry ransomware attack cost the British National Health Service (NHS) nearly £100 million, but they were not alone in being targeted. WannaCry affected over a quarter of a million machines across the globe in companies as diverse as Telefonica, FedEx, and LATAM Airways. Internet security company McAfee revealed in 2016 that there had been separate WannaCry attacks in America, Britain, Germany, Canada, and South Korea, and the global cost was estimated overall to be £6 billion. In the particular case of WannaCry, the virus was delivered by email, which tricked the recipient into opening an attachment that then released malware, an approach known as phishing. Once the malware is in the system, it locks up files and cannot be unlocked unless a payment is made, usually in bitcoin, to regain access.

Although it had not been specifically targeted, the NHS was brought to a standstill.[12] The cyberattack resulted in the cancellation of hundreds of thousands of appointments, together with the frantic relocation of emergency patients from affected centers. Staff were forced to revert to paper and pen, and to use their own mobile phones, as the system affected key infrastructure including the telephone system. The ransomware spread though the NHS N3 network, the internet system connecting all the NHS sites in Britain. NHS reported that at least 80 of their 236 Trusts were affected as well as 603 other primary care and other organizations.

In technical terms, the cyberattack exposed a specific Microsoft Windows vulnerability as opposed to being an attack on unsupported software. Before the event happened Microsoft had identified the problem and had issued a security bulletin, and security patches had been released for all Windows versions that were supported at that time. In fact, the NHS had been made aware of the risk of cyberattack a year before the incident occurred. At the time, the NHS was criticized for using outdated systems, in this case Windows XP, which was 17 years old and which Microsoft had stopped supporting in 2014. Unusually, Microsoft also issued a security patch for what was an unsupported system.

What transpired was that the NHS was not only unprepared for a national cyberattack but had not carried out any rehearsals. As a result, it was unable to adequately communicate the issue throughout the organization as the emails themselves were either infected or were shut down. Additionally, although there was a National Recovery Plan, there was no provision for an incident of this scale. To add to the problem there were no clear relationships between the individual Health Trusts affected.

The cyberattack was stopped by an accidental "kill switch" discovered by a computer security programmer named Marcus Hutchins, who had registered a domain that the ransomware was programmed to check or invade. A kill switch is a feature that instantly turns off the internet connection if it detects any disruptions or failures of a virtual private network (VPN) connection. (A VPN extends the private network of an organization across a public network, and allows users to send and receive data across shared or public networks as if their computing devices were directly connected to the private network. Among the main functions of a VPN service is the protection of data and privacy online.) The domain that Hutchins had registered was attacked by powerful botnets (a string of connected computers) that were hoping to disable the domain and start another outbreak but instead was stopped by Hutchins's kill switch, ultimately giving him the description of being an accidental hero.[13]

The National Crime Agency advises that ransomware is the most common cyberextortion in the UK and some incidents have been viewed as being so severe that they had to be reported as a potential breach of data protection or confidentiality laws. British universities and local authorities are also receiving threats and in 2020 at least 23 British universities received ransomware threats with demands of up to £2,200. Security experts warn that the health service is a lucrative target, as health records are worth up to 10 times that of banking details. Such is the sensitivity of the topic that many health organizations are reluctant to provide information about ransomware attacks.

In 2016, the Hollywood Presbyterian Medical Center in Los Angeles paid $17,000 to unlock data that had been encrypted and left systems inaccessible for 10 days. Hospital management said that they had been left with no alternative but to pay "as it was in the best interests of normal operations."[14]

NHS Digital is the body that oversees cybersecurity for the National Health Service in the UK. In 2015 they unveiled a program to help Trusts defend against cyberattack. In terms of why the WannaCry attack happened, security experts pointed to the problem of insufficient funding, which had led to the NHS using old unsupported systems. Furthermore, in the nine months after the WannaCry attack, a survey by NHS Digital found that none of the 200 Trusts passed a cybersecurity test. In 2015 the National Audit Office concluded that continued deterioration in finances was not sustainable and that financial problems in the NHS were endemic. Because of this, the Wannacry event resulted in a boost of finance from the Government, but overall it is suggested that a lack of understanding of the risks involved was one of the main reasons that there had been insufficient funding.

A more recent hacking event happened in 2021 involving the Irish Health Service, which was described by the chief executive, Paul Read, as being callous and stomach churning, and an attack on health workers who had been working relentlessly during the pandemic. As a result, over 80% of appointments were affected as staff struggled to maintain the system using paper records.[15]

A 2019 study by software security company Sophos[16] pointed to the fact that there is a communication gap or disconnect between leaders and those frontline staff charged with maintaining data privacy in the public sector. The Sophos report noted that:

- 55% of public sector leaders believed that their data was less important than that of the private sector.
- 36% of public sector IT leaders say that recruitment is their biggest challenge.
- Only 14% of frontline public sector IT staff recognized that they are underresourced.
- 76% of senior public sector IT leaders said their organization had been affected by a ransomware incident over the past year but only 16% of frontline IT practitioners were aware of such an incident.

According to Jonathan Lee, UK director of Public Sector Relations at Sophos:

The kind of data held by public sector organizations could cause extensive harm if exposed to cyber attackers. Sensitive data for up to 66 million UK citizens could become available to the highest bidder on the dark web or among other criminal groups that buy and sell personally identifiable information (PII) like names, addresses, National Insurance numbers, tax returns, confidential medical records, passport details, and more. Cybercriminals can then use this data for spear-phishing, identity theft, breaching networks, or extortion.

Lee goes on to say,

Our survey results show that there is a real chasm in perception about security issues between different IT-related roles across the UK public sector.

Pointing to the need for better, multilayered security products to safeguard the public sector, Lee considers the problem to be due to:

- Misunderstanding about the level of risk involved
- Failure to prepare for that level of risk
- Need for better communication and knowledge sharing
- Necessity for more clearly defined processes

With technology expected to transform the NHS, the use of AI can create areas of greater risk but also can help provide important step-changing solutions. This is not an issue confined to the Health Service. Surveillance records and tactical plans could also be at risk and would have major consequences for national security if data were to be leaked or lost from those areas.

The Solarwinds operation was a cybercrime that severely compromised security and that insurance expert Aon described as "one of the most devastating events in cyber history." In that operation, US federal agencies were targeted, with hackers gaining entry through a tainted software update. In effect, this comprised the theft of cybersecurity tools from globally recognized cybersecurity firm Solarwinds. UK newspapers reported that at least 200 organizations around the world had been affected including NATO, the European Parliament, and government agencies in Washington, DC. In the UK, the National Cyber Security Agency NCSA also identified a low single-digit number of UK public sector organizations that had been targeted.[17]

12.6   PREVENTION OF CYBERCRIME AND PROTECTION FROM IT

In a book of this nature, it is impossible to adequately cover all elements of the prevention of cybercrime. It may be helpful, however, to mention a few tactics that can be considered in addition to the more generic actions mentioned earlier in this chapter.

12.6.1   Air Gapping

Otherwise known as an airgap or airwall, this is a way of ensuring that a network is secure from unsecured networks such as the internet. The intention is to build some sort of hypothetical roadblock to keep hackers from attacking a network. For data (and therefore malware) to be moved from outside the network into it, the data needs to be physically transferred through the use of a USB or removable disk drive. The approach is used in military applications, energy, and in aviation, but the approach is not foolproof as sophisticated viruses can still be transferred in this physical process. Also, the risk of physically losing a USB or removable drive cannot be overlooked.

12.6.2   Supply Chain Vulnerability

In 2021 cyber ransomers took the major Colonial Pipeline Company offline, interrupting 45% of the US East Coast's oil, diesel, and aviation fuel suppliers. The pipeline runs for 5,500 miles, from Texas to New York, and travels through 14 states. This was not, however, a direct attack on Colonial, as the cyber attackers targeted a third-party supplier of electronic data interface (EDI) services, Latitude Technologies, which provides the computer-to-computer exchange of documents, which enables companies to do business with each other.[18] According to Fred Kneip, CEO of cyber risk consultants CyberGRX:

There is a good reason that hackers have been attacking weak links in targets' digital ecosystems for years: it's often the easiest path to accessing data or distributing malicious content. It doesn't matter how well an organization protects its own perimeter if third parties with weak security controls create vulnerabilities that can be easily exploited.

12.6.3   Impact on Insurance Coverage

One way organizations can protect themselves against cyberattack is through insurance, but things are getting more difficult in terms of obtaining coverage at an affordable price. The cost of obtaining insurance in the public sector is passed on to the taxpayer at least in part. In a 2021 review by insurance experts Aon, cybercrime is now reported to be the fastest-growing form of crime in the United States.[19] Aon predicts that cybercrime will be more profitable for criminals than the global trade of all major illegal drugs combined at a cost of US$2.0–$6.0 trillion.

From an insurance point of view, the global cyber risk insurance market of US$5.5 billion in 2020 was expected to grow to an estimated US$18.2 billion in 2022. Aon also describes ransomware as having become truly weaponized. The result is that some insurers are now beginning to walk away from the risk or are imposing new, more stringent terms that include placing more pressure on organizations to improve their cyber risk management and be able to fully explain their cybersecurity arrangements. The increased move toward working from home has also added to the risk, with a recent report emerging of a US$50 million ransomware demand against a hardware/electronics company.

12.7   THE USE OF AI IN MANAGING RISK

This chapter has focused on the risks that attach to the introduction of advanced analytics and AI into the public sector. It might imply that the scale of the risks are such that this should not be done, but this is not the intention. Risk can hopefully be effectively managed and there are almost certainly service improvements that are possible at the same time as cost efficiencies. This final section therefore considers how risk management can be improved through the use of AI and, in so doing, mitigate any risk that might occur through its usage.

"Regtech" describes the use of technology to help manage the plethora of different rules and regulations not only across the globe but also across different industry sectors. The focus of regtech tends predominantly to be in financial services, especially among organizations with an international footprint. Public sector organizations, on the other hand, are mainly national, rather than international, so for them the problem of compliance with international regulations is not such a big problem. The use of AI in regtech is relatively in its infancy, although there are potential opportunities to automate functions. The role of blockchain in public services has not been discussed in this book, yet there are natural blockchain opportunities in the public sector in multiple areas such as finance and the supply chain. There is an increasing convergence between some of blockchain's capabilities and the use of AI.

Regtech has a place in the public sector, especially in the areas of:

- Financial and budgetary control tools
- Anti-money laundering and other financial crimes
- Policy implementation
- Legislation analysis and reporting tools, especially where a public service might work across different legislative jurisdictions

The public sector is in a stage not only of redevelopment but also possibly complete reinvention. It will ultimately require tooling that reflects the increasing complexity of the modern age but automates solutions in a coordinated way. The use of capabilities such as IBM's Open Pages[20] is one example of how AI might support automated systems that measure, monitor, analyze, and manage operational risk. Their system brings together risk and control assessments, internal and external events, key risk indicators, and action plans all within a single platform. The ability to infuse AI-based systems within the platform allows regulatory requirements to be intelligently mapped against organizational policies and ultimately to be complied with.

12.8 CONCLUSION

In considering not only the current uses of advanced analytics but also AI in the context of the public sector, it is critical that issues of risk are considered. This chapter has considered the various categories of risk, ranging from those relating to simple human error to those that are much more organized and malicious in nature through the impact of cybercrime in all its forms. The reality is that as the public sector increasingly moves toward and embraces a digital form of operation, the management of all these risks becomes not only more prevalent but also more critical. The risk of system failure in policing, social services, or security has consequences at a personal level, a societal level, or, in many cases, both.

Increased digitalization as a result of 5G and the proliferation of devices will only add to the risk. Greater dependence by the community on a networked, data-intense solution makes the consequences of failure more likely and also more catastrophic. In many cases, where one of the debates is that of insourced rather than outsourced services, the risk to an organization may not exist within that organization but rather within the outsourcer. The breadth of the exposure to risk might not be within the public sector organization itself but rather in the entire ecosystem or virtual organization, which may have multiple entry points of weakness.

That is not to say that digitalization should stop, if that was ever possible, nor should it be used as an argument for inertia. Experience of the use of digitalization should serve to continually remind the sector of the scale and extent of risk, the impact of systematic failure, and the constant threat of aggressive attack by third parties. In an environment of increasing dependence on data, there needs to be even greater emphasis on risk management controls within the public sector. The relatively traditional three lines of defense approach remains true:

- Unit or management control of risk
- Risk management and compliance functions
- External evaluation of the risk defense strategy

The stakes in the public sector are, however, arguably much higher than in the private sector. The public sector avoids effective risk management at not only its own peril, but at the peril of society and ultimately at the peril of the citizens it is intended to protect.

12.9 NOTES

1. Zurich Municipal. (2019). "What Are the Risks of Using AI in Social Housing?" Zurich Marketing, November 5. https://www.zurich.co.uk/news-and-insight/what-are-the-risks-of-using-ai-in-social-housing.
2. HM Government. (2017). "Management of Risk in Government: A Non-Executives' Review." https://assets.publishing.service.gov.uk/government/uploads/system/uploads/attachment_data/file/584363/170110_Framework_for_Management_of_Risk_in_Govt__final_.pdf (accessed December 7, 2021).
3. BBC News. (2013). "NHS IT System One of 'Worst Fiascos Ever,' Say MPs." September 18. https://www.bbc.com/news/uk-politics-24130684.
4. Richards, Neil M., and King, Jonathan. (2014). "Big Data Ethics." *Wake Forest Law Review*, May 19. Available at https://ssrn.com/abstract=2384174.
5. van Duin, E. (2021). "GDPR in the Public Sector: The Biggest and Smallest Changes." Deloitte. https://www2.deloitte.com/nl/nl/pages/risk/articles/cyber-security-privacy-gdpr-in-the-public-sector.html (accessed December 7, 2021).
6. PwC. (2011). "Fighting Fraud in the Public Sector." June 11. https://www.pwc.com/gx/en/psrc/pdf/fighting_fraud_in_the_public_sector_june2011.pdf.
7. Kock, N. F, McQueen, R. J., and Baker, M. (1996). "BPR in the Public Sector: A Case of Successful Failure." *Proceedings of AIBSEAR Conference*, edited by V. Gray and V. Llanes. Dunedin, NZ: University of Otago, 485–490.
8. Davenport, T. H., and Stoddard, D. B. (1994). "Reengineering: Business Change of Mythic Proportions?" *MIS Quarterly* 18 (2): 121–127.
9. Igniyte. (2015). "Reputation Management in the Public Sector." Ignyte blog, January 14. https://www.igniyte.co.uk/blog/reputation-management-public-sector/.
10. Wæraas, A., and Byrkjeflot, H. (2012). "Public Sector Organizations and Reputation Management: Five Problems." *International Public Management Journal* 15, 186–206.
11. Department for Digital, Culture, Media and Sport. (2019). "Cyber Security Breaches Survey 2019." Crown copyright, April 3. https://www.gov.uk/government/statistics/cyber-security-breaches-survey-2019.
12. Smart, W. (2018). "Lessons Learned Review of the WannaCry Ransomware Cyber Attack." Department of Health and Social Care, February. https://www.england.nhs.uk/wp-content/uploads/2018/02/lessons-learned-review-wannacry-ransomware-cyber-attack-cio-review.pdf.

13. Whittaker, Z. (2019). "Marcus Hutchins, Malware Researcher and 'Wannacry Hero' Sentenced to Supervised Release." *TechCrunch*, July 26. https://techcrunch.com/2019/07/26/marcus-hutchins-sentenced-kronos/.

14. Milmo, C. (2017). "NHS Cyber Attack Is Just the Latest 'Ransom' Hack in a Worrying Trend." iNews, May 12. https://inews.co.uk/news/dozens-nhs-hospitals-targeted-cyber-blackmailers-24703.

15. Black, R. (2021). "Hack of Health IT System Has Had 'Catastrophic' Impact, Says HSE Chief." AOL, May 20. https://www.aol.co.uk/hack-health-system-had-catastrophic-141248901.html?soc_src=aolapp.

16. Sophos. (2019). "UK Public Sector Information Vulnerable to Cyberattack Due To Awareness Gap Between IT Professionals." Press release, November 19. https://www.sophos.com/en-us/press-office/press-releases/2019/11/uk-public-sector-information-vulnerable-to-cyberattack-due-to-awareness-gap-between-it-professionals.

17. Landi, M. (2021). "UK Faces 'Moment of Reckoning' over Rising Cybersecurity Threats." *Evening Standard*, May 11. https://www.standard.co.uk/news/uk/cyber-security-gchq-china-russia-director-b934417.html.

18. Muncaster, P. (2018). "US Gas Pipelines Hit by Cyber-Attack." *Infosecurity Magazine*, April 4. https://www.infosecurity-magazine.com/news/us-gas-pipelines-hit-by-cyberattack/.

19. "'Staggering, Concerning': Aon Says Ransomware Now 'Truly Weaponised.'" InsuranceNews.com.au, April 15. https://www.insurancenews.com.au/daily/staggering-concerning-aon-says-ransomware-now-truly-weaponised.

20. "IBM OpenPages with Watson." https://www.ibm.com/products/openpages-with-watson?utm_content=SRCWW&p1=Search&p4=43700069900865820&p5=e&gclsrc=aw.ds&gclid=CjwKCAjwi6WSBhA-EiwA6Niok8BnjM-Y1Rd2aE3Z9H09R-4BNblVMfLyviG2BzPwKeDl_w9jq8yDVRoCRzQQAvD_BwE (accessed December 12, 2021).

CHAPTER 13

Implementation – Leadership and Management

13.1   INTRODUCTION

Although multiple different and quite diverse public sectors have been considered, it becomes possible to draw out some generic issues of implementation across all of them. There are many complications related to the execution of an AI program, and traditional practitioners in the public sector are unlikely to have deep expertise relative to the ins and outs of the detailed technologies of machine learning and, for instance, that of neural networks. Technologists equally are unlikely to understand the key operational drivers of organizational success in the public sector.

Therefore, the following elements in this chapter and the next are aimed at the "non-techie" who wishes to consider an AI-infused program of transformation and to be able to have sensible conversations with deep technical experts.

There are principally three components to implementation:

1. **What** needs to be done, especially measured in terms of the organization's mission statement.
2. **How** it will be done, by creating the management framework and creating the critical capabilities to deliver success, including talent management.
3. **Where** resources will be allocated, and where efforts need to be prioritized.

With particular regard to the public sector, each stage requires two further elements:

1. How will these actions be undertaken within the constraints of the public purse?
2. Does it meet the tests of not only satisfying public consent but also gaining public support? These tests may not be equal across the whole of the public sector but may be more important in certain areas, such as policing, than in other functions.

In this chapter, four important and complementary elements of the change process will be considered:

1. Leadership with specific regard to the public sector, and how this differs from management.
2. The second area is what is described as "managing the mission."
3. The third is managing resources, which also deals with team building.
4. The fourth deals with key stakeholders, particularly in this case the area of employee representation, which is a particular issue for the public sector.

13.2 LEADERSHIP

One of the most important elements of transformation is the management of leadership and cultural change. In the public sector, leaders have a threefold challenge, as they are required to win the hearts and minds of:

1. The public
2. The senior teams
3. Frontline staff

As a result, an effective communication strategy becomes a critical component of the transformation program.

Many of the leaders we are usually familiar with are either from the private sector or political in nature. As a result, few citizens tend to be aware of who might be "organizational" leaders in the public sector. The need for effective leadership is recognized as a key enabler for transformational change within public sector services, but there are important challenges to overcome. Business Research Methodology (BRM), an educational portal, suggests that there are five key differences between leadership in the public and private sectors, as summarized in Table 13.1.[1]

In its 2019 article "A New Mindset for Public Sector Leadership," Deloitte invited readers to take the #TenYearChallenge.[2] It was a process where an individual photo of a leader (as a participant to the process) from 10 years earlier is placed alongside a photo of that same participant today, and contributors are invited to make comparisons. They use this personalized approach as an example of how much (or how little) the public sector has changed in the past 10 years and how it needs to change in the next. It's quirky, but the point is well made.

Leadership in the public sector is a "broad church." It ranges from medical officers to police chiefs; from government officials to chief executives of local government. Some roles are highly technical whereas others require advanced levels of stakeholder management as to how budgets and relationships are managed. Deloitte suggests that there need to be five shifts in thinking in leadership in the public sector, as summarized in Table 13.2.

TABLE 13.1   Differences in Public and Private Sector Leadership Characteristics

Key Characteristic	Differences between Public and Private Sector
Differences in organizational aims and objectives	In essence, the private sector focus on shareholder value whereas the public sector focus on service.
	BRM suggests that private sector employees are generally clearer on their mission than are those employees in the public sector. This almost certainly is related to better use of internal communication and brand awareness.
	While external branding appears at first sight to be mainly for the benefit of external customers, there is some evidence that shows that it also has a beneficial impact on internal employees as well.
Different stakeholder sets and their expectation	There are both internal and external stakeholders in both the private and public sector, but they differ in nature.
	In the public sector, stakeholders are more generally the public, whose expectations are related to the fact that funding is mainly through taxpayer money. Additionally there are other major stakeholders, for example, employee representative bodies such as trade unions.
	In the private sector, by comparison, stakeholders usually comprise stockholders (or shareholders) who expect an adequate financial return on their investment; customers who expect an adequate service; and to some degree employees who expect adequate remuneration.
Degree of scrutiny	Public sector organizations are usually subject to greater scrutiny than private sector organizations, which is a by-product of taxpayer funding. This is not always the case; for example, some private industries such as banking are heavily regulated.
External environment	The public sector is especially affected by the political external environment.
	By comparison, although private sector organizations are also affected by the external environment such as politics and the economy, in the main the greatest influence for the private sector is the marketplace.
Sources of motivation	It is suggested that public sector managers are motivated more by safety and security, whereas private sector motivations are more related to career progression, financial compensation, and autonomy.

The overall suggestion is that public sector leaders will not only need to develop and maintain new capabilities but also need to generate a completely new mindset. This new and different approach is similar to that which already exists in the private sector, where there are already greater citizen (or customer) expectations, continued pressure on budget and finances, and heightened scrutiny.

Technology insights also form a key part of that new mindset, but public sector leaders of the future who leave this element solely to technologists do so at their peril. For example, public sector leaders need to be as aware of the problems of data security

TABLE 13.2   Five Shifts in Public Sector Leadership Thinking

Essential Shift	Implication and Requirement
Greater creativity	The ability to find creative and innovative solutions to public sector delivery issues that might be found in forming new partnerships or in embracing new technologies.
Greater personal resilience	Current, and almost certainly future, challenges for public sector leaders require considerable personal inner strength, especially when decisions are subject to public scrutiny.
	A strong personal sense of duty appears to be one of the most important critical success factors.
Blurring of boundaries	The recognition that the old segmented way of thinking is less valid than before. Traditional boundaries are increasingly blurring, for example, between health and education, and between homebuilding and homelessness.
	The impact of this apparent convergence is forcing public sector leaders to adopt a more collaborative approach than before and to replace the traditional hierarchical way of leading.
Greater complexity	New challenges in the public sector have created new complexity. This requires leaders not only to be able to recognize ambiguity but also to operate using a much broader set of capabilities.
	This may well be unfamiliar territory for those leaders who have risen through the ranks from a more technical or managerial route.
	Complexity brings with it some of the traits more likely to be seen in the private sector such as an excessive focus on operational efficiency, which for many is considered to be the zeitgeist of the modern age.
Mastery of teambuilding	The multilayered and diverse nature of this form of "new" leadership in the new model means that all these tasks and competences needed are almost certainly beyond the scope of one individual.
	Public sector leaders of the future will increasingly need to learn how to build and retain effective teams, and to prioritize tasks more effectively.

as they are of the political environment. They also need to be aware of the impact of technological change, not only in the hearts and minds of their own workforce but on the mix of employees within their organization, especially as many of the administrative jobs are likely to disappear and be replaced by automation. According to Deloitte in its 2019 article, "automating tasks using artificial intelligence could free up 96.7 million working hours annually in the US Federal Government – and that is a conservative estimate."

With an opportunity of this size, the move toward greater digitalization of the public sector will be compelling, especially where financial pressures exist. This type of change will also be accelerated by more technologists entering the sector. This shift of skills in itself will create its own problems in terms of recruitment and ensuring that the right capabilities are in place to successfully deliver on the mission. The public sector has always been known to be a relatively poor payer compared to the private sector when it comes to salaries, although often this has been offset by other benefits such as more generous pension provisions. The reality is that those generous pensions are less likely to be available in the future and, as a result, the public sector will have to compete for resources with the private sector by being able to offer not only comparable but also more competitive reward packages. To do this might require additional savings elsewhere in the budget, which could place pressures elsewhere in the system. There are likely to be hard choices for public leaders to make.

For employees, the traditional attractiveness of the public sector may also be in jeopardy. Public sector organizations may start to look more and more like commercial organizations, which may be less appealing, especially to those who principally join the sector through a sense of duty. Full-time employees will increasingly find themselves working alongside part-timers, outsourced organizations, and participants from the so-called gig economy who work in the public sector as part of their portfolio of part-time roles. How these roles are filled will also be the subject of detailed attention to avoid accusations of cronyism and bias. The mood of the workforce may also change from one that is focused on duty to one where working in the public sector is "just another job." Effective communication both inside and external to the organization will become increasingly critical as leaders try to manage their internal and external stakeholders.

How all this looks in the eyes of the public remains to be seen. When everything is fine there will be no complaints, but in such a complex and broad sector this is an unlikely scenario. The whole of the public sector may be at risk of being measured by the lowest common denominator, wherever it occurs.

13.2.1 Transfer of Private Sector Leaders to the Public Sector

As the public sector assumes more of the characteristics of the private sector, public sector leaders will acquire private sector leadership attributes. As an alternative, and perhaps as a shortcut to progress, there is likely to be greater opportunity for transfer of private sector leaders into the public sector.

This was previously attempted in the UK National Health Service, but the new management system ultimately was the subject of considerable condemnation. The move by the government to create commercial characteristics within a public sector healthcare function led to an increase in managers in the NHS of 16% between 2013 and 2017, but this did not compare favorably to an increase in doctors of 8% and in nurses of 2% over the same period. In many cases the introduction of more managers was viewed as being another layer of unnecessary administration and control that added to cost without adding significantly to value, although some of the complaints were political in nature rather than operational.

In their 2021 article "How Managerialism Took Over the NHS," *Tribune* newspaper argued that the role of social home care was taken over by "a cadre of management specialists: accountants, consultants, auditors and the legal advisors who design 'provider' contracts or organize 'purchaser' strategies."[3] The authors of the article also suggested that a decade of austerity had resulted in the NHS being unable to manage the business itself. This had opened the door to private sector management techniques including outsourcing and had led to 26% of the total NHS expenditure being allocated to private sector companies.

Conversely, rather than a flood of private sector managers entering the NHS, the movement of skilled people seems to be in the opposite direction as NHS managers and executives increasingly join private healthcare companies. The exact cause is unclear but it may reflect public sector pressures on the reward system, expected productivity, and lack of funding. While at face value this could be seen as a worrying trend, it could ultimately prove to be beneficial, as the private sector might gain a greater understanding of the sensitivities of the public sector. The impact may be that as a result of this migration of talent, the private sector could well end up in a better position to undertake a function that better mirrors the current public sector.

13.3   LEADERS OR MANAGERS?

One particular concern is that it is suggested that staff at the top of the public sector are primarily managerial in nature rather than exhibiting leadership. To that extent, it might be argued that leadership and management reflect opposing values, so one of the key issues is how to translate leadership into more effective management. Most are familiar with the charismatic type of leader, but in his 2002 paper "Rethinking Leadership for the Public Sector," Australian author and leadership consultant Don Dunoon suggested that one way forward is for leadership in the public sector to be more "collaborative" and "collective" in nature than charismatic.[4] Although much of what has been written about collective leadership tends to relate to the healthcare sector, the principle appears to apply to many other parts of the public sector.

Being "collective" means that leadership does not rest with a single individual; rather, the leadership resides with the overall team and individual team members share in leadership responsibilities.

> *In collective leadership cultures, responsibility and accountability function simultaneously at both individual and collective levels.*
>
> *They breed regular reflective practice focused on failure, organizational learning and making continuous improvement an organizational habit.*
>
> *By contrast command and control leadership cultures invite the displacement of responsibility and accountability onto a single individual, leading to scapegoating and a climate of fear of failure rather than an appetite for innovation.*[5]

In their report "Collective Leadership for the Health Sector,"[6] health charity the Kings Fund suggests the following important approaches:

- That in collective leadership everyone takes responsibility for the organization as a whole as opposed to just focusing on their own job or sector functions.
- If leaders create a positive environment for staff then staff will in turn create a positive environment for patients (and presumably, if adopting a broader public sector viewpoint, of all citizens).

- Where there is a culture of collective leadership then all staff will intervene to solve problems and to innovate safely.
- Performance of the organization does not rely on the number or quality of leaders but rather reflects their commitment and sense of direction.
- The vision and mission need to be effectively communicated to all levels of the organization.

The starting point for the concept and implementation of collective leadership rests at the Board level, where complete commitment to the approach is required from senior members. A strategy for collective leadership is one that focuses on the skills and competencies across the entire team, creates shared behaviors, and is also a process for leaders working together. It's a model that has been promoted elsewhere by the UK Government, with approximately 300 chief executives and equivalents across the UK's public sector already participating in their Collective Leadership program.[7]

However, collective leadership may not be for everyone and there is a case for more traditional approaches to leadership in some parts of the public sector. For example, the UK Fire Service applies a four-stage approach to leadership:[8]

1. **Leading the service**, which focuses on developing skills to support and lead corporate change.
2. **Leading the function**, which focuses on setting direction and vision for the function or department, including performance management and well-being.
3. **Leading others**, which focuses on people management, personal skills, and personal resilience.
4. **Leading yourself**, through personal development.

One different approach to leadership, again from the fire service, is that of "servant leadership." This is a model that places the needs of the team above those of the leader. It follows the U.S. Marine approach of "officers eat last." According to Bruce Bjorge of Lexipol, himself an experienced fire service leader, "If there isn't enough water for everyone, the servant leader will make sure the crew drinks first. If you are an effective servant leader, chances are your crew won't let you go thirsty either."[9]

13.4 MANAGING THE MISSION

13.4.1 Creating the Mission

The mission statement of an organization is a concise explanation of its purpose and intention, and can often include reference to its culture, ethics, and values. Deloitte indicated that there are four elements to creating the mission, generally as shown in Table 13.3.

Initial building blocks may additionally require:

- The need to revisit the mission on an iterative basis, especially as progress may depend on effective and sustained funding and if transformation is likely to be a lengthy process.

TABLE 13.3 Creating the Public Services Mission

Mission statement	Implication for Public Sector
Breadth of the mission	A clear explanation of the breadth of the mission or service. For example, the mission could be deep and focused or it could be broad and all encompassing.
	Whether any intended changes in the mission deal with an entire sector of a public service, or just a particular function within it.
Establish the level	To establish the level that the mission is to attain, usually through some sort of benchmarking.
	This goes beyond simply a rhetoric-based comment such as "We will create a world-leading public service" but rather defines detailed performance targets against which progress can be measured.
	These benchmarks or targets might be used to make comparisons with other similar successful projects, either elsewhere in the country or even internationally.
Public perception	To ensure that the mission fits with the public perception of the service, which may need to take into account the challenge of differing public expectations regarding priorities.
	In an AI context, this might mean that the public recognizes that transformation (for example, through the use of chatbots) is being undertaken to maintain and enhance service, rather than save money.
Ethical element	This relates in part to political promises but can equally reflect what is feasible to attain the mission.
	In the context of AI, this may include the need to ensure that there are adequate safeguards in place to manage and maintain safety and security of data; that issues of bias have been considered and managed; and that there is appropriate regulation and oversight.

- The identification of quick wins that will identify demonstrable success within the funding available, in order to pacify stakeholders and reassure key sponsors.
- Gaining a stakeholder consensus of what is being promoted not only in terms of the mission but in the context of AI, and how this will be achieved.

13.4.2 Prioritization: Where to Start?

Many public sector organizations have broad aspirations, so it becomes essential that any agreed mission statement is linked in some way to prioritization. There is a more practical aspect to prioritization and that is the question of what is actually achievable, as opposed to merely being political rhetoric. In many cases of public service such as healthcare, there are strong emotional issues involved. Additionally, in an AI context there may also only be certain limited data sets that are available for use, although increasingly one trend is that of using "synthetic data" to model and test new ideas.

Prioritization may also require some degree of flexibility, as providing more effective AI-informed services at the front end could create a backlog at the back end. The use of chatbots to improve the efficiency of the initial citizen interaction may require a better follow-up service such as benefit management or health treatment. At a macro level, governments also need to understand where the priorities rest in terms of the allocation of funding. In 2017 the UK Government created the HM Treasury's "Decision Making Framework," which sought to assess and rationalize future spending decisions.[10]

13.4.3 Communicating the Mission Statement

Many will have different ideas as to what the end result of a digital transformation might look like. Perhaps there are visions of automation, robotics, and some sort of authoritarian regime from the realms of science fiction. Alternatively, others might simply view the digital transformation of public services as comparable to that of media and entertainment, that is, public services being provided in the same way that we have digital entertainment on demand or through a subscription service. These different ideas of the future can lead to ambiguity and uncertainty that ultimately may be unhelpful.

As a result, it becomes critical that business leaders are able to effectively explain what the potential end result will look like in terms of digital transformation. This requires the use of appropriate language that is understandable to all key stakeholders, many of whom will not have either academic or technical backgrounds. This means that technology jargon should be avoided.

The ability to create a clear message is crucial. Leaders may decide to use professional advice to help them craft a message with appropriate appeal, and this typically will come from a marketing professional. For many public servants, using a marketing professional is likely to be unusual as the public sector has not tended to need such services in "normal" business. Some might well argue that there should be no need to market public services, suggesting that marketing per se is a way of driving greater usage, which is not normally the case in public services. (If anything, the public sector probably wants fewer people to use the services.) The reality is that not only do consumers benchmark the public sector against the private sector, but also that marketing expertise:

- In the form of market research, is a way of better understanding the needs of the end user.
- Helps organizations create products and solutions that are actually needed in the market.
- Raises awareness of the benefits available to citizens who might not normally be aware of their entitlement.

Table 13.4 shows the key elements of effective marketing strategies, which have been extrapolated to apply to the public sector.

TABLE 13.4 Marketing Strategies for Public Sector Transformation

Key Fundamentals of Private Sector	Key Fundamentals of Public Sector
Identify the target audience	Understand the group most likely to be affected by any change or transformation.
	Craft a communication strategy so key messages can be appropriately shared.
Create and document the strategy	Create a single documented strategy to provide clarity in creating any internal and external communications for all key stakeholders, and to avoid ambiguity.
Make the strategy personal	Keep stakeholders engaged, especially with citizens by using personal messages: "What does this mean for you as an individual?"
	Create emotional touches and an emotional connection to the service involved.
Maintain focus on content marketing	Create and maintain effective, timely, and relevant content on websites.
	Reuse generic content where possible, especially as some content might be capable of being used across different sectors or departments.
	Improve ease of navigation on websites.
Build marketing partnerships where two companies collaborate to the benefit of both	Marketing partnerships are an effective way of promoting a marketing campaign and building key alliances.
	In the public sector, internal partnerships can be created between departments by recognizing and promoting key synergies.
Collaborate with influencers	The use of key influencers can help in sharing aspirational content, or to take specific actions (such as preventive treatment).
Help customers solve a problem	Place greater focus on the customer or citizen rather than focusing on the public service itself.
	Public services are, in effect, a form of problem-solving ecosystem, so the essence of any change is to provide ways of solving those problems in a more timely and effective way.
Use customer forums	Use customer or citizen forums to contribute to any program of change. This not only helps with engaging the stakeholder base as a whole but may add a different perspective to key issues.
Get other employees involved	Allow employees to be effective advocates of change, including employee representative bodies. Frontline public servants will invariably see things from a different angle than that of management and the views of frontline staff need to be taken into account as part of effective stakeholder management.
Use data to predict trends	Use data and information to constantly engage with customers in a transparent, reliable way, so that they are aware of key trends and developments. Use effective visualizations to communicate key information.

13.5 MANAGEMENT OF RESOURCES

The creation of an effective team with different tiers of capabilities is a critical component in successful implementation. In this section three elements will be considered:

1. Technical skills versus traditional skills
2. Specialist skills versus generalist skills
3. Training and education, and their impact on capability

13.5.1 Technical versus Traditional

In most public sectors, many employees will continue to undertake a traditional function, but there will be others who are primarily engaged with technology. With progress toward a more technology-enabled public sector it is almost certain that the latter category of technology experts will grow and may perhaps even start to dominate as they deal with highly technical issues such as technology transformation and data science.

This is likely to create some problems at a time when there is widespread movement across all industries, both public and private, toward the better use of technology and where there are already skill shortages. The private sector has historically relied on the transfer of staff from one sector to another to satisfy their need. Even within the private sector there is a form of pecking order based on those types of industry that are best able to afford relatively scarce skills, such as in banking. The public sector in the form of government will need to create an effective strategy for recruitment, training, and staff retention.

There are broader considerations. Through the investment of venture capital and the sheer size of the opportunity, the private sector is likely to become more adept at developing and implementing new forms of technology and systems that meet the needs of the public sector. As this happens, the natural consequence is that governments will discharge their public sector obligations more readily by outsourcing. The ability of governments to move staff off the balance sheet while maintaining the same level of service will, notionally at least, be very attractive financially. There may, however, be strong political and ethical consequences to consider, not least the outsourcing of national core public activities and importantly, the public reaction to it.

13.5.2 Specialist versus Generalist

Another key area is that of determining whether data scientists and other technology experts working in the public sector will be generalists or specialists. Being a technical expert will no longer be adequate, and the most effective operators will have a working knowledge of both the technology and the key organizational drivers of the sector they are working in. A comparison can be made in the private sector where there are analytical experts who have digital marketing skills specifically for the retail sector. In the public sector, new hybrid analytical and AI experts will have specific skills in policing, healthcare, and other public sector functions. The possibility of a downside cannot be overlooked, as it has been suggested that the increased use of algorithms in the police and justice systems has resulted in a fear of deskilling among police, prosecutors, and judges.

Not all sectors are of equal weighting or importance, and even within those particular sectors there may be specializations. These niche areas may not be able to afford or be able to compete for specialist skills. This may in turn lead to collaboration between sectors or regional departments, or could even lead to greater public/private collaboration. The impact of this may be to increase centralization, create new collaborative models, or both.

13.5.3 Training and Education

Talent management through training and education is not an optional extra but rather is a critical component. There is a growing need to create data literacy training for the public sector with content that is specifically aligned to the public service they are undertaking. Data management and analytical capabilities are important, as they ensure that resources are focused on the most critical areas and the simpler processes can be left to automation and self-service. The topic of data science in the public sector is especially challenging, as it is one of the areas where a high level of transparency is needed to ensure that fair decisions are made without bias and in accordance with ethical standards.

Already individual public sector organizations are responding to the challenge. The United Kingdom, for example, has created a campus managed by the Office of National Statistics and universities, proposing curricula in data science especially for public administration applications. Distance learning courses are open not only to civil servants but also to the public. This creates an opportunity for administrations to recruit graduates who will have been trained on data science with specialization related to public issues.[11] An international example of this is the South Korean Customs forces. They have implemented a training course for customs officials on data science tools. Their course is led by academics but is relevant to their own specific needs in terms of border control.[12]

Required key skills are not all related to data science. Successful implementation of any project usually requires a wide range of capabilities and this will affect the type and amount of workforce allocated to any particular task. In terms of individual simple pilot projects, these usually need to comprise a combination of public service leaders, technologists, and project/program managers operating as a multidiscipline team. Each can and will bring their own perspective to the table in order to provide a comprehensive, integrated solution (Figure 13.1). In an AI environment, additional key capabilities may be required, such as:

- The ability to conduct a more sophisticated relationship with end users, which Deloitte describes as citizen relationship management (CRM). CRM is an approach adopted by governments that aims to improve the speed, accuracy, and quality of responses to citizen requests for answers to questions and general information about policies, practices, and procedures.[13]
- A new form of the organization relating to changes within the workforce, often called Workforce Relationship Management. A workforce relationship management system helps organizations ensure that the staff are working in the right roles, which increases staff satisfaction, as their skills are used more efficiently, but also decreases operational cost, as employees are more efficiently deployed.[14]

■ Relational, influencing, and collaborative capabilities that reflect the need of organizations to work with many other stakeholders outside their direct organization such as partners, outsourcers, and other agencies.

One key challenge is that there is a vast gap between those charged with delivering public services and those who ultimately will provide technological solutions in the future, and who are usually outside the organization. The language of both parties is often different, and it might be argued that their motivations are different as well, one being motivated by duty and public service and the other being commercially-minded. Ultimately traditional public sector practitioners have to be able to understand more about the technological solutions that will form an *inevitable* part of their future. By the same means, those with deep technological insight must recognize the very deep and often personal pressures and sense of duty of those working in the public service.

The reality is that public sector workers could potentially fear technologists, especially if the technologists create a threat to the existing status quo. In many cases, these technologists will be viewed as jobbing contractors with no ongoing sense of responsibility. Because of this worry and the needs of the public sector, one starts to imagine a new breed of technical expert who has a sense of duty and purpose to the wider community rather than to their own personal interests. This is not contradictory, and the impact of the gig economy may also result in even temporary workers having a different, more moralistic approach to the importance of work in the public sector.

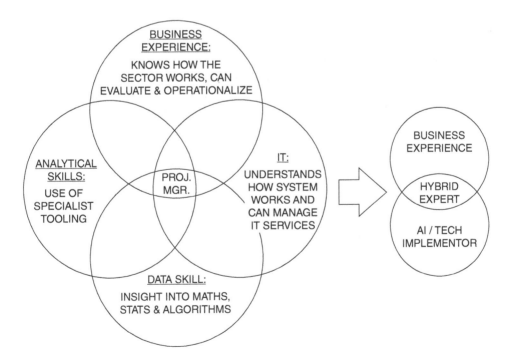

FIGURE 13.1   Evolution of Capabilities

Finally, it is also worth reminding ourselves of the Seven Principles of Public Life, which consider issues such as:

- Selflessness
- Integrity
- Objectivity
- Accountability
- Openness
- Honesty
- Leadership

These are dealt with in more detail in Appendix A, and represent a framework for behavior for *all* those working in the public sector.

13.6 MANAGEMENT OF KEY STAKEHOLDERS

A stakeholder is an individual or group that has a vested interest in an organization, and can either affect or be affected by that organization's operations and its performance. The matter of "stakeholder dynamics" is critical in the implementation process. It is a role that is usually managed by the project manager with stakeholder feedback collected and analyzed. In many countries there are legal issues of employee representation where this relates to any changes that could relate to job losses over a certain number of employees.

In any AI or information system implementation, there is likely to be a large and complex network of stakeholders, at different levels and that changes with time. These stakeholders may have either formal or informal roles, be internal or external to the organization, and be individuals or act in groups. Overall a "stakeholder relations influence" framework may be used to map their power and influence (Figure 13.2). The stakeholder ecosystem in the public sector is so complex that there are even some specialist companies that offer to map these for individual organizations.[15]

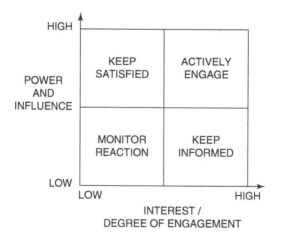

FIGURE 13.2 Stakeholder Relations Influence Framework

The public sector generally needs to manage a broad collection of stakeholders that comprise:

- Internal: management, staff, contractors, and employees and their representatives
- External: citizens, regulators, media, political, and local representation

The issue of communication to staff and end users was dealt with earlier in this chapter and it is recognized that it is a key element of stakeholder management. In the next chapter we will further consider how best to influence the general public toward the use of AI and analytics through the use of behavioral management, or what is known as nudge theory. Initially the matter of internal stakeholders especially needs to be considered and in many, perhaps most, public services, employees are represented by collective employee groups that are usually in the form of trade unions. It is this area that we will particularly focus on.

13.6.1 Worker Representation and Trade Unions

One of the key stakeholders in any change is likely to be that of workers' representation or, more specifically, trade unions, which have continued to grow throughout the twentieth century. In the United States, in what was called the "Little Wagner Act," New York Mayor Robert Wagner gave trade unions exclusive authority to represent all New York City workers whether or not they were members, and in the 1960s and 1970s this was expanded to include teachers, clerks, firemen, police, prison guards, and others. Later, President Kennedy upgraded the status of unions of federal workers and by 2009 trade union membership of US public sector workers had outstripped that of private sector workers.

In other countries where trade unions are allowed, the size of these unions and therefore their influence remains significant. They remain key stakeholders, especially in respect to any substantial change in the operating model of public services, but the reality is that the unions are themselves in a challenging position. On the one hand, they naturally want to represent the best interests of their members. On the other hand, as AI takes greater effect and more simple jobs are automated, then the size of the workforce (and therefore the unions' membership and associated fee income) is set to be reduced.

One of the great achievements of unionization is obtaining better pension rights. This particular benefit itself is under threat because, as life expectancy increases, the pressure on the pension book for the public sector is likely to become increasingly unsustainable. Automation and AI may reduce the size of the workforce and reduce the overall pension burden, and of course robots don't expect pensions, but they don't contribute to the pension pot either. Perhaps that money will need to come from technology companies in the form of changes in taxation. Automation may become an essential component in ensuring the affordability of pensions in the short term but there are likely to be longer-term implications.

It may be useful to take a moment to look back at history, specifically, the impact of the Luddites, who were named after their alleged leader, Ned (or General) Ludd.

Although characterized by their destruction of textile machinery, they were not anti-technologists; rather, their complaint was with changes to their terms and conditions of employment, and a lack of consultation. Put another way, the Luddite movement occurred as a result of poor stakeholder management. The main point, however, in the current context of AI transformation of the public sector is that trade unions remain key stakeholders and need to be engaged in the discussion. Neglecting this will lead to inevitable conflict. By the same measure, however, unions are aware of the march of time and of their need to keep pace with technological developments.

In their 2017 paper "Shaping Our Digital Future," the UK-based Trade Union Congress (TUC), which represents all the major UK unions, recognized that "We are living through a period of profound and rapid technological change."[16] They accept the inevitability and eventual operational advantages of these changes and make the point that the unions cannot afford to "be passive recipients," calling for "government employers and policy-makers to seriously engage unions in shaping Industry 4.0."

Overall, it is a very positive viewpoint. The TUC says that "rather than attempt to hold back the technological tide, the UK should plan how to use it to enhance productivity, jobs, and wages, particularly in the areas which previous waves of industrial change have left behind." As might be expected with an organization that represents employee rights, their focus is on protecting those workforces and communities that are at greater risk. If there are benefits, they say, then these should be fairly shared. By this they mean, for example, that if there are major productivity savings, then these savings should go toward Universal Basic Income. The TUC also refers to the need to reconsider the matter of the pension age, or age of normal retirement, suggesting that it be brought forward.

Beyond this, the TUC's aim is for a "fairer, more equal society." The concept of digitalization is placed side by side with globalization and climate change as being a major contributing factor of change. The famous economist John Maynard Keynes had previously addressed the issue of technological change in the 1930s, seeing it not as a curse but rather that it would create a new "leisure class." He even suggested a working week of 15 hours. It appears to create a view of great optimism for the future but the reality seems to be that this has not happened, even if there has been a reduction in weekly working hours over the past century from 70 hours per week to 30. These figures may in part be misleading. Changes in the nature of work means that there are more part-time workers than before and that there has been a shift from industrial work to professional work, including education and healthcare. This in itself is an interesting issue as these two areas are likely to be substantially affected by AI going forward.

Elsewhere, on the topic of wages, it has long been held that there is a link between wage levels and productivity. While productivity has increased as a result of automation, wages have not matched those increases. The union movement generally is concerned about what is known as the "labor share"; that is, the proportion of national income that ends up in workers' pockets, and that it is decreasing. There appear to be several reasons for this decrease, including:

- Globalization
- Taxation policy, with incentives being more in place to invest in technology than in workers
- The impact of technology, on both productivity and on the number of jobs that can be automated

The TUC also draws a strong correlation between trade union membership and inequality in the UK, where inequality is defined as how wages are distributed, as measured by the gap between the highest and lowest paid. This book is not intended to be a political statement, but it is feasible that AI-infused automation could lead to some sort of reemergence of stronger employee representation, perhaps through the union movement. Some specific unions in the UK are already looking at how AI will change the working landscape. Unite, the UK's largest trade union, is working with the automotive sector to look at the potential impacts of automation and the digital revolution in manufacturing on the future of the industry, as well as the impact of automation on other sectors.

In their 2013 report "The Future of Employment: How Susceptible Are Jobs to Computerisation?" Carl Frey and Michael Osborn looked at the types of jobs that may be lost as a result of digitalization.[17] They compare the overall impact on jobs to a hanging catenary chain (mentioned earlier in section 10.2). Transportation and logistics occupations, the bulk of office and administrative support workers, and labor in production occupations, services, sales, and construction occupations all show high probabilities of digitalization. These, say the authors, are the jobs most likely to be initially at risk.

It's not a clear picture. An alternative report, "The Risk of Automation for Jobs in OECD Countries," challenges that view, suggesting that only 9% of jobs are at risk, but it uses a different methodology.[18] In yet a different review, PWC estimated that "around 30% of jobs in the UK are at potential high risk of automation, compared to around 38% in the US."[19] On the matter of wages, while the unions are aiming to reduce inequality, there seems to be a real risk that the opposite could result. Those at the lower end of the skills set, whose jobs are most likely to disappear, could see even greater competition for work and, as a result, their wages might even fall.

13.6.2 US Policy Recommendations

In their 2017 document that frames AI policy, the US White House set out a series of recommendations that deal with both the positive and negative impacts of AI: [20]

Technology is not destiny; economic incentives and public policy can play a significant role in shaping the direction and effects of technological change. Given appropriate attention and the right policy and institutional responses, advanced automation can be compatible with productivity, high levels of employment, and more broadly shared prosperity.

There is a focus on education, not only for young people but also with a broader agenda of lifelong learning that significantly expands the availability of capability training to meet the anticipated need. Beyond this, the aim is to help workers by providing strategies that strengthen the social security net. This includes unemployment insurance, raising the minimum wage, and modernizing US regulations with regards to overtime.

Beyond this, the White House report declares,

> *Growing and sustaining the middle class requires strong labor unions. Labor unions help to build the middle class and have been critical in restoring the link between hard work and opportunity so the benefits of economic growth can be more broadly shared. Unions have been at the forefront of establishing the 40-hour work week and the weekend, eliminating child labor laws, and establishing fair benefits and decent wages. Policymakers should explore ways to empower worker voice in the workplace through strengthening protections for organizing and creating new and innovative ways for workers to make their voices heard.*

13.6.3 German Policy Recommendations

The process adopted in Germany is called "Re-Imagining Work." The title in itself reflects the *Re-Imagine!* book by Tom Peters[21] and specifically invites answers to six key questions:

1. Will digitalization enable everyone to have a job in the future?
2. What will new business models look like?
3. How can employees' entitlement to data protection be safeguarded?
4. If humans and machines work together, how can machines support humans in the way that they work?
5. What do solutions to flexibility look like?
6. What will the modern company of the future look like?

These are general expressions related to the entire marketplace rather than just the public sector, and that reflect on what there is called "Industrie 4.0," which also comprises a recognition of a broader view toward the monitoring and development of technology skills needs going forward. Four key ideas that emerge from that program, which is specifically targeted at their local market, are:

1. The gradual transformation of the current *un*employment insurance into an employment insurance, aimed at giving more support to workers. In Germany, unemployment insurance is mandatory for all workers.
2. The Working Time Choice Act, which gives greater choice to employees about work time and location,
3. The extension of the collective bargaining system,
4. A Personal Activity Account relative to the use of new technologies that is described as a form of "social inheritance," which is the set of beliefs (and prejudices) that individuals are given as they grow by parents, schools, and the wider society.

While both the United States and Germany focus on a digital future, they seem to slightly differ in that the United States recognizes and aims to engage the unions in discussion as a key stakeholder, whereas the German model integrates existing union ideas and especially any scope for avoiding worker exploitation. Perhaps these are just nuances of the same wider ambition. Two examples of German union case studies provide an indication of the degree of worker protection that exists in an era of AI transformation and greater automation:[22]

1. IG Metall is Germany's metalworkers' union, with about 2.2 million members. Their view is that unionized workers need have less fear than others, partly because it is more difficult to sack them; there are also cultural issues: "In order to lay off workers with permanent contracts, there must be a business reason for it."
2. Airbus Works Council, Hamburg-Finkenwerder employs about 12,500 people. According to Jan Hinz, who is vice chair of the General Works Council, "We told management that we will play our part but at the same time we want to make sure that you take care of the defence of the job."

The challenge for both these employee representative bodies is that they recognize the changes going forward but are also keen to protect the interests of their employees. They take the view that worker replacement by automated systems might best be resolved in part through natural attrition or alternatively through reduced working hours.

13.6.4 "Dignity at Work" and Working from Home

In their March 2021 paper "Dignity at Work and the AI Revolution,"[23] the British-based TUC also made a further alignment between the impact of the pandemic and the introduction of AI. They suggested that the pandemic has provided a stimulus for the acceleration of AI specifically linked to home working, and their manifesto focuses on the impact of home working through issues such as isolation, creation of inequalities, and unsafe working practices. The approach is what they describe as values-based, and is grounded on what they consider to be the key elements that they consider to be important for those working from home in a technology environment, including worker voice, equality, health and well-being, and human connection.

One notable right is the concept of data reciprocity. This relates to the right or entitlement of the worker to collect and use their own data, such as how long they have been active on their home computer. The TUC makes the point that trade unions are uniquely placed to help achieve that right. This is of particular interest as, for many, workplace data and analytical insight are owned by the employer and therefore are in the employer's control. After all, employers might argue, it is *they* who own the storage and software where the data is held and analyzed, and one might imagine that employers could even insist on that entitlement through work contracts. Data reciprocity suggests a wider approach to the idea of data democracy, whereby information about worker behaviors should be bilaterally shared.

In order to ensure employer delivery against these values, the TUC presents a set of proposals as summarized in Table 13.5.

TABLE 13.5 Key Elements of Value in Workplace Dignity

Proposed Value	Description of Value
Targeted high-risk decisions	Particular focus on high-risk AI/automated decisions at an industry-by-industry level, which includes (according to the TUC) issues such as "selecting candidates for interview, day-to-day line management, performance ratings, shift allocation and deciding who is disciplined or made redundant."
Worker voice	Collective bargaining and a new statutory duty to consult employees in the deployment of AI and automated decision making.
Equality	Amendments to legislation to manage issues of discrimination, bias, unfairness, and impact assessment.
Human connection	A right to human review decisions that are automatically made, including an express entitlement to "analogue intervention" where important decisions are made.
	This also includes the "right to disconnect," which is the right of people to disconnect from work, and not to engage in work communications such as emails when they are not at work.
Data awareness	The right to challenge data processing in specific circumstances and to obtain greater clarity of workers' data rights in the context of GDPR.
	It also recognizes that trade unions might have specific roles in the workplace to monitor the use of AI and automated decision making (ADM).
Ethical collaboration	To encourage ethical behavior at all parts of the supply chain and to establish ethically-focused principals in the use of AI and ADM.

According to TUC president Frances O'Grady, this is "a crucial moment in the AI-driven technological workplace revolution." She adds:

> *Artificial Intelligence is transforming the way we work and, alongside boosting productivity, offers an opportunity to improve working lives. But new technologies also pose risks: more inequality and discrimination, unsafe working conditions, and unhealthy blurring of the boundaries between home and work.*
>
> *Our prediction is that, left unchecked, the use of AI to manage people will also lead to work becoming an increasingly lonely and isolating experience, where the joy of human connection is lost.*

There are some fundamental issues related to these requirements and expectations, especially when associated with the public sector. The sector has a higher proportion of union members than does the private sector, and as a result, there are greater opportunities for collective bargaining and representation. Of course, not all countries and territories have rights as regards these issues and UNISON president Josie Bird described a "need to plug the gaps in protections."[25] In a way, perhaps what is now emerging is a sort of post-Luddite approach whereby the unions are aware that technological change is inevitable but that it is important to recognize and represent the needs of workers during this transformation. It is hoped (and expected) that employers will similarly see that need.

13.7 CONCLUSION

Traditional textbooks on project implementation might fail to take into account the particular aspects that relate specifically to the public sector, especially when set against a background of accelerating technology and financial pressure. The focus in this chapter aims to counter this.

In this chapter, the first of two chapters on implementation, the key issues of leadership, communications, team building, and stakeholder management have been considered. These are not mutually exclusive but rather aim to provide an indication of the key issues and how they relate to each other. It is not easy to place one of these above another in terms of importance. Even the most effective and charismatic leader with a strong record of transformational success in the private sector will find problems if they do not win the hearts and minds of employees and representatives from their unions.

Managing the mission and being able to set a clear statement of intent is also important, but needs to be effectively communicated in a form that is close to being marketed, especially as many of the same techniques are likely to need to be used.

The complexity of implementation also demands the effective recruitment of a skilled team. Success depends on more than technologists and data scientists, and there are other capabilities such as project management that need to be brought to the table. These skills usually go beyond what leaders themselves can personally deliver.

In the next chapter, some other elements of implementation, including theoretical and operational approaches to transformation, will be explored, including the application of behavioral science in persuading change.

13.8 NOTES

1. Dudovskiy, J. (2013). "Leadership Differences between Private and Public Sector Organisations: Literature Review." British Research Methodology, November 8. https://research-methodology.net/leadership-differences-between-private-and-public-sector-organisations-literature-review/.
2. George, R., and others. (2019). "A New Mindset for Public Sector Leadership. Take the #TenYearChallenge." Deloitte Insights. https://www2.deloitte.com/us/en/insights/industry/public-sector/public-sector-leadership-changing-mindset.html.
3. Dutta, S. J., Lovering, I., and Knafo, S. (2021). "How Managerialism Took Over the NHS." *Tribune*, March 6. https://tribunemag.co.uk/2021/03/how-managerialism-took-over-the-nhs.
4. Dunoon, D. (2002). "Rethinking Leadership for the Public Sector." *Australian Journal of Public Administration*, December 8.
5. West, M., Lyubovnikova, J., Eckert, R., and Denis, J.-L. (2014). "Collective Leadership for Cultures of High Quality Health Care." *Journal of Organizational Effectiveness: People and Performance* 1 (3): 240–260.

6. West, M., Eckert, R., Steward, K., and Pasmore, B. (2014). "Developing Collective Leadership for Healthcare." London: The Kings Fund, May 21. https://www.kingsfund.org.uk/publications/developing-collective-leadership-health-care.

7. Gov.UK. (2017). "Collective Leadership." HM Cabinet Office, September 27. https://www.gov.uk/guidance/collective-leadership.

8. National Fire Chiefs Council. "NFCC Leadership Framework." NFCC Programme Office. https://www.nationalfirechiefs.org.uk/write/MediaUploads/NFCC%20Guidance%20publications/Workforce/NFCC_Leadership_Framework_Final.pdf.

9. Bjorge, B. (2019). "Why We Need Servant Leadership in Today's Fire Service." Lexipol, September 23. https://www.lexipol.com/resources/blog/why-we-need-servant-leadership-in-todays-fire-service/.

10. Barber, M. (2017). "Delivering Better Outcomes for Citizens: Practical Steps for Unlocking Public Value." HM Treasury, November 17. https://www.gov.uk/government/publications/delivering-better-outcomes-for-citizens-practical-steps-for-unlocking-public-value.

11. Data Science Campus. (2021). "Data Science For Public Good." https://datasciencecampus.ons.gov.uk/ (accessed December 7, 2021).

12. Mikuriya, K., and Cantens, T. (2020). "If Algorithms Dream of Customs, Do Customs Officials Dream of Algorithms? A Manifesto for Data Mobilisation in Customs." *World Customs Journal* 14 (2).

13. TechTarget Contributor. "Citizen relationship management (CRM)." What Is.com. https://whatis.techtarget.com/definition/citizen-relationship-management-CRM (accessed December 7, 2021.

14. Heuer, C. (2018). "Workforce Relationship Management." Monday, October 22. https://medium.com/mymonday-co/workforce-relationship-management-7e660718736b.

15. Oscar Research. (2020). "Public Sector Geo, Organisational and Stakeholder Feeds." https://www.oscar-research.co.uk/directories/stakeholder.php (accessed December 7, 2021).

16. Trades Union Congress. (2017). "Shaping Our Digital Future." London: TUC. https://www.tuc.org.uk/sites/default/files/Shaping-our-digital-future.pdf.

17. Frey C., and Osborn, M. (2013). "The Future of Employment: How Susceptible Are Jobs to Computerisation?" Oxford Martin Programme on Technology and Employment, September 17. https://www.oxfordmartin.ox.ac.uk/downloads/academic/The_Future_of_Employment.pdf.

18. Arntz, M., Gregory, T., and Zierahn, U. (2016). "The Risk of Automation for Jobs in OECD Countries: A Comparative Analysis." *OECD Social, Employment and Migration Working Papers*, No. 189. Paris: OECD Publishing. https://doi.org/10.1787/5jlz9h56dvq7-en.

19. Hawksworth, J., and Berriman. R. (2017). "Up to 30% of Existing UK Jobs Could Be Impacted by Automation by Early 2030s, But This Should Be Offset by Job Gains Elsewhere in Economy." PWC, March 24. https://pwc.blogs.com/press_room/2017/03/up-to-30-of-existing-uk-jobs-could-be-impacted-by-automation-by-early-2030s-but-this-should-be-offse.html.

20. Feldman, M. (2017). "White House Frames AI Policy: Technology Is Not Destiny." TOP500, January 2. https://www.top500.org/news/white-house-frames-ai-policy-technology-is-not-destiny/.

21. Peters, T. (2004). *Re-Imagine!* London: Dorling Kindersley Ltd.

22. Trades Union Congress (TUC). (2017). "Shaping Our Digital Future." https://www.tuc.org.uk/sites/default/files/Shaping-our-digital-future.pdf.

23. Trades Unions Congress. (2021). "Dignity at Work and the AI Revolution." London: TUC, March 25. https://www.tuc.org.uk/research-analysis/reports/dignity-work-and-ai-revolution.

24. UNISON. (2021). "New Manifesto Defends Workers' Rights from Artificial Intelligence." March 25. https://www.unison.org.uk/news/article/2021/03/new-manifesto-defends-workers-rights-artificial-intelligence/.

14

Further Implementation Issues

14.1 INTRODUCTION

In this final chapter before the Conclusion, some more academic and practical issues of change will be considered. There is even an argument for including the theoretical aspects earlier in the overall text, especially as it is important to understand the reason for change rather than just the matter of financial pressures or the availability of new technologies. Even so, this content probably sits conveniently with other wider implementation issues, especially those of leadership.

Additionally we will further reflect on some key issues such as the management of bias, the way in which stakeholders might be influenced (otherwise known as "nudge"), and finally, the issue of supply chain management.

14.2 A THEORETICAL APPROACH TO CHANGE

The introduction of AI and advanced analytics to the public sector will be viewed by some as being somewhat radical, definitely disruptive, and perhaps even dramatic. In this section, as a preamble to examining some more issues of operational transformation, the topic of change as a conceptual or theoretical model is considered. The intention is to allow readers to understand some of the deeper change management issues, especially in an area as complex as public services.

In his 1986 book on operational dynamics, Dr. Amir Levy describes two distinct types or levels of change.[1] Levy studied at the University of California and researched success and failure factors in implementing organizational change. He called these two levels of change first-order change and second-order change. Although Levy was mainly focusing at the time on international politics, additional insight can be gained by comparing his research with how change happens in what is a quasi-political public sector.

He describes these two elements as follows:

- **First-order change:** A form of transition where there is no material change to what he calls the deep rules of the game.
- **Second-order change:** Where "rising actors" are no longer happy with the current deep rules and try to establish a replacement or create a new model.

Levy describes the deep rules of the game as a series of pillars, which might alternatively also be described as undisputable truths. Table 14.1 sets out those tenets and compares the impact of change in international politics to that which might happen in the public sector.

Levy's suggestion is that if any of these pillars are subject to alteration in the form of tinkering or minor adjustments, then these changes would fall within the category of evolutionary or first-order change. Alternatively, if holders of power seek to make major changes and recraft these pillars or truths, then the changes are likely to be considered as second-order change and be more wide-ranging, radical, and relatively unpredictable.

TABLE 14.1 Pillars of Change and Comparison of Political and Public Sector Impacts[2]

Pillar	Political Pillars in International Politics	Comparable Pillar in the Public Sector
1	The existence of an open market economy that maintains peace by allowing cross-border trading.	Using advanced analytics and AI to provide services to all citizens at a global level, especially using transfer of knowledge and international supply chains.
2	The social bargain that implies that the success of the state is dependent on the safety of citizens.	The need to introduce advanced technologies to provide effective support to citizens at an affordable cost, and to provide them with safety and security.
3	The existence of multilateral organizations that provide regulatory control.	The provision of safeguards to protect the citizen against unfair and unreasonable use of analytics.
4	Shared security to offer shared protection, such as NATO.	The provision of cross-border agreements that allow data to be safely and securely transferred across borders.
5	Democratic solidarity, which reinforces the ideal that democracy is critical to maintain peace.	The idea that the outcome of effective use of data and analytics is a shared benefit and accessible to all. This is sometimes known as the democratization of data.
6	Human rights	An avoidance of bias.
7	Global leadership	The provision of an analytically-driven way forward that is nonpartisan.

In the 1980s, two researchers, Greenwood and Hining, also looked at the way organizations change.[3] They set out a number of different approaches to change, which they called pathways, which are summarized in Table 14.2.

TABLE 14.2 Organizational Pathways to Change

	Change Path	Characteristics	Public Sector Consequence of This Change Path
1	No change	The current rules of the game are not challenged.	Continued stress on the existing system, leading to failure and frustration.
2	Incremental change	Small evolutionary changes that are made by current and evolving participants. Any changes are by agreement and there is no conflict.	Incremental improvement but no real difference to the status quo.
3	Transformation	A new set of rules emerges, with change happening either in a linear way or through stepped changes. Change will be peaceful even if there is a dominant party, provided the other parties are in agreement.	The use of collaborative leadership that creates a shared vision of the future, adequately describing a shared mission as well as shared and agreed values.
4	Splintering	New methods emerge. Some stay with the old rules of engagement while others push forward, perhaps with a degree of experimentation. There may be local conflicts of approach.	Different paths to transformation occur at different speeds. These different paths may occur between different sectors of the broader public service, or within different departments of the same public service. Pilot ideas might be carried out, which may (or may not) be sustainable.
5	Conflict	Changes happen in an attempt to move to a new way of doing things, with single-minded determination on behalf of the dominant player to impose their will. In this approach, other players who were historically dominant will resist, resulting in conflict.	The use of AI and analytics are forced on the public sector, perhaps by a government that is a dominant party especially, as key sponsor and principal funder. This causes disquiet and disruption among employees and their representatives, and can lead to potential strike action.

(Continued)

TABLE 14.2 *(Continued)*

Change Path		Characteristics	Public Sector Consequence of This Change Path
6	Unsuccessful assault	Those engaged or in charge may overestimate their power. Their "attack" that attempts to force change on the existing dominant force will be resisted.	The use of AI and analytics is successfully resisted by employees, their representatives, and perhaps even by citizens who seek to return to the traditional but unsustainable model. Some elements of the transformation remain that represent incremental improvement, and there are other reforms in the process.

The issue therefore in the transformation of the public sector is whether the greatest progress in the adoption of advanced analytics and AI is most likely to be made by gradual evolution, or by some form of more radical "assault" on the traditional approach. It is a potentially complex situation.

It is important also to consider issues of motivation. Why would any leadership want to encourage change to the point that there might be an element of conflict? Maslow reminds us that people are generally most attuned to change and innovation when they are feeling safe and secure. At that point they are most open to self-actualization (the realization of human potential and where the development of talent is likely to take place). In a world where public services are at potential risk of forced change as a result of government austerity, perhaps coupled with political disruption, the normal human reaction is most likely to be one of trying to maintain the status quo as far as practically possible. It is sometimes suggested that humans are hardwired to resist change as it is unsettling and ultimately we all desire stability. At the same time there is an entitlement to basic public services such as public order and healthcare, which in themselves provide a different type of safety. Because of this apparent trade-off in requirements, some compromises will probably need to be made by accepting change if only so that order can be maintained.

What then are the apparent triggers that will provide appropriate signals that transformation will need to take place? The following are suggested:

- When the benefits outweigh the cost, in this case of public services, a combination of demonstrable hard and soft benefits is required.
- When the resources available to the traditional approach have been reduced to a point that traditional public services cannot effectively fulfill its obligation.
- When the status and capability of the traditional approach has been reduced to such a degree that it forces traditionalists to take a different way forward, as they have no other option.

- When the traditional rules of the game have been effectively challenged, are no longer valid, and are ready for change.
- When the capacity and will of the traditionalist to resist change has been reduced or removed, which may include removal of any power base.

In these circumstances, successful implementation is almost certain to need a top-down/bottom-up approach. The implication is that public sector leaders will have identified from a top-down viewpoint that there is a need for reform, whereas lower down the hierarchy there is a recognition of the fact that existing systems are not adequately serving the purpose. This is especially the case where there are continued and almost certainly future pressures on finance, leading to frustration by both users and employees and, increasingly in modern times, continual adverse reaction in traditional and social media channels.

The adoption of AI with a promise of real (or even perceived) benefits could act as some sort of rallying call for change, especially when accompanied by other economic and environmental pressures. Even if the benefit case for full-blown transformation has not been adequately made, or the risks and consequences of change are not fully understood, the need for some change might still remain compelling. In such an environment, the onus will inevitably pass from one of why to take action to one of how to implement these changes operationally.

14.3 MANAGING THE PROBLEM OF BIAS

The removal of ethical bias is of concern in all areas of AI but perhaps of greatest concern in the public sector due to the nature of the services provided. Machine learning systems must ensure that automated outcomes are not biased or distorted, either consciously or unconsciously, and the adequacy and accuracy of inputted information is critical. Outcomes might accidentally relate to ethnicity and place of natural origin even if that information may not have been specifically inputted in the data sets. In May 2021 the UK Government published a suggested framework for ethics, with particular reference to the use of automated decisioning in the public sector.[4] The need for such a framework arose from a recommendation by the Committee on Standards in Public Life in 2020. The framework is aimed at:

- Senior owners of all major processes and services
- Process and service risk owners
- Executive and senior leaders
- Operational staff, including those in digital data and technology roles
- Policy makers and government ministers, when considering an algorithm or automated system

The Committee invited the UK Government to consider a series of recommendations that comprised a seven-point framework (Table 14.3).[5]

TABLE 14.3 Seven-Point Framework for Removal of Ethical Bias

Point	Recommendation	Explanation
1	The creation of tests to avoid any unintended outcomes or consequences.	The need to test the algorithm or system to ensure that it is fully robust, sustainable, and delivers the right policy outcome. These tests include risk assessment, independent testing, and red team testing (a form of testing where there is a deliberate simulated attack on a live system without the owner's knowledge).
2	The delivery of fair services for all users and citizens.	This can be undertaken by using a multidisciplinary team to spot and eliminate bias, prejudice, and discrimination. This includes doing an equality impact assessment, which is an evidence-based approach to ensure that policies, practices, events, and decision-making processes are fair and do not present barriers to participation or disadvantage any protected groups from participation. The tests might also use (safe) hackers to identify bias.
3	Clarity as to who is responsible.	This works on the assumption that every significant automated decision needs to be agreed by a minister and that all systems and processes have a senior owner. The document also recognizes that there are stricter rules about decision making in the public sector. On a daily basis, officials make decisions on behalf of the secretary of state, and any decision-making system needs to be signed off by them.
4	The safe handling of data and protection of citizens' interests.	This requires that the system or algorithm complies with all appropriate regulation and the Data Protection legislation. It specifically draws attention to the need for extra care in cases where data is used for decision-making purposes that it was not intended for.
5	Compliance with the law.	To ensure that the algorithm or system complies with all legislation, and also that it has been signed off on by the relevant government legal advisor. The framework recommends that legal advisors should be involved from the outset, and that they should be consulted not only on existing legislation but also on forthcoming changes.

(Continued)

TABLE 14.3 *(Continued)*

Point	Recommendation	Explanation
6	That the system is future proof.	This requires the use of continuous monitoring, with regular review points (which are suggested to be quarterly). Also that the system is checked for compliance with all the points in the framework on an ongoing basis.
7	That users and citizens are able to understand how the system impacts them.	Owners should advise users that an automated system has been used, with plain English explanations, and that users need to be able to explain them. This means that a user has to be able to explain how an automated decision has been reached, in simple terms, and should avoid bias or groupspeak.

Notwithstanding the very good intentions in this framework, it has some other challenging issues to contend with, especially that of being able to explain to a layman how an algorithm works and how it has reached a certain outcome or decision. To do this effectively requires users and decision makers to be able to interact effectively with those in digital and technology roles, and to be able to converse with end users without resorting to jargon. This involves having a common lexicon of language and terminology, but already there are multiple interpretations of the same word. For instance, even the term *artificial intelligence* is widely misused and already encompasses different forms of automation and prediction as well as including the different attributes of AI such as facial recognition, for example.

14.3.1 Data Exclusion from Marginalized Communities

In the public sector, the management of "exclusion" is an especially important aspect and relates also to the issue of bias. AI and data analysis assume that all the population are equal contributors to information on which the algorithm calculates a decision, but this is not necessarily so. Problems of social exclusion, where people are not contributors to the data set, can lead to the outcome being skewed. These exclusions may be on the basis of location, distance from the urban center (i.e., rural), poverty, or even something as relatively simple as a failure of the individual to register within the system.

This is of particular concern in respect to the use of AI to implement effective social programs that provide help and support across the entire community. The implication is that there may be a need to identify marginalized communities and specifically obtain data from them. A comprehensive AI solution needs, by default, to be inclusive, but this requires a strategic approach to inclusivity, including sourcing data perhaps from groups least likely or willing to provide it. Many of these socially exclusive groups quite deliberately live "outside the net."

While synthetic data is increasingly becoming common in model outcomes where there is a shortage of information, using this approach to represent marginalized communities may be questionable and some form of data collection program that represents the interests of the digitally excluded probably still remains the best option.

14.3.2   Locational Data Issues

There may also be specific locational issues to contend with, especially as public services need to serve both the urban and rural communities. For example, there may be certain geographical areas where there are higher demands for a particular type of public service such as flood defenses. One way forward is to adopt the approach of having a minimum standard of service across all geographies but with the ability to enhance that service in key geographical areas.

Location analytics is a methodology that allows both people and assets to be geographically placed through an approach called geocoding. It is an important part of the analytics suite, especially as everyone and everything is somewhere. Location analytics not only can help with the optimal placement of assets but can also assist in tracking the movement of individuals and vehicles.

14.4   OPERATIONAL CONSIDERATIONS

This is not intended to be a comprehensive textbook on implementing a complex project, but rather to highlight some of the key operational concerns during the implementation process, especially with regard to the public sector, which has certain particular attributes. This section will consider some of them and will build on earlier comments within this book, typically:

- The use of pilot schemes
- Measuring improvement
- The need for independent review
- Risk management aspects of implementation
- Data security and transparency

Students of complex program implementation will, without doubt, wish to consider other sources of information about project management, but need to recognize the particular characteristics of the public sector, meaning that generic implementation advice that is commonly available should be viewed through a public sector lens, and modified accordingly.

14.4.1   Piloting and Test Running the System

One of the main problems of AI is that with so much data, machine learning systems may discover correlations and rules even where the relationship is at best spurious and difficult to check. Systems are created to provide smartness, but at the same time the system can prove to be too smart for adequate checking. Additionally, an automated system may self-create rules based on incomplete or distorted information, so it becomes critical that it is provided with enough correct information to ensure that any rules are wisely developed, and that outcomes are sensibly created.

The essence of an AI system is that it should create outcomes that are indistinguishable from human decisions. One obvious way might be to take the same set of information and provide it both to a machine and to a human, and to see if the same outcome is delivered by both. There will inevitably be borderline decisions, but there should generally be some degree of matching. The essence of a reliable, trustworthy system is that it provides reliable, trustworthy results. AI systems are no more than sophisticated automatic processes that identify correlations between variables and from these create some sort of a model that makes predictions. There are often inherent weaknesses or flaws both in the models and in the data being used, and some argue that *all models* are intrinsically incorrect insofar as they are only approximations.

The only sure way to identify systemic weakness is to create a pilot scheme or "dummy run" that establishes whether the system performs as well as and in the same way that it was expected to do. A small-scale trial can be used to check the reliability of the system before rolling it out fully, but there is still a need to be cautious. Even a successful trial may be due as much to fortune as to technological expertise, so it is suggested that there should be a number of different pilots of the system in multiple scenarios as opposed to a single test.

Getting it wrong is more than a simple technology blunder. The public sector deals with the most vulnerable in society and as a result are disadvantaged more than others in the event of systemic failure. By way of an example, an automated but incorrectly rejected asylum application may have disastrous implications at a human level.

All that aside, in an area of potentially significant disruption, one difficulty with pilot schemes is that they seldom guarantee commitment to full-blown implementation. A pilot may well be at the whim of a key stakeholder, who may leave the organization or move on to other responsibilities. Pilot schemes may also prove a limited delivery of benefits, but skeptics will still argue that the pilot was not adequately representative of the whole opportunity. Failure of the pilot for whatever reason may simply provide ammunition to those resisting change. It is for this reason that many test runs are better described as being a proof of concept and that the process adequately carries appropriate caveats to ensure that all stakeholder expectations are carefully managed.

These important considerations should not be rushed. The German Society for International Cooperation, in their 2019 report "AI in Social Protection – Exploring Opportunities and Mitigating Risks," advise:

> *The cost and time requirements of extensive testing may be high, but the costs of large-scale failure would probably be higher.*[6]

14.4.2 Measuring Benefit

One of the important aspects of any cost–benefit analysis is the ability to accurately measure any financial impacts. The key requirement is measurable improvement in terms of soft (qualitative) and hard (quantitative) benefit. Although this book is written in the context of the application of AI and other advanced technologies, it is usually important to have relatively straightforward business intelligence (BI) tools or financial controls in order not only to measure the status quo with a degree of certainty, but also to be able to measure any improvements (often described as the *delta*).

Often benefits are not immediately realized due to the degree of disruption through the implementation process; this can put pressure on pilot programs. Many organizations struggle to define what real advantage has been obtained and often restrict this to reductions in headcount, which is the most obvious tangible benefit – but this is a simplistic approach. Organizations need to be clear about the complete benefit they are hoping to achieve and to have an effective tracking process in hand to ensure that all the outcomes obtained are in line with those anticipated.

It is possible to measure accrued benefits from pilot schemes, but any trial run needs to be representative of the wider picture and does not simply reflect a limited viewpoint. It is important to ensure, especially in a public sector implementation, that any benefits take into account the successful delivery across the whole population (as applicable) and that measured improvements from any pilot scheme are not skewed in some way through accidental exclusion or bias.

A different approach might be to recognize that in some parts of the public sector, benefits may not indeed be evenly spread and that historically excluded groups might even ultimately receive a disproportionate benefit. Similarly, implementation *risks* across the entire population may not be evenly distributed and this should also be taken into account in any evaluation of success.

14.4.3   Independent Review

There is an inevitable worry that technological capabilities such as those being discussed have the potential to become political tools. Because of this, the relative sensitivity of any systematic approach on key groups should not be overlooked, especially where solutions are automatically generated, because of the adoption of specific systemic rules. These rules might have strategic, financial, or political objectives.

In the area of social protection, for example, it is possible to see that changes made to rules could create distortions and create either planned or accidental consequences. This might disadvantage those who are already in need and may even make the problem worse. On the other hand, perhaps improving the situation of some could result in antagonizing others who are already financially secure, as funds are diverted to other causes.

The reality is that continuous review of outcomes is critical with a need for independent, external oversight. One key element is that of who makes the appointment of these independent overseers and whether they also have a political or even an emotional viewpoint to accommodate.

14.5   OUTSOURCING, PARTNERING, AND SUPPLY CHAIN MANAGEMENT

Whereas this section may not provide a comprehensive text on the issues of outsourcing, partnering, and supply chain management, it can at least draw out some of the key issues as they relate to the public sector. In the context of hosting, maintaining, and, in some cases, operating advanced analytics and AI systems, in many cases the technical competencies needed are far outside the core capabilities of most public sector organizations, with perhaps the exception of only the largest. Even they might struggle to deal with rapidly evolving technologies and, as a result, they will probably need to depend on third-party suppliers to either support or assist them in any transformation.[7]

There is no commonly accepted definition of supply or delivery chain. The following definition covers the main points.

> *A delivery chain is the complex network of organisations, including central and local government agencies, and bodies from the private and third sectors, that need to work together to achieve or deliver an improved public sector outcome.*[8]

In almost all cases the end user, in this situation the citizen, will be unaware of any of the individual parties within the supply or delivery chain, as the process is mainly invisible to them. Traditionally in the public sector, external suppliers have been used principally to provide operational efficiencies and value for money. Governments usually give guidance into procurement and management techniques, recognizing particularly that there is a need for accountability within the public purse. Effective supply chain management has the following benefits:

- **Cost reduction**, especially as the dynamic and competitive nature of outsourcing forces competitive pricing.
- **Risk transfer**, although ownership of the output ultimately will remain with the public sector client.
- **Greater opportunities for innovation**, comprising a better quality of solutions when compared to that which the public sector can provide itself.

There will always be a debate around the topic of "build or buy" with regard to technology solutions. Many technical officers in all types of organizations balk at the costs involved in outsourcing and the fact that external technology experts need to be brought in. Internal advisors are also likely to emphasize the degree of dependence on a third-party system that might be otherwise avoided if the project is brought in-house. By the same measure they need to be realistic regarding the in-house capability of their own organization, and in any event having a third party to blame should there be failure is often a very useful asset.

A new trend is currently emerging, under the name AI as a Service, which leaves business management in the hands of the client but the technology platform in the hands of other differently qualified experts. It is important to differentiate between those technology providers who offer an integrated, that is, "joined up," capability, as opposed to an IT company that provides individual technical products but leave the client to implement them themselves. In technology, one of the most difficult issues is integrating different systems and products.

In the case of an AI transformation, alternative operating models are possible (Figure 14.1), typically:

1. A single relationship with a principal (Tier 1) "managing" supplier, who then takes on the responsibility to manage multiple (Tier 2) subcontracted suppliers but where the client is able to intervene directly with the subordinate organizations to exercise commercial buying power. In such a situation, the managing supplier might be prone to accusing the client of interfering.
2. An alternative model is where the client might have an individual arrangement with the managing supplier, who takes on full responsibility for all other suppliers. In this approach, the lines of risk and authority are clearer but the overall cost may be greater.

MODEL 1 : DIRECT INTERVENTION BY CLIENT

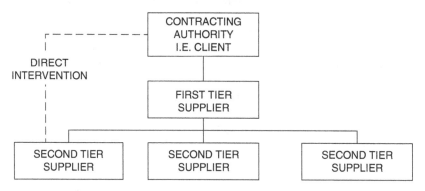

MODEL 2 : FIRST TIER SUPPLIER AS SUPPLY CHAIN MANAGER

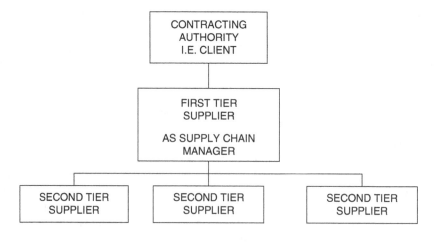

FIGURE 14.1　Alternative Subcontracting Models
Source: Office of Government Commerce. "Supply Chain Management in Public Procurement: A Guide." Crown copyright, June. https://sovz.cz/wp-content/uploads/2016/11/supplychain-managementguide.pdf.

There are pros and cons to each approach, but the ultimate test is where accountability will rest in the event of possible failure. This is not a matter of planning for failure but rather being able to effectively and realistically handle all parts of a complex implementation. Prudent client organizations should also consider an exit strategy in relation to any supplier or supplier chain. This is not a matter of accepting defeat or failure from the outset, but rather appreciating that third-party proposals can be either oversold or underdelivered.

Partnering as an alternative model is more than an approach to distribute benefit equitably between a client and a system provider; it is also one that presents a more amiable way to resolving differences.[9] One issue is that the client might consider themselves as being dominant in the relationship, which tends to undermine issues of perceived equality.

In their briefing paper "Public Sector Supply Chain: Risks, Myths and Opportunities,"[10] authors Zurich Municipal insurers point to some of the myths in terms of supply chain management, namely:

- **Myth 1.** Outsourcing makes life easier, as risk can be delegated. Zurich reminds readers that failure can have major impacts in multiple areas, including reputational risk. Elsewhere in the briefing paper, the issue of contagion is mentioned, noting that a failure by one part of the public sector might adversely affect other parts of the sector.
- **Myth 2.** Relationships manage themselves. This is never the case and requires appropriate professional attention and skill.
- **Myth 3.** Due diligence provides all the answers. Many technology providers are experts in being able to satisfy procurement processes but sometimes deeper issues are only exposed when operations are underway.

Supply chain management in the technology sector is different from other forms of supply chain management and, as a result, requires specialist competences. As discussed in the previous chapter, in the creation of an effective team, it is essential that appropriate supply chain skills are included if a third party is to be used in any capacity. Supply chain professionals should be involved at the outset to get the process started on a firm footing and to ensure that the right metrics are adopted in terms both of adequate remuneration and end user satisfaction.

The use of proprietary third-party algorithms or "black boxes" where algorithms are not transparent also presents some issues. Third parties are unlikely to want to disclose proprietary knowledge and intellectual property, especially regarding the inner workings of a system or algorithm, because of the competitive nature of such systems. On the other hand, users need to have full transparency so they can manage issues such as bias and discrimination, which is critical to do in the public sector.

One area of particular consideration is "surge management," which is when demand exceeds supply. Public services need to be able to respond to surges in demand for, say, healthcare issues and it is critical that procurement processes and ultimately operational systems are able to cope with extreme levels of operational demand.

Perhaps the most important of all supply chain considerations is the matter of the public sector ethos or ethical approach relative to that of the private sector. The public sector normally considers their principal duty as being to the citizen whereas private sector players principally have a duty to their stockholders or shareholders. While these issues can never be perfectly reconciled, the best way forward to manage outcomes is through a robust performance management environment.

14.6 THE CONCEPT OF "NUDGE"

The concept of "nudge" relates to behavioral management and manipulation, and is relevant in the context of this book as it helps to provide a mechanism whereby stakeholders can be directed toward making important decisions. The approach may well prove to be a key tool in the transformation journey as public services increasingly adopt an AI-infused transformation that some might view as controversial and unnecessary.

> *"Nudge": Verb (used with object), nudged, nudg-ing; to push slightly or gently, especially with the elbow, to get someone's attention, prod someone into action, etc. Noun, a slight or gentle push or jog, especially with the elbow.*[11]

In his book *Thinking, Fast and Slow*, Thomas Kahneman identified two elements to the cognitive brain, which he described as:

- **System 1:** The part of the brain that is relatively fast, automatic, effortless, and responsible for intuitive processing.
- **System 2:** The part of the brain that is relatively slow, controlled, effortful, and responsible for conscious reasoning.

The concept of nudge theory was introduced by Richard Thaler (who went on to win the Nobel Prize in Economics) and Cass Sunstein. It's an approach to behavioral management that can affect people's intuition (System 1) or appeal to their logic (System 2). The idea can appeal both to the irrational and to those who consider themselves to be rational, although with a particular bias. A nudge can be either positive or negative. In effect, the concept is that by providing the right "choice architecture," people can be influenced to make better (or at least different) choices in their own interests.

Influencing people's behavior is nothing new in government and has been used in areas such as legislation, taxation, and regulation. It was recognized to be beneficial especially in the area of health management, where new ideas needed to be adopted. In 2010 the Institute for Government set up the MINDSPACE report, which suggested that both the messenger and the message matter.[12]

That report identified a series of key behavioral influences that correspond to the mnemonic MINDSPACE (Table 14.4).

TABLE 14.4   Nudge and MINDSPACE

	Key Influence	Impact
M	Messenger	We are heavily influenced by who communicates information.
I	Incentives	Our responses to incentives are shaped by predictable mental shortcuts such as strongly avoiding losses.
N	Norms	We are strongly influenced by what others do.
D	Defaults	We "go with the flow" of preset options.
S	Salience	Our attention is drawn to what is novel and seems relevant to us.
P	Priming	Our acts are often influenced by subconscious cues.
A	Affect	Our emotional associations can powerfully shape our actions.
C	Commitments	We seek to be consistent with our public promises, and reciprocate acts.
E	Ego	We act in ways that make us feel better about ourselves.

In the UK, the so-called Nudge Unit was set up in the Cabinet Office in 2010 by Prime Minister David Cameron, with an aim of influencing the implementation of public policy through applying behavioral science techniques.[13] Since then, it has been spun off and is now in shared ownership between the Cabinet Office and NESTA (a UK innovation foundation) and its employees. The Nudge Unit has worked in a range of policy areas, including tax payment, increased organ donation, and autoenrollment of young people for pensions.

In a 2020 YouTube presentation, the Behavioural Science Unit explained how these principles were also used to encourage citizens to take essential precautions during the coronavirus pandemic.[14] They recommended that to prevent the spread of the virus, singing the song "Happy Birthday" would provide an appropriate behavioral trigger to ensure that hands are washed for the requisite 20 seconds. The approach is subtle and, some might argue, manipulative, but also provides an insight into how change can occur without head-on conflict or by issuing directives.

Their presentation also provided some key approaches to the application of nudge (Table 14.5).

AI transformation in the public sector is unlikely to be easy, especially in the context of potential job losses, new processes, and the real challenge of outcome uncertainty. For many already in the public sector, their attitude to change of this type might already be hardwired by their existing habits and behaviors. When issues such as bias and ethics are added, then it seems that every methodology available, including nudge, could be likely to be considered to ensure effective implementation.

TABLE 14.5   Three-Step Approach to Behavioral Science

Step	Purpose	Functional Aspects
Step 1	Identify the key barriers to changing behavior	■ Personal beliefs ■ Lack of motivation ■ Social pressures ■ Culture and normalization ■ Environmental aspects
Step 2	Apply behavioral principles in defining communications	■ Make the message simple and easy to understand ■ Place the key actions at the top of the message ■ Use precise advice and shorter text ■ Use images and graphics ■ Create social commitment by placing the individual into the context of interacting with the wider societal structure ■ Encourage altruism, which is the belief in or practice of having selfless concern for the well-being of others ■ Provide rationale for change in behavior ■ Help people plan their time to achieve change
Step 3	Test the process	■ Recall: To what degree does the reader remember the message? ■ Comprehension: Does the reader understand the message? ■ Behavioral indicators: Does the reader say that the message will change their behavior? ■ Sentiment: What is the credibility of the message and how does the reader feel about it?

14.7   GLOBAL CONSIDERATIONS

Many of the issues that are dealt with by the public sector, such as security, welfare, and healthcare, transcend global boundaries. With aging demographics and rising life expectancies almost everywhere, there is an increasing need to look after old citizens in Europe, the Americas, and Asia, even if different cultures might have different ways of solving this problem. Traditions are a bedrock of society, but nowadays there seems to be an easing of tradition in many areas of life. However, it remains essential that where traditions are forgotten, there is something better to replace them with. Many are convinced that technology does not in itself provide that better alternative.

On the issue of healthcare for the aged, for example, some countries seem to have a higher regard for the elderly than others:[15]

■ In Greek and Greek-American culture, respect for elders is central to the family.
■ Much of the Korean regard for aging is rooted in the Confucian principle of *filial piety,* which is a fundamental value that dictates that you must respect and look after your parents in the same way that they looked after you as a child.

- Similarly, in China, abandoning one's family is considered deeply dishonorable.
- Many Indians live in joint family units where elders are still the head of the household, and sending them to an old-age home is considered to have a social stigma.

As different technological ways to provide, manage, and support public services are considered, including looking after the elderly, it should be remembered these new approaches do not have geographic boundaries. Robots are capable of helping healthcare workers anywhere in the world, provided that the technological infrastructure exists to support them. Better knowledge transfer will help that happen, but the rate of adoption of these innovations may not rest just with technology providers but also with the state. Perhaps some time should be spent considering the importance of "the state" in this context.

The "state," that is, the concept of a land mass with physical borders, was first recognized by the Treaty of Westphalia in 1648, which is a law thought by historians to be one of the fundamentals of international relations, especially as it drew to a close both the Thirty Years' War (1618–1648) and the Eighty Years' War (1569–1648). According to US author Phillip Bobbitt, whose focus is on constitutional law and theory, the primary reason a state exists is to maximize the wealth and safety of its citizens, but he suggests that fulfilling those functions is increasingly growing beyond the ability of the state, especially in a globalized, technology-driven world.[16]

Bobbitt and others go on to suggest that the nation state as we currently understand it may well be reaching the end of its traditional definition, as it is being affected by a number of globalization challenges, as shown in Table 14.6.

TABLE 14.6   Factors Affecting the Nation State

Globalization Challenges of the Nation State	Impact
Human rights	There is an increased emphasis on human rights, which has created a framework for expected and allowable norms of behavior that applies across national boundaries.
Terrorism and weapons of mass destruction	The growth of both of these has not only changed our understanding of war between nations but rather brought conflict to a micro, localized level that often requires cross-boundary cooperation to resolve. The problem of cybercrime also fits into this category.
Pandemics and other transnational threats	The experience of COVID-19 has especially highlighted the international nature of disease and natural disasters. The reaction by many countries seemed at times to be xenophobic and inward-looking, altruistic and outward-looking, or both, depending often on political and economic pressures.
Economic influence	The free flow of money across national boundaries and the degree of interdependence has increasingly reduced the ability of a single country to influence its own economic future.

(Continued)

TABLE 14.6 *(Continued)*

Globalization Challenges of the Nation State	Impact
Free flow of information	Although information and new technologies are able to flow more readily between countries and across sectors, constrained in some cases by data laws, the true ownership of key technical capabilities rests with those who have developed it. Ownership is usually held in the form of patents and copyrights rather than with nation states.
Legislation	The "state" has increasingly found it difficult to truly protect its citizens who are in foreign territories without needing to resort to statecraft and quid pro quo measures.

This does not entirely assume that the nation state, which is the usual source of funding for public services, is on its last legs, even if there are growing views that there are likely to be changes in the evolution of a world order. Some of these might be predictable. In a scenario-planning session with MBA students at a London business school, it was suggested that traditional national boundaries could even be replaced by a different way of looking at things. This alternative model for a nation state equivalent might perhaps reflect the way that individuals are treated, where there is alignment between citizens around cultural values and the way in which capital is consumed. This new type of thinking suggested that nation states might somehow even be replaced by, hypothetically, a global network of aligned cities.

It seems entirely feasible that the technological approaches ultimately adopted by, say, public services in New York, Paris, and London might in some way be replicated even if they are adapted to some degree for local circumstances. We should not overlook the influence of technologists and other suppliers in supporting the creation of a subtle, nonconspiratorial new world order that might comprise smart cities that are networked together in some way. On the other hand, we cannot overlook the importance of the state as we currently know it in terms of its political and financial power and that even smart cities would find it difficult or even impossible to act independently.

Implementation of transformation in public services at a global level – for example, a common global approach to looking after old people – is clearly more difficult than change at a local level. Perhaps this process might be eased in some way through the application of "soft power." This is an approach understood to have the ability to influence others and persuade them through a combination of culture, which is expressed in how we behave socially and measured by our social values, political positions, and foreign policy.

One way forward, in what is known as the Golden Arches Theory, comprises an approach whereby multinational technology (and other) companies might even be able to influence national policies by investing only in peaceful rather than warlike countries. In other words, the technology potentially exists to help peaceful countries look after their old people in a better way. This could seem to many like an unnecessary convergence of public services and political power but the public sector has always been quasi-political in nature, looking after the old is expensive, and perhaps such a potential development should not really come as a surprise.

14.8 CONCLUSION

Although this chapter is not intended to provide a comprehensive summary of how to implement a project involving advanced analytics or AI, it should provide some insights and techniques that are particularly relevant to the public sector, including the controversial aspect of behavioral management and the challenges of supply change management. These have also been represented in Appendix B, Transformation Roadmap for Public Services, which may, in itself, serve to act as a form of checklist for practitioners.

AI implementation in the public sector has two key differences when compared to the private sector, first in the ethos of the provider, which is public-spirited and dutiful by nature, and second in respect to the vulnerability of the end-user base.

The public sector has traditional values but can also be burdened with traditional attitudes. These create an important bedrock of service through a set of well-established beliefs and values but also bring with them an inertia that makes change difficult. Understanding some of the theoretical aspects of change may help. The use of behavioral manipulation or nudge may be controversial but might in some circumstances assist in repositioning some of the important parts of any debate, especially if there is a need for change due to pressures on the public purse.

How the public sector chooses, relates to, and manages third parties is also important. The former usually will have different values than the latter, although the transfer of staff from one "side" to the other can help break down those differences. Perhaps the use of temporarily transferring staff or "secondment" may be a useful approach.

Finally, the idea that public sector challenges are domestic rather than international issues opens the door to a broader international response. This may partly be through knowledge transfer, and many examples of implementations across the globe are given throughout this book. Additionally, it may be possible to take advantage of common ground, recognizing, for example, that the concept of smarter cities exists in many places on the map. Knowledge transfer will continually and perhaps even naturally happen, within the bounds of commercial confidentiality, and this could comprise smart cities with similar values sharing both their ideals and their data across boundaries in a legal way. Perhaps there are even opportunities to take this to a different and higher level that somehow works in parallel with our current understanding of the nation state.

14.9 NOTES

1. Levy, A. (1986). "Second-Order Planned Change: Definition and Conceptualization." *Operational Dynamics* 15 (1): 5–17, 19–23.
2. Davies, Robert W. (2012). *The Era of Global Transition. Crises and Opportunities in the New World*. London: Palgrave McMillan.
3. Greenwood, R., and Hining, C. (1988). "Organisational Design Types, Tracks and the Dynamics of Strategic Change." *Organisational Studies* 9 (3): 293.
4. Gov.UK. (2021). "Ethics, Transparency and Accountability Framework for Automated Decision Making." Crown copyright, May 13. https://www.gov.uk/government/publications/ethics-transparency-and-accountability-framework-for-automated-decision-making.
5. The Committee on Standards in Public Life. (2020). "Artificial Intelligence and Public Standards. A Review by the Committee on Standards in Public Life." Publishing Service, UK Government, February 10. https://www.gov.uk/government/publications/artificial-intelligence-and-public-standards-report.
6. Ohlenburg, Tim. (2020). "AI in Social Protection – Exploring Opportunities and Mitigating Risks." Bonn: Deutsche Gesellschaft für Internationale Zusammenarbeit, April 20. https://socialprotection.org/sites/default/files/publications_files/GIZ_ADB_AI%20in%20social%20protection.pdf.
7. Office of Government Commerce. (2006). "Supply Chain Management in Public Procurement: A Guide." Crown copyright, June. https://sovz.cz/wp-content/uploads/2016/11/supplychainmanagementguide.pdf.
8. National Audit Office and Audit Commission. (2006). *Delivering Efficiently: Strengthening the Links in Public Service Delivery Chains*. London: The Stationery Office.
9. European Construction Institute. (2015). "Partnering the Public Sector." http://www.eci-online.org/wp-content/uploads/2015/11/ECI-ARC15-Partnering-in-the-Public-Sector.pdf.
10. Kaye, David. (2009). "Public Sector Supply Chain: Risks, Myths and Opportunities." Zurich Municipal. https://www.ncvo.org.uk/images/thebriefingpaperfullversion.pdf.
11. "Nudge" definition. https://www.Dictionary.com/browse/nudge.
12. Institute for Government. (2009). "MINDSPACE: Influencing Behaviour through Public Policy." UK Institute for Government. https://www.instituteforgovernment.org.uk/sites/default/files/publications/MINDSPACE.pdf.
13. Rutter, Jill. (2020). "Nudge Unit." Institute for Government, March 11. https://www.instituteforgovernment.org.uk/explainers/nudge-unit.
14. The Behavioural Insights Team. (2020). "Crafting Effective Communications During a Crisis: Applying Behavioural Insights to COVID-19 Comms." April 29. https://www.bi.team/our-work-2/events/webinars/bit-webinar/.
15. *HuffPost*. (2014). "7 Cultures That Celebrate Aging and Respect Their Elders." February 25. https://www.huffpost.com/entry/what-other-cultures-can-teach_n_4834228.
16. Bobbitt, Phillip. (2003). *The Shield of Achilles: War, Peace and the Course of History*. London: Penguin.

CHAPTER **15**

Conclusion

15.1 REFLECTIONS

This book considers the impact of advanced analytics and AI on the public sector. It's a journey that is not likely to be directly comparable to the impact of AI on private sector industries (as covered in one of the author's earlier books) because of the very special nature of the public sector. Instead, it recognizes the difficulties of offering a continued and effective service to the public against a backdrop of financial and operational pressure brought on by events such as the Covid pandemic, increased customer expectation, and the continued impact of technology. In reality, many of the issues affecting the public sector such as underfunding are longstanding in nature, and while the pandemic cannot be viewed as a cause of the problem, most certainly it has brought these issues to the forefront and exacerbated them. Intertwined with these elements is the quasi-political nature of the public sector, and the recognition that the sector can at times become a political football.

The intention was not to create any political statement and while the author might have his own personal views, these, in the overall context, are irrelevant to this book. What matters most is not only how best to ensure the effective operation of these services but perhaps in some situations even to maintain their continued existence. It is inevitable that we might turn to technology as a panacea, although it may not be the only answer. Increased taxation and deeper national debt will always remain alternatives but in most cases will be unacceptable at the ballot box.

The march toward the use of data, analytics, and ultimately to AI in any or all of its forms is now unstoppable. The technology genie is out of the bottle and its eventual impact will be felt not only by the providers of the service but by citizens as end users. Any effect is likely to occur not just in terms of organizational and process changes but also at an individual and therefore personal level as employees come to terms with the consequences.

Advanced analytics and AI will almost certainly play a major part in the systematic change of the public sector. In its current condition, urgent action needs to be taken to protect the well-being of vulnerable citizens as a result of:

- Increased levels of stress and anxiety caused by the pandemic and its aftermath, which has substantially increased the number of people suffering from mental health issues.
- The aging demographic, and the fact that the elderly no longer can depend on having an extended family on their doorstep to provide care for them in old age.
- An increased and seemingly continuous threat of terrorism and cybercrime.
- The challenges already faced by an overstretched welfare system, which, if some experts are to be believed, will be made worse by greater unemployment following more automation.

The topic of technological change was also considered by comparing the present situation with the infamous Luddite movement – but *their* complaints were not with the technology itself but rather with how it affected their terms and conditions of work. Elsewhere the topic of stakeholder management recognized the importance of employee representation in the sector, usually through trade unions. Unions themselves are not blind to the march of change but remain true to their own beliefs that the protection of workers' rights is their raison d'être.

One key question will be the degree to which employee representation in the form of unions will be the critical factor in the speed of the public sector's transformation. If they are supportive, then the passage of change will be much simpler and therefore quicker. Governments, and perhaps more so nonsocialist ones, may even need to form effective alliances with those who were previously unlikely bedfellows. Chapter 14 provided some insight into some of the theoretic elements of change, including how conflict can occur, but conflict is not likely to serve the public sector or its dependents very well.

15.2   AI AND THE REAL PACE OF CHANGE

Perhaps this particular section might be alternatively named "Why Things Don't Change as Quickly as Expected." One element to reflect upon is that, on the whole, there is a general expectation that things should happen much more quickly than they actually do. We can often see this from our own personal experience. For example, improvements to personal laptops might not seem much when looked at on a year-by-year basis. Laptops may remain the same thickness and weight as before but over the course of a decade or two their operational capability will be considerably greater.

This predominantly consumer-led approach to digital transformation of the public sector might expect there to be change almost on a monthly rather than annual or even 10-year basis. In his 2021 article, Felix Holzapfel suggested that this expectation of the rate of change is primarily due to two reasons:

1. The first is what he calls the networking effect. This is due to the fact that many of the changes are mainly influenced by the impact of social networks, and community attitudes not only stimulate change but provide shared expectation.

2. The second key reason is what he calls the converging effect, that is, as new technologies such as mobile and cloud increasingly converge, these themselves will trigger more speedy innovation and change. The rapidly approaching 5G/6G communication network is a good example, as it will be not only used to support new systems and devices, but new use cases will inevitably be created.[1]

There is always the potential for change to happen much more quickly than expected. Accelerated change is often associated with the idea of the burning platform, which is an expression used in business to signify the need for rapid and sometimes dramatic change.

Metaphors such as a burning platform are a good way of getting a message across. In the case of the public sector, there is no physical fire but there is recognition that changes need to be made, especially as a result of the massive amounts of finance that have been plowed into the public sector in an effort to maintain services throughout the pandemic. While there are options to raise taxes or increase national borrowing, neither of these is likely to be sustainable in the long run. As a result, the public sector will need to learn some of the lessons of the private sector and incorporate some of their ideas about transformation even if they are at times painful. Even so, the special nature of the public sector might mean that some private sector techniques are not readily transferable. Can (and should) desperate citizens be analyzed in the same way as retailers analyze brand-aware consumers, especially as different emotional triggers are involved and the consequences of failed pilot schemes are much more traumatic and life-changing?

15.3 MEASURING ROI – MORE ART THAN SCIENCE?

There is a massive challenge of being able to distinguish between the reality of a situation in terms of benefit and opportunity, compared to market hype. Those who are less emotive will prefer their decisions to be influenced by numbers and projected return on investment (ROI) rather than by narrative. It's natural that third-party case studies will be considered and investigated for what outcome was obtained. The optimist uses these case studies as an example of the "art of the possible." The pessimist might alternatively say that any benefit from a particular case study was based on its particular merits, might be unique, and, as a result, is not comparable.

The science of AI is still in its early stages, and organizations such as Deloitte suggest that three elements are critical:

1. The ability to scale, which allows successful experiments (or pilots) to be able to be expanded on an enterprise level. In the case of public services, this might need to extend to a regional or national level.
2. The need to fully account for both hard and soft benefits to measure cost, strategic, and nonfinancial improvements, perhaps even creating new measurement metrics.
3. Commitment to long-term investment and expenditure in practices, technologies, talent, and business processes.[2]

All these are fundamental truths in respect to progress, and perhaps might equally have been considered in the implementation section of this book. Regarding the third element, that of commitment, Deloitte describes this as being "In it to win it." Perhaps that particular expression seems to lend itself more to the private sector, which is more competitive in nature, than to the public sector. In a public sector context, then, the ultimate winner is likely to be the citizen as main beneficiary, either by way of being a recipient of the service, or as funder, in the role of taxpayer. Conversely, a different view of the winner might constitute those key financial stakeholders in private sector companies who might provide outsourced services to governments, and through technological innovation will be able to place themselves in a prime position to win lucrative contracts.

It is important to recognize that in the public sector, there is a real likelihood, or even a probability, that a better service for the citizen can be provided at lower cost. The traditional public sector approach is already burdened with frictional processes and layers of hierarchy that both add to cost and are inefficient, and are inappropriate to a future more streamlined age of technology.

Some might argue that moving forward in the absence of proven data, which demonstrates operational improvement and provides a clear return on investment, requires a leap of faith. Nowadays, experienced executives apply analysis, experience, and (hopefully) judgment in their decision making, and an ability to make leaps of faith is not usually included in their job description.

15.4   AI AND STIMULATION OF WIDER REFORMS

This may not be simply a technology issue. There are some cutting-edge techniques that will readily transfer from private sector to public sector usage. Many foundational change management elements, such as business process reengineering (BPR), can make a substantial difference to existing processes. The introduction of advanced analytics and AI does not simply mean digitalization of the way things are currently done but should challenge existing approaches. These might include:

- Collecting data in a more systemized way but without adding an additional burden to already overworked and exhausted employees.
- Better integration of existing data and databases held in different departments and silos (all within the limits of data privacy, data protection, and avoiding misuse).
- Discovering new insights and how they can be used to help understand some of the key issues behind social need.

Perhaps one has to ask what might happen if the data and AI "revolution" either does not take place or does not happen quickly enough. The public sector almost certainly needs to become more digital in nature, especially as paper-based systems are beginning to reach the end of their lifespan, even if from time to time paper becomes the administration system of last resort in the event of cyberattack.

The ultimate aim of using AI to improve service at lower cost may be the target operating model, but substantial changes will nevertheless need to happen. Both the threat and expectation of AI may be sufficient in their own rights to stimulate these reforms.

15.5   THE ROLE OF GOVERNMENT IN PUBLIC SECTOR TRANSFORMATION

Public service transformation will not happen in some sort of isolated bubble but has to be encouraged through wider governmental support at a national level. Governmental involvement is critical in leading the way for transformation, especially as the sector itself is highly unlikely to feel the need for change without senior encouragement, or until some type of tipping point is reached, which might even comprise the breaking down of the existing system.

Implementation will not and cannot happen overnight. Successful change will require a prioritized transformation program comprising an integrated set of individual projects that, when combined, serve to provide a single overall strategy. Forward planning is essential, but the rapid and unforeseen cost impacts of the Covid pandemic and other financial shocks may have created acute financial pressures, leading to the acceleration of any planned AI program.

There are a number of key issues that any government needs to address:

1. The first issue is that of education and training so that there are enough trained and qualified people that can contribute to, facilitate, and sustain the extent of change needed. If the demand for trained technology specialists is so great that it extends across both the public and private sectors, then the private sector is almost certainly going to be winners, as it is they who are most likely to offer the best remuneration packages and attract the best candidates. Any government needs to make it attractive for people to join and remain in the public sector.
2. The second issue is that of preparing the ground for change. This needs to happen inside the various parts of the public sector but also with the user base, which ultimately is the citizen. Governments need to gauge how citizens will react to increasing levels of automation such as in healthcare and dealing with chatbots as first point of contact, for example, rather than dealing with a general practitioner. Part of this will be the matter of raising public awareness, and of explaining not only what is planned to be done but also why and how.
3. The third and perhaps key issue is that of leadership, that is, someone who will bear responsibility for the successful implementation of a program. Potential leaders might come from any one or more places or sectors, and all these origins have their strengths and weaknesses. The public sector carries a particular work ethos and sense of duty, and "parachuting" someone with a predominantly commercial mentality from the private to the public sector might not provide a panacea. By the same measure, existing public sector leaders may not be sufficiently risk-minded to take such chances with their career, academics may understand the theory of change but have limited practical implementation skills, and politicians may be seen as being insufficiently neutral in terms of their views and the quasi-political nature of change.

Perhaps there is no need to worry about how such a leader will become ultimately available, for, as the saying goes, "Cometh the hour, cometh the man" (or person). Nevertheless, it still requires a prime mover, and that impetus almost certainly will need to come from the very highest level of authority.

15.6 MOVING THE GOALPOSTS

Transformation of the public sector is important in terms of creating a new public sector that is both fit for purpose and affordable. The public sector, in the form of policing, for example, has been around for several centuries and will continue to endure, but it has changed with the times and responded both to the needs of the public and the systems (and powers) available to it.

A fully effective public sector will almost certainly need to be more integrated, and will require the movement of data and information about both individuals and groups from one operational silo to another. It is something that citizens will need to be prepared to live with, although there will always be some people who prefer to live outside the system. One key ethical question is whether those who aren't prepared to participate in the provision of this information as part of a greater, more integrated model of social support should be entitled to benefit from it fully.

Even those who choose to live outside the system may find themselves at least partly caught in the wider data net. Governments will increasingly rely on advanced systems to monitor the population, principally as a way of managing their safety and security. Some might suggest that this monitoring provides the most effective way of maintaining the power of the state as the principal concern, and with the interests of the populace as a secondary consideration. Many countries already have ID cards with the potential to hold biometric details, and in some countries there has been a move toward the usage of "vaccine passports" that prove that individuals have been inoculated to agreed standards. This degree of monitoring naturally plays strongly to those who are concerned about a more highly controlled surveillance society, and further reinforces the need to carefully manage change through effective messaging and communications. At the same time, citizens will need to be sure that they are not manipulated or nudged into accepting change that is either undemocratic or oppressive.

Pursuing an agenda of automation in order to reduce costs, albeit while improving efficiency, also needs to be weighed in part against the impact of providing social benefits to a larger number of people who have become unemployed (and unemployable) through automation. Matters of individual taxation and the retirement age all form part of a wider consideration that reinforces the need for a comprehensive strategy covering many different and interconnected angles.

One level of expectation might be that change within the public sector could look a little like those changes in our personal laptops, as mentioned in an earlier paragraph. Year over year the difference might look small, but the aggregate effect over a decade will be substantial. That is all well and good, and almost certainly true, but financial pressures might force a more aggressive program.

At the end of the day, there will inevitably be those skeptics who are fearful of some sort of data-controlled, dystopian state that has all the characteristics of a Hollywood movie or literary work like *1984*. Perhaps we might usefully attempt to picture a public sector not in 2084 but at least in 2048, which is a little more than two decades into the future. Children of today, often described as digital natives, as they have been born into a digitalized era, will by then have grown into adulthood. For them, so many things will be different from what we experience today, yet there are equally likely to remain many similarities. It is almost certain that the public sector will retain some sort of role that remains principally centered on duty and service to the citizen, even if discharged in ways that to us currently might be almost beyond imagination.

15.7 NOTES

1. Holzapfel, Felix. (2021). "What Will Happen if AI, Biotech, Quantum Computing, and Robotics Combine?" Thinkers360, May 18. https://www.thinkers360.com/tl/blog/members/why-the-future-comes-more-slowly-than-we-think-at-least-most-of-the-time.
2. Jarvis, David. (2020). "ROI from AI: The Importance of Strong Foundations." Deloitte Insights, October 21. https://www2.deloitte.com/us/en/insights/industry/technology/artificial-intelligence-roi.html.

Appendix A: The Seven Principles of Public Life

In May 1995, in the first report of the UK Committee on Standards in Public Life, which was chaired by Lord Nolan, the Seven Principles of Public Life (also known as the Nolan Principles) were drafted.[1] These principles create a framework for behavior in the public sector.

These ethical statements were deemed to apply to all holders of public office in the United Kingdom who serve the public in any way, including those elected or appointed to public life. The principles are applicable, nationally and locally, to all people working in the UK Civil Service, local government, police, courts, health, education, and social services. They are also relevant to all those in other sectors delivering public services, including occasional and volunteer workers such as school governors (and might presumably therefore also extend to technology and other providers).

1. **Selflessness.** Holders should act solely in terms of the public interest.
2. **Integrity.** Holders must avoid placing themselves under any obligation to people or organizations that might try inappropriately to influence them.
3. **Objectivity.** Holders must act and make decisions impartially, fairly, and on merit.
4. **Accountability.** Holders are accountable to the public for their decisions and actions and must submit themselves to the necessary scrutiny.
5. **Openness.** Holders should make decisions in an open and transparent manner.
6. **Honesty.** Holders should be truthful.
7. **Leadership.** Holders should exhibit these principles in their own behavior and treat others with respect.

NOTE

1. Smith, C. (2020). "The Nolan Principles." Good Governance Institute, June 1. https://www.good-governance.org.uk/publications/insights/the-nolan-principles.

Appendix B: Transformation Roadmap for Public Services

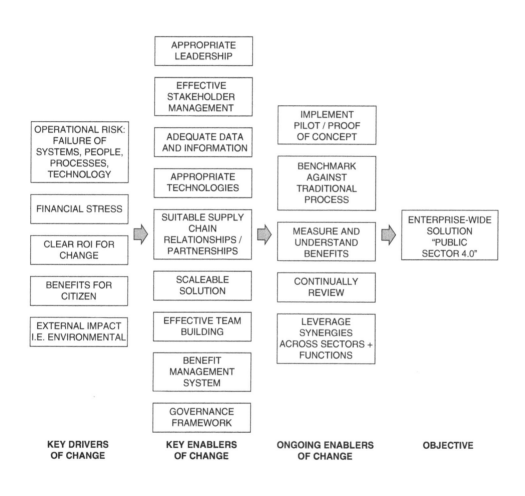

KEY DRIVERS OF CHANGE	KEY ENABLERS OF CHANGE	ONGOING ENABLERS OF CHANGE	OBJECTIVE
OPERATIONAL RISK: FAILURE OF SYSTEMS, PEOPLE, PROCESSES, TECHNOLOGY	APPROPRIATE LEADERSHIP	IMPLEMENT PILOT / PROOF OF CONCEPT	ENTERPRISE-WIDE SOLUTION "PUBLIC SECTOR 4.0"
FINANCIAL STRESS	EFFECTIVE STAKEHOLDER MANAGEMENT	BENCHMARK AGAINST TRADITIONAL PROCESS	
CLEAR ROI FOR CHANGE	ADEQUATE DATA AND INFORMATION	MEASURE AND UNDERSTAND BENEFITS	
BENEFITS FOR CITIZEN	APPROPRIATE TECHNOLOGIES	CONTINUALLY REVIEW	
EXTERNAL IMPACT I.E. ENVIRONMENTAL	SUITABLE SUPPLY CHAIN RELATIONSHIPS / PARTNERSHIPS	LEVERAGE SYNERGIES ACROSS SECTORS + FUNCTIONS	
	SCALEABLE SOLUTION		
	EFFECTIVE TEAM BUILDING		
	BENEFIT MANAGEMENT SYSTEM		
	GOVERNANCE FRAMEWORK		

Appendix C: List of Tables

Appendix D: List of Figures

Index

Page numbers followed by *f* and *t* refer to figures and tables, respectively.